EBURY PRESS

SOLO

Indrajeet More is a Mumbai-based film-maker and illustrator who loves documenting people, languages, food and cultures. In 2021, he completed his BA in philosophy from Ramnarain Ruia College. After four years of directing food shows, travel series and sketch comedies for a Marathi content platform, he transitioned to independently creating content. His works range from films to comics and writing.

From working as a bartender in South Goa to filming the daily life of a seventy-year-old Himachali weaver, learning to tango in Auroville, painting walls in Varanasi, sharing food with fellow passengers on train journeys, pretending to work in cafes and following camel herders in the Thar desert—backpacking fuels Indrajeet's curiosity and helps him understand people with more empathy. *Solo* is his debut book.

You can reach him at indrajeetm22@gmail.com. He also shares his journey stories on Instagram @my_blue_backpack and showcases his work on www.indrajeetmore.com.

SOLO

MY YEAR OF BACKPACKING AND UNPACKING

WRITTEN AND ILLUSTRATED BY

INDRAJEET MORE

EBURY
PRESS

An imprint of Penguin Random House

EBURY PRESS

Ebury Press is an imprint of the Penguin Random House group of companies
whose addresses can be found at global.penguinrandomhouse.com

Published by Penguin Random House India Pvt. Ltd
4th Floor, Capital Tower 1, MG Road,
Gurugram 122 002, Haryana, India

Penguin
Random House
India

First published in Ebury Press by Penguin Random House India 2025

Text and illustrations copyright © Indrajeet More 2025

ISBN 9780143469841

Typeset in Adobe Caslon Pro by Manipal Technologies Limited, Manipal
Printed at Thomson Press India Ltd, New Delhi

www.penguin.co.in

CONTENTS

Preface   vii

1. Home   1
2. Gokarna   6
3. Hampi   26
4. Jaipur   47
5. Rishikesh   71
6. Dharamshala   89
7. Auroville and Puducherry   114
8. Varanasi   134
9. North Goa   157
10. Shillong   175
11. Kolkata   195
12. Darjeeling   220
13. Nagaland   236
14. Kochi and Alleppey   265
15. Souvenir   291

Acknowledgements   305
References   309

PREFACE

We are free to buy a hand wash of our choice; we can choose our leaders (although arguably); and our Subway sandwiches can have veggies of our choice. Although these notions of self-determination make us feel like the world revolves around us, there is a bigger power that drives us—the Power of Randomness. Some things fall into place in such a way that they surprise us most unexpectedly. No matter what the odds are. Does it sound stupid? It absolutely does! It is mad. You happen to be at a place at the right time when something is already waiting for you. It might not have been there if it was someone else instead of you. Or even if you aren't there at that time and are somewhere else. It is a puzzle that gets solved with nothing but absolute belief. It is this 'randomness' that intrigues me about travelling. It puts one in an involuntary process of inquiry where the inference is (most of the time) devoid of biases and wholly yours. If nothing, it takes away the mental burden of having things in your control and leaves you in awe of your most humble, innocent and truest self.

While I am writing this, there is a nationwide lockdown. Covid-19 cases don't seem to be decreasing and we still don't know what's ahead of us. But looking at the brighter side, I have decided to utilize this time to write a book! Just kidding.

I'm actually just doing my best to keep myself occupied and not succumb to another existential dread. Amid the gruelling anxiety of everything around us changing so quickly, my mind circles around one thing I can't afford to do in the given situation, or don't know when I will be able to—travelling. Feeling strongly for things in their absence rather than when we had them is a naivety that we humans have barely been able to evolve from. They exist and grow in our minds more vividly. I wouldn't say I particularly miss travelling but I'd trade any day of my life for the feeling of it!

In 2018, accepting an offer to host a YouTube travel series led to a year-long journey of backpacking across various parts of India. The following year, 2019, was filled with travelling like never before. On my last trip to Kochi, in the middle of a canal, my boss suggested, 'You should write about it.' And I instantly agreed as the two of us continued rowing our canoe. I am sure she meant a blog or something on similar lines. But in the same month, I visited my school principal too. I had prepared myself to have a small talk with him, and as I was telling him about my Kochi trip, he asked, 'Why don't you write about it?' The very next day, in a textual banter, my ex-girlfriend said, 'If you ever write a book, you should write about how forgetful you are.' I saw a clear pattern here and took it as a sign.

This was about writing. As for the illustrations in the book, they're just an attempt to compensate for my substandard writing. They're also for potential clients looking for a young, talented illustrator, but mainly for readers like me who pick up books only if they have pictures in them. If you are among the former, please drop an email and if you're one of the latter, we should definitely be friends in real life.

I have stayed home so little that I barely have any muscle memory for all the switches in my house. Although the YouTube travel series is available on the Internet and has already been watched by many of you, a big part of this journey remains mine. Its experiences remain a catalyst for several fundamental changes and paradigm shifts. This book is a reflection on all those experiences, narrated from my absolutely biased point of view. The ones that are just videos on YouTube wouldn't do them justice. It is about all those missed buses, weird food, painful diarrhoea nights, strangers-turned-friends, long walks, cheap adventures, mountains climbed, tents pitched and beaches sat on for hours.

I don't know who should read this book and why, but for me, the reasons are quite personal. I do not have the habit of collecting or preserving mementos and memories for long. This is my attempt to keep all those memories in one place. I hope this book inspires someone like me to travel and put themselves out of their comfort zones just to realize how capable they are. There are still many questions unanswered and many actions unquestioned. I hope to inquire about them in the process of writing this book and, most importantly, to be mindful and open to exploring whatever this expression unfolds. This is a reminder for me to never stop seeking, expressing and evolving.

I invite you to take a look.

ONE

HOME

In the middle of a forest, during a frenzied shoot, a sudden phone call from Anusha excited me. 'Hey Indrajeet,' she began in her usual perky tone. (I had known her for more than four years by then, and still her tone hadn't changed one bit.) 'We wanted to discuss a new project; could you visit the office soon?' Anusha is one of the co-founders of the company where I interned. Although she was the closest person I worked with, getting a call from her wasn't frequent, which made me even more curious.

The evening light was slipping away, and I remember frantically searching those dark woods for better connectivity. I wanted to ask her what the project was about and why she was calling me, a newly joined intern, of all people. But I didn't want to risk losing the network in the middle of a big reveal. (At least that's what I wished for. A rational part of my mind knew it'd be for some super trivial work.) 'Sure, I'll be there on Friday,' I complied.

The shoot was for my first pitch video, an indie project. After two days of excruciating editing, the video was finally ready. I had decided to present it on Friday itself.

On my way to the office on Friday, I kept mulling over the mysterious project that Anusha had mentioned.

I tried my hardest to not get my hopes up because, in our field, the only jobs under the profile of interns were sitting at the merchandise desk, designing Instagram posts, holding reflectors or co-ordinating with the actors to make call sheets. I got associated with Bharatiya Digital Party (popularly known as BhaDiPa) when its office was just a 1BHK apartment in Bandra. It was probably the only content platform in Marathi that ventured beyond the stereotypical family daily soaps. Of whatever that was made in Marathi, BhaDiPa's content stood out. They were the only people trying to put regional content into mainstream.

My friend and I applied at BhaDiPa as stand-up comics. But after three bombed jamming sessions and a threat call to my friend, both of us decided to rethink our choices. We, however, still stuck around interning as assistant directors. We did everything that was given to us.

A few weeks later, a small part of our team got busy setting up a sister channel for non-fictional content, mainly related to food, travel and culture. It was named Bharatiya Touring Party (aka Bha2Pa). My job vaguely revolved around writing voice-overs, supervising edits, posting stories on Instagram and replying to collaboration messages. For a new YouTube channel with 500 subscribers, getting more than 10k views excited us more than anything.

That day, I reached the office quicker than ever before. The trains were on time, the ticket counters had no queues and the streets were free of traffic jams. At the office, Sarang and Paula, the other two co-founders, watched my pitch video. Both of them have the habit of giving 'sandwich feedback', but this time, it was outright appreciation. An involuntary sigh of satisfaction calmed down my anxious fidgeting.

'Good job with handling social media,' Sarang said, making himself comfortable on the couch for a long conversation. 'We've been thinking about producing in-house travel content for Bha2Pa . . . something new.' He continued, 'I read your travel stories on Facebook.' (Yes, I used to do that when Facebook wasn't taken over by prejudiced uncles.) 'I like how cost effectively and spontaneously you travel. It was totally my thing when I was your age.' Sarang does this a lot. He is a twenty-year-old fitted in the body of a thirty-year-old but is practically forty.

'Oh, yes, that post,' I responded as calmly as I could, while internally jumping on a trampoline, because SARANG SATHAYE READS MY FACEBOOK POSTS! It was valid for me to get this excited because he is precisely who nineteen-year-old me wished to be, a few years down the line.

He is this bearded, hat-wearing hipster with the wit of a wise old man. He lives with his Canadian life partner Paula and his two cats, Ma Anand Sheela and Mogambo, in a cute apartment in Bandra. He collects lapel pins everywhere he goes and is responsible for my coffee addiction. He is skinny, wears coloured clothes, smiles widely and enjoys eccentricity. The way he embraces his masculinity makes me feel accessible to mine.

Sarang went on, oblivious to my excitement, 'Yeah, so Anusha and I had something similar in mind. How about you make short travel videos for Bha2Pa? Essentially about backpacking on a budget. Travel vlogs work great on YouTube.'

'I am down for this!' I replied instantly. Usually, in such scenarios, my indecisiveness does its best to sabotage the opportunity, but this time, I was proud of my rare impulsive reactions.

Also, why me? I was the closest person associated with travel in the team. I had recently switched from being a trek volunteer to venturing out on solo journeys. That was where most of my stipend money was being spend.

Sarang continued in a calm demeanour, 'Awesome, so this is how it is going to be. You go and film, and we'll cover your expenses.' He said it as a matter of fact.

I could not believe what I was hearing, however clichéd it might sound. 'Was I getting an offer to travel . . . for FREE? AND to make videos?' I wish I had a writer's vocabulary to describe how it felt. At that moment, it did feel surreal, but over time, I also realized how rare it is to have the freedom to choose your favourite project so early in your career.

After brainstorming for various names for the series, we ultimately settled on our first option, 'Budget Backpacking with Indrajeet'. (Just because it was direct and had an alliteration. I have a thing for alliterations.) The basic structure of the show was to have a five-minute vlog of a three-day trip on a budget of Rs 3000, with the cost breakdown explained at the end. Also, why Rs 3000? Again, alliteration—'3 days in 3000'.

Chinmay (the then content head of the channel) said, 'But let's keep it easy. Let's experiment with the pilot episode and see how it goes.' At the end of our last meeting, every single part of it excited me—travelling, a one-person team, experimenting and hosting. It was going to be Bha2Pa's first in-house intellectual property; although not a big-budget production, it was full of possibilities.

For almost a week, I still wasn't able to process the idea of getting to run an entire show. It was unimaginable how it would materialize. A surge of excitement, nervousness and curiosity kept me on my toes.

Barely a year into junior college, I was among a group of gullible teens in the college theatre circle, absolutely unsure of what to do ahead. To look up to, all we had were seniors barely making it to their graduation. They gave us sermons in the auditorium before we found them in the quadrangle talking about dicks and vaginas. For an entire year, I was part of a play titled 'Laila on the Rocks'. I wasn't given a role, but since I could draw, I stuck with the set department.

Before joining the internship at BhaDiPa, I spent almost an entire year in my college auditorium. I'd take an early morning train from Dombivli, reach Matunga at 9 a.m., sign my attendance for the first lecture and head to the auditorium in the senior college building. The rehearsals would end at 10 p.m., and a group of fifteen to twenty kids would travel together back home only to show up again at 9 a.m. the next day. It took me another year to figure out what the play was about and why I was doing it. My plan was to assist directors on shoots and work on my independent material in the meantime. Life ran on a trial-and-error basis.

However, now I had something substantial to work on— something that was mine. I was very insecure about how I looked back then. Why would anyone watch an eighteen-year-old in braces? But more than that, I was finally able to do the two things that mattered the most: visiting places and filming them. Vaguely loitering around, life suddenly got into a pace. I had gone to pitch my work and came back with a new one.

TWO

GOKARNA

A town so little, you'll see each traveller at least twice.

A deserted bench on Madgaon railway junction, 1 a.m. I was struggling to fit my flimsy, crackling emergency blanket into the packet in which it had snugly resided before. Since Goa was on the way, I managed to squeeze out a day to attend the ongoing Serendipity Arts Festival in Panaji. I had spent an eventful day among grey-haired Fabindia-adorned women at art galleries, tasting tribal food and praising anything that was entitled 'contemporary', 'immersive' or 'nuanced'. Art festivals are the best places to meet creative people and learn different styles of expression, though most of the time, it's just figuring out the 'nuances' of the 'nuanced'. At the end of a hectic day, I was awaiting the train to Gokarna to begin my first backpacking shoot.

A nervous frenzy of kick-starting something new emerged in me as I began to count down my days. As I finally saw my train to Gokarna arrive, it dawned on me that now there is no going back. Although I have been to Gokarna once before, this time it felt different. Very unusually, I had made a checklist of things, charged all my equipment, chalked out an itinerary and scribbled a shot list for the shoot. It consisted of a list of B-roll shots, such as shooting myself while walking, establishing shots of temples and inserts of people and shops. To calm my fidgeting, I kept reminding myself, 'Look at it as just another backpacking trip.'

Gokarna is a quaint little town situated in the north of coastal Karnataka. Almost like the one described in R.K. Narayan's *Swami and Friends*. The place is mainly known for its Mahabaleshwar Shiva Temple. According to folklore, Ravan was once passing through this town, carrying a Shiv lingam (Shiva's symbol) in his hands. He asked a boy to hold it for him while he went to practise his cleansing rituals. He had instructed the boy to not place it on the ground, as the lingam would stick to it and could not be moved again. The boy, who was Shiva's son, Ganpati, in disguise, kept it there and left. Ravan was furious at seeing the Shiva lingam on the ground. He could not move it and had to leave, dejected. The spot where Ganpati had set down the Shiva lingam is exactly where the Mahabaleshwar Temple exists today, with the town of Gokarna built around it.

Running parallel to the coastline, the Western Ghats occupy a major part of Gokarna. The thick canopy of deciduous trees on these hills houses one of the most biodiverse ecosystems in the world. Apart from the laidback local life, backpackers who have had enough of Goa come down to settle in Gokarna. Hence, the majority of travellers coming here are foreigners. Here, they attend Saturday yoga sessions, sign up for mandala-making workshops and get chakras tattooed on their backs. I chose this spot for my first video mainly because I had been there before and Gokarna, not being a very popular tourist destination, would add novelty to the series. But also, honestly, due to the same reason, if I missed shooting anything, I could get away with it easily.

From Madgaon Junction to Gokarna Road railway station, it was only going to be a four-hour rail journey, so I didn't bother getting a reservation. I can only dare to do this in south India, as the railways here are comparatively cleaner and usually devoid of brash fellow passengers. Carrying a general ticket that cost me some Rs 230, I boarded the train. Upon negotiation, the TC (ticket checker) let me curl up in my sleeping bag in the passage in between two berths. I had my backpack on me for almost the entire day; it had almost become one of my body's organs. I felt levitated as I took it off. The hum of the rocking train lulled me to sleep in anticipation of the big trip.

Day One, 23 December 2018

The trip hasn't even begun and . . .

My eyes opened to an almost empty bogie. It woke me up in shock. I checked my watch, and it was 5 a.m. I HAVE MISSED MY STOP! The train had left two stations from Gokarna Road already. It was running very fast, and I couldn't do anything about it. The trip had not even begun yet, and something had already gone wrong. I hastily stuffed my sleeping bag in the sack and got down at the very next station, Murudeshwara. After the train left, the platform got dark, silent and deserted. I sat on a bench under the blank indicator with a numb brain and an unpacked rucksack. 'Where would I have been right now, had I woken up on time?' I would probably be at a nice cafe, having idli for breakfast. I badly wanted to brush my teeth, take a bath, change into a dry pair of clothes and maybe have some coffee. Here I was, sleep deprived, with a sore back and an empty stomach. None of the incoming thoughts added to what could be done next.

After gaining enough energy to process the mishap, I walked to the ticket counter and had to wake the person at the desk. On inquiring, I got to know that the next train to Gokarna was at 9 a.m. 'One of the tallest Shiva temples is just a few kilometres from here; it's a very good place to visit . . . Very tall. Will you be sitting here for hours waiting for the train?' The ticket guy offered a plan. We both low-key smiled at each other. That made me feel less lost.

I could think of no reason not to visit the temple. Sitting at the station and fidgeting anxiously was not helping at all. Dropping all my scepticism, I left in the early light of dawn. National Highway 66 ran endlessly till the horizon as the morning got clearer; trucks passed and disappeared in the mist, leaving behind the echoes of their exuberant honking. The only sound in these waves of silence was that of my coffee mug rocking in my backpack. It was just me walking alongside this long stretch of highway. The tip of the temple grew more visible as the sky changed its hue, and in no time, I was walking among several other pilgrims following the same path.

A thirty-minute meditative walk, and we stood in captivity, gazing at the giant, twenty-storey *gopuram* (entrance) of the holy Murudeshwara Temple. Behind this expansive structure lay an equally enormous statue of Shiva, meditating in *padmasana* (lotus pose). His half-closed eyes reflected compassion. Between these two massive structures was the holy sanctum, gleaming in the morning sunlight. It resembled the sun itself, rising through two massive mountains, right on the shore. The enchanting imagery involuntarily brought my palms together. In the melody of the washing waves and the hymns, all of my unhappiness over failing to stick to the plan faded away. My bare feet touched the cold rocks and were finally breathing out of my shoes. I was glad to be alone and not having to speak a word the whole time. That felt like true serendipity.

* * *

By 9 a.m., I got a lift back to the station, and a passenger train finally dropped me off at Gokarna. However, my staying arrangements still needed to be figured out. I often travelled during off-season and since most of my plans were tentative, I never really pre-booked anything. I tried to do it consciously for this episode too. For someone who isn't really organized while travelling, a perfectly planned itinerary would dilute the candidness of the video. Pretence is easily noticeable in any sort of content, and every time I had not been entirely confident about something, the output had turned out awfully fake. Backpacking was something I *was* confident about, so gambling on this micro-adventure seemed alright.

I had a budget of Rs 3000 for this trip. Surely, I could manage my trip with that much money, because the last time

I had visited Gokarna, I had spent half the amount. The cheapest options for accommodation were these little shacks by the beach. They are run by local people and are often filled with Russians who rent it out for months. If you check out ten shacks, you will probably find one or two decent ones. Sitting at an eatery, as I looked up some shacks online, I got my second shock of the day—all the hotels, shacks and homestays were full due to Christmas! How did it slip my mind?

This was still less bothersome than missing the station, though. When you backpack, it never happens that you have no place to crash in; there is always some alternative. I was prepared to bunk at the bus stop in the worst-case scenario. At that age, even my backup plans were driven by the sheer excitement of the unknown. I expected that as I got older, I'd prioritize comfort, but to my surprise, I never have.

'Do you know of any homestays nearby?' I asked the shack owner while paying my bill.

He gave me a clueless stare in response and then started explaining something to me in Kannada, assuming I lived next door. I tried asking him in Hindi, even English and finally resorted to sign language. Everyone in the eatery was staring at our frantic gesticulations. I returned to my table downcast, donned my backpack and stepped out in search of a place to stay. The language problem, usually not that bothersome, suddenly made me feel like an absolute foreigner. It didn't take much time for everything to turn so unfamiliar.

Eben, the stranger

'I think my place could have a spare room; I can check if you want,' said a person at the gate, in a Middle-Eastern accent, as

he lit his cigarette. He was white
and tall; had brown eyes and a
pointy nose; wore brown baggy
pants and a loose tank top and
carried a sling bag.

'Umm . . . sure,' I replied. He
pulled out an old button phone
and made a call, and to my utter
surprise, he started speaking in
Kannada, the local language!

'Yes, they can accommodate you. I am staying at a shack on
the main beach. It's a twenty-minute walk. So, do you maybe
want to check that out?' he offered. I didn't know what to say.

I had no other option. Or perhaps I did, but I was
too tired to hunt for one. I evaluated my options: 'I don't
know this guy; he could take me anywhere. He even knows
Kannada. Is he part of some local drug-peddling gang? But I
really want a place to crash in. And on what basis do I refuse
him? That I don't know him? I didn't even know the people
whom I called on the Internet a while ago.' I finally agreed,
even though I was a little sceptical, and we left for my new
lodgings.

He introduced himself as Eben from Israel. On the way,
Eben waved at six people and greeted them in Kannada. They
too joyfully waved back, as though he were some local hero
who had saved kids from drowning in a well.

'Hey man, I'd prefer it if you don't record me . . . Not
very comfortable,' he said, as I pulled out my GoPro to record
snippets for my vlog. The thought of him being a psychopath
staying off grid overpowered the actual possibility that he
probably just didn't like being filmed. However, I naively

dismissed every suspicion and decided to place my faith in his seemingly genuine helpfulness.

I did score a room at that shack for the night, proving that Eben was probably neither a serial killer nor a drug peddler, but just another traveller who could speak Kannada. The price we settled for was Rs 200 per night, and the shack was just as expected—like a typical Konkani house. The walls were made of laterite rock and covered by palm leaves on top. Inside, the floor was nothing but beach sand; a mosquito net hung on the stinky bed, damp with what I liked to assume was beach water. I quickly replaced it with my sleeping bag. The only electric gadgets were a crippled bulb and a socket board hanging off the wall like a delicate chandelier. They had better rooms too, but this was the only vacant one, and it directly faced the beach, filling the space inside with the cool ocean breeze. The other guests were German, Israeli and Russian. The owner and his wife were the only Indians I could spot there. For Rs 200, the room seemed like a fair deal. This was my first expense out of the budget of Rs 3000; so I had Rs 2800 remaining—I made a mental note.

I spent the rest of the day in Eben's room, which was MUCH better than mine but also highly messy with his things strewn all over the place. Only he knew what was kept where. It seemed like he had been staying there for quite a while. He made us coffee using his little electric kettle and quite generously let me use his charging sockets and cables.

'What work do you do?' I asked him inquisitively.

Eben raised an eyebrow. 'I am on vacation and all you ask me is about work?' he questioned back as he rolled himself a cigarette. Looking at the way he was settled in that shack and judging by the greetings he made in Kannada, it didn't seem like he was on vacation.

'All I will say is if a country had more people like me, its economy would face a downfall,' he contemplated.

Eben spoke very vaguely. He started with a topic at one moment, and in the next, he jumped onto something completely different. Although we talked for hours on various subjects, I couldn't quite get to know Eben. He spoke a lot, but that didn't add up to enough information for me to form a definitive opinion about him. But then I wondered, do I even need to have an opinion? Especially about someone whom I am not going to meet again? It seemed like he had nobody to talk to for days. I listened to his sermons, sipping on the bitter coffee he made for us.

* * *

Subconsciously, the fact that I had trusted a complete stranger and it paid off made me have a little more faith in my intuition. The same night, I befriended my neighbours—a Russian guy and his mom. The three of us spent the night on the veranda in the comfort of a cool sea breeze and some herbal tea his mom made for us. Amid the annoying humidity and brutal mosquitoes, there still was a sense of comfort. All of us—Eben, the Russians, the locals and I—spoke a mix of terrible Hindi and English to each other, but by the end of the day, we were just happy to at least be understood.

This entire day, almost nothing went as I had initially planned. Whatever went wrong now feels like it couldn't have been better any other way. This truly was a perfect first day for a backpacking series!

Day Two, 24 December 2018

Rerouting . . .

Today's plan was simple and sorted: hike to Paradise Beach, pitch my tent there and spend Christmas Eve camping solo!

Anyone who has been to Gokarna cannot stop going gaga over Paradise Beach. They say it is so secluded that at night glowing phytoplankton make the shore look exactly like the starry sky. Covered with forested hills on all three sides, Paradise Beach is cut off from the nearby villages, Gokarna and Belekan, by dense shrubs. This makes the beach inaccessible by vehicles, and the only way to get there is to either hike all the way through the woods over the hills or take a boat from any of the adjoining beaches.

Hiring a boat was out of question as it would eat up a good chunk of my given budget, so the only option left was to hike. Buckling up my backpack with high enthusiasm, I filled my water bottle and stocked up on four bananas for dinner. I first hitchhiked my way to Om Beach and then started hiking at around 5 p.m. My aim was to reach there before it got dark. Acting all cool, I would occasionally track my route on Google Maps as the trail appeared to have faded in some parts. Slowly, the trail started to fade for a few metres and eventually vanished completely. I realized that it was taking a bit longer than I had calculated to reach my destination. Dubiously, I pulled out my phone to check the GPS and realized that I had been hiking in the wrong direction the whole time! The bloody GPS had lost its signal 500 metres back! 'NOT AGAIN!' an instant bout of panic rushed through my body. I could see the sun going down, which made me even more anxious. I had no time to process any of this. I was in no mood to die in a forest without ever having sex or tasting baklava or even seeing a whale, just because I had lost the damned GPS signal!

My brain was whizzing away, trying to find a way out: 'What options do I have? I could cry for help, but it was probably going to be futile because there was absolutely nobody around. Maybe I could camp in the forest? No way! Or . . . could I go back to the point where I lost the signal and start from there? Yes!'

I started running back as fast as I could, but the GPS still couldn't latch onto a signal. By this point, I had totally forgotten about filming the vlog. I needed to find a way out of this mess urgently. Compelling my brain to not assume extreme scenarios, I started to think of a way out of the forest. Mindlessly, I started following the sound of the waves and began descending from the woods onto the rocks, hoping to find a path that parallelly ran to the rocky shore. It was a tough walk, especially with the heavy backpack on. There were times when the rocks were so steep that I had to ascend, fixing my toes and fingers in the cracks, while the gigantic waves crashed just a few feet apart. I didn't know if that was the right way or the wrong one, but at that moment, I was operating solely on instinct. The red wash of the sky melting down into the ocean at the horizon strangely helped calm my racing heart.

There it finally was! Not more than 100 metres away, in the dark, this fine patch of sand nestled in a nook between the mountains. A grove of coconut trees swayed between the beach and the cliff. It would have made the perfect spot for hanging up a hammock and listening to some light Hindustani melodies. There were no shops or cafes here, but just one man, setting up some fruit on a tiny table. Paradise Beach was just like its name—nirvana, totally cut off from the rest of the world. How could anything be so perfect?

My wonderment was instantly ruined when I heard someone yell, '*Abey chutiye, apna tent yahaan hain!*' (Our tent is over here, you asshole!) a few metres away, to which another voice replied, '*Susu karne ja raha hu! Aaega?*' (I am going to take a leak; want to join?) It was a group of IT engineers from Bengaluru, occupying the coconut grove with twenty to thirty tents! My idea of solace broke into pieces. This was the last place I wished to see an engineer, and there they were in abundance, calling each other in slang, flashing torches, playing Bollywood music and peeing in corners.

There is no recreational activity left unexploited by the IT people as a compensation to their presumably miserable jobs. I had seen the worst of them when I used to volunteer as a trek leader in 2016. You suppress a kid for years and leave them in a new city with a decent package. What else are they going to do? I really wanted to empathize with them, but when you trek for three hours carrying a heavy tent on your back, cross forests and climb rocks and see this, it becomes really hard to do that.

I walked to the other end of the beach, as far from the crowd as possible, at an elevated part of the cliff. As I started to unpack, the lamplight attracted many moths. To make matters worse, the bananas I had carried all this way had turned soggy. Sweaty and irritated, I managed to set up my campsite in whatever minimal light my head torch provided.

'Are you with them?' a guy asked as he collected dry wood a few feet apart, near his tent.

'Nope, camping solo,' I replied, as I pitched mine.

'Amazing, I am travelling solo too. I am from Kerala,' he said, and we shook hands. 'Where are you from?'

'Mumbai,' I replied.

'Cool, let me know if you need anything, bro,' he said, as he continued collecting dry wood. We had the same tents— Quechua Arpenaz 100.

As I sat by the bonfire with the Kerala guy, we bonded over our shared disdain for the IT crowd who earned twice our salaries—myself with none. I recalled being taught that 'man is a social animal' but the more I observed, the more I was puzzled by what happens when people gather. Individually, people are sharp and full of independent thought, but together, their collective intelligence seems to dilute into a less insightful version of itself. Their actions become something none of them would choose alone. It makes me wonder about the nature of group dynamics that blurs individual clarity—be it society meetings, religious gatherings, commuters, politicians, college reunions, kitty parties, corporate conventions or the neighbouring IT squad.

The Kerala guy pulled out his pouch and rolled a joint. We sat in silence, each on our own journey. It was 25 December. Merry Christmas to us.

* * *

Day Three, 25 December 2018

I awoke to the sound of the ebbing waves. It was pretty hot inside the tent by now. The rays of the sun falling directly onto my face through a small opening in the zip was what finally woke me up. I was unable to sleep well the previous night, but at least it was not as bad as the night before or the one even before that. As soon as I got out of my sleeping bag and opened the zip, a cool breeze rushed in filling the tent. On the other side lay the majestic blue ocean; beneath the clear sky, mild waves wiping the shore in a mystical rhythm. The sun rose from behind, illuminating the ocean, making it brighter and clearer. I came out of my tent and felt the cool sand brushing over my feet. The beach was empty. The group had left, and so had the camper from Kerala. It was just me and the fruit vendor.

For another half hour, I did nothing; I just sat outside my tent and relished the solace. My senses were at their sharpest, feeling the cool breeze brushing my arms, legs and face listening to all of the minute sounds that usually blend into the white noise—the crashing waves, rustling palms, a fruit vendor cracking open a coconut, a lapwing calling from a distance. Nothing felt so humbling as a human experience. To have the ability to absorb all the artistic wonders of nature; to think beyond survival. My tent was right in the middle of the vast, raging ocean and the calm mountains. This conversation needed no words while I was just a bystander.

I took off my shirt and started walking towards the water. The water was still cold; I let out a deep breath after it touched my feet. I kept walking until my feet lost contact with the land and the water floated me on the surface of its dancing waves, staring at my tent as it got tinier and tinier, until I reached a point where I had to squint to see it. I plunged into a dive as a long wave approached, and it pushed me back towards the shore. I swam against the flow, and each time, an incoming tidal wave pushed me back. The seals do this when they don't have to go on hunts or mate. This kept on going for quite a while. This freedom felt earned and tasted salty. Stupid me, contemplating whether or not to laugh like an idiot, I actually did it after realizing nobody was watching.

Moments after coming out of the water, my bliss turned into extreme irritation from the salt drying up on my skin. Unwilling to walk again on the dreadful trail I had taken yesterday, I decided instead to hike south up to Belekan and take a bus back up to Gokarna. The fruit vendor gave me the bus timings and warned me to reach on time, as their frequency was quite poor. I left with the vendor himself, as he had no reason to stay back after me. I followed him all the way through the shrubs, watching him walk barefoot in a lungi, chopping off twigs with his sickle.

An empty road ran parallel to the coast, along with the vibrantly coloured Konkani houses of the fishermen. Boats, filled with fishnets, were docked on the shore. A few fishermen sat in them, preparing their nets for the day. Observing their chores from the shed of a roadside shop, I waited for the bus. It arrived thirty minutes later and took me back to Gokarna in another thirty. The ticket barely cost Rs 20. The 'luxury' of public transport!

Gokarna town was setting up for the day. Vendors selling fruits, priests holding up their dhotis and rushing from temple to temple, fish markets in full swing, courtyards

being washed and decorated with
the traditional *kolam*, or rangoli.
I was back in the noise, but it
was still nowhere close to the
one in cities. It had the charm
of comfort. The one that you
feel after visiting your native
town after years to rarely see anything changed. An uncle
in folded lungi sat on the veranda solving the Sudoku in his
newspaper. Occasionally, he tucked the pen behind his ear
to sip his coffee. If I manage to live long enough, I'd choose
to have such a slow-paced life.

My raging hunger grew unbearable. Upon inquiring, I
was guided to a local house that served nothing but fish meals.
From the outside, one couldn't make out that this place served
food. It had neither a board nor a menu card, but just two tables
laid out in the courtyard of a single-storey house. I assumed it
was run by a family and not some proper staff. This was the
exact kind of place I was looking for—extremely local and very
homely.

A sumptuous meal consisting of two freshly fried mackerel,
the iconic Konkani prawn curry (the orange-coloured coconut-
based one), beetroot salad and a generous
amount of steaming hot rice was on my table.
A spoonful of curry mixed in rice, a few strands
of beetroot and a big piece of the mackerel's
belly—I gathered a wholesome morsel. The
flavour was smooth, savoury and slightly
tangy. The abundance of fresh coconut was
a plus too. It had that pampering, homely
essence I was craving. I believe that apart

from the fantastic preparation, the food tasted great due to the fact that I had been starving to death and wasn't expecting something like this. I remember having three rounds of rice and six cups of curry. Such surprises occur only when you aren't expecting them. Not even the fanciest of the fancy restaurants can deliver half the authenticity, comfort and satisfaction that these household eateries do. On top of this, I only had to pay Rs 70 for the whole meal. This felt like a cosmic reward for solely surviving on bananas the previous night.

Walking outside, I saw the old man was still sitting on the veranda; he was done solving his puzzle and sipping his coffee. His wife came from within and took his empty coffee tumbler inside. He was glued to his seat.

My train back home was at 4 p.m. the next day, and I badly needed some rest. In order to include various accommodation options in my video, I had tried out a cheap beach shack, camped on a beach and it was now time to check into a hostel. I had saved more money than planned.

I got to know what a hostel is from a fellow trekker a few years ago. Back then, Zostel, a chain of backpacker hostels, had started to expand their properties across India. They had one in Gokarna too, where I had stayed the last time. Their dorms are affordable and clean. Their common areas used to be crawling with solo travellers gleefully mingling. That was also the time when it felt delightful to spot another solo traveller; now, in most cases, I escape those groups. The conversations have become too predictable, and everything eventually boils down to who gets laid with whom.

I made a walk-in booking at Zostel and settled in my dorm. Their tariffs usually range between Rs 600–700, but since it was the Christmas season, they were selling bunk beds for almost the price of an entire room. I paid Rs 900 for that night. Given the way I had spent my last two nights, I couldn't really complain.

I somehow resisted the urge to crash on the bed before unloading my backpack and taking a shower, for I knew it would be too hard to get up after that. Although my phone network was back and buzzing with notifications, it was the last thing my brain wished to engage with. I can't remember when I slept. The enthusiastic chatter of my dorm mates woke me out of my slumber, only to realize it was dark by now. They couldn't stop sharing about their day. I happily listened, having almost no ability to drive the conversation. It was one of those moments when you are just happy to be around other people without having to actively participate. We continued our conversation as we made our way to the cafe at the hostel and sat until late. Three sleepless nights in a row and a lot of walking were compensated with beer and fries that breezy night.

* * *

On the train back home, I went through the footage of all three days, browsing through every clip and chuckling at some really silly ones. As I had no idea how the video was going to turn out in terms of the structure or the narrative, I had rampantly shot every single moment in the worry of not missing out on anything. I could not wait to get everything on the edit table and watch the first cut; release was out of the question. I did not know how anyone would perceive this content, but for me, this shoot was pure, raw and devoid of any compromises made for the sake of the 'audience'.

On this trip, not all of my plans had turned out well, but the spontaneity and surprises that the journey bore made it memorable. I don't know how sane it is to not have a plan. But I realized that something or the other always worked out. At the time, the stakes were low, so this spontaneity felt enjoyable, and I thought it's best to just go with the flow. I am sorry, do I sound like a hippie already?

THREE

HAMPI

Some rocks, some gods.

In search of his abducted wife, Ram, along with his brother Laxman, arrives in Kishkindha,* the kingdom of monkeys. Travelling a long way from the dense forest of Chitrakut

---

* Ruchi Pritam, 'On the Ramayana trail—Kishkindha at Hampi', *Pragyata,* 6 February 2018, https://pragyata.com/on-the-ramayana-trail-kishkindha-at-hampi/

(central India) to this vast rocky plateau, they come across a monkey as if it were destined to happen. He informs the brothers of spotting a woman being taken through the sky. They have collected the ornaments fallen from above. 'It's her,' Ram confirms. After several days of frantic search, for the first time, hope restores among both the brothers.

In this story, the abducted wife is Devi Sita, the monkey is none other than Hanuman and the arid land of Kishkindha is today's Hampi.

Reference from *Ramayan, Kishkindha Kand*.

Day One, 17 February 2019

We have all had our love–hate relationship with autorickshaw drivers. Coming from a city where auto drivers treat you like shit, it's overwhelming when you travel to a different place and the auto drivers there actually acknowledge your presence. And not just that, they even make sure that you acknowledge theirs too.

Soon after alighting the bus, half a dozen auto drivers rushed towards the bus, asking for rides and grabbing people's luggage. Battling them was a clueless and annoyed East Asian guy. At 7 a.m. on the empty streets of Hospet, there didn't seem a better option than taking an auto to Hampi. Assuming the foreigner too wanted to go to Hampi, I offered to share a ride and save money for both of us. The Chinese guy introduced himself as Chang. Putting his suitcase at the back of the rickshaw, we rolled.

The first episode got a massive response. Backpackers could finally find content they could relate to, while for others, it was a fascinating novelty. A college kid travelling solo *and* on a budget of Rs 3000 apparently sold the show. The tagline '3 days in 3000' became a thing. The show had the highest audience retention of all the videos on the channel. The team decided to roll out an episode every thirty to forty days. More than the success, the fact that I'd get to travel every month cheered me up. Even before we could sit down to plan our calendar, we had requests pouring in for Hampi. Without giving it a second thought, I booked tickets for Hampi two days after the release of the first episode. As I was imagining everything I'd do differently on this shoot, the auto hit a speed breaker, bringing me back to my trip. I was in Hampi in no time.

The auto dropped us in the main market right next to Virupaksha Temple. The rows of single-storey houses in the market were slowly setting up shop. Women of the houses had bathed the roads in turmeric water and were making kolam, although short-lived until the shops opened. The aroma of fenugreek seeds from bubbling hot sambar and M.S. Subbulakshmi's *Suprabhatam* chants set the tone for a perfect morning.

The main market was abundant with homestays. I found a room priced at Rs 600 per night at the house of an old man who had just swept his veranda with a broom. Chang too had a room booked nearby. Craving for breakfast, among the closed shops, we found a lady setting up a dosa stall. She looked old yet tossed the dosas like a sport. A little girl with pigtails helped her collect cash; a handsome amount had been earned at the beginning of the day itself; also, her calculus was brilliant. The sizzle and aroma gathered quite a herd of customers. In taste, it was definitely the fiery podi (also known as 'gunpowder') elevating the flavour of the soft, fluffy dosa. We washed it down with a tumbler full of coffee each and began our day.

The heritage sites of Hampi are spread across the area in clusters. We started from the nearest one, Virupaksha Temple, one of the oldest structures in the area that has stood the test of time.

Groups of tourists kept up with their rushing guides, who explained various interesting scientific facts about the temple like magicians. Unlike the adjoining market, Virupaksha Temple was already bustling with pilgrims and tourists. Hiring a guide was out of my budget, so we chose to follow bigger groups and overhear their guides. The whole time, I kept rolling the camera, so much so that most of the Virupaksha Temple I saw was through the viewfinder. Dodging the crowd and filming the space, I could barely spare myself a moment to take in the beauty of all those intricate carvings.

Looking back

In history, Hampi saw both extremes. It was a crucial standpoint for a lot of historic plot twists.

If you had visited Hampi in the thirteenth century, you'd be assumed to be an offbeat traveller. Roaming around, you might have come across people discussing politics at temples. Most of the stories would have been of the Sangama* brothers Harihara and Bukka and how they were giving it back to the

---

* Shreya Suresh Kumar, 'The Fascinating History and Story of Hampi And Vijayanagara Empire', *India.com*, 19 December 2019, https://www.india.com/travel/articles/the-fascinating-history-and-story-of-hampi-and-vijayanagara-empire-3231767/

powerful Muslim forces of the north. The youth might have been fanboying them.

If you'd visited Hampi in the fifteenth century, it'd be the best trip of your life because you would see the city in its golden days. You'd find yourself at the bazaars bargaining for some fancy item, and traders from around the world would be outbidding each other for a rare stone. If you were an artist or an architect, you would be spoiled. Perhaps you would hear good remarks from the great King Krishnadev Raya[*] himself.

But after 1565, Hampi definitely wouldn't have been a great place to be. The great Vijayanagara Empire, which had its boundaries from the east coast of the peninsula to the west, had collapsed. As a citizen, you'd have either been killed, raped or had to seek refuge in a nearby village with your house in ashes. The allied armies

THE ROYAL EMBLEM OF VIJAYANAGAR EMPIRE

of the neighbouring Deccan Sultanates[†] would have looted everything. You'd experience nothing but extreme panic.

You'd either have to be crazy or a culture-hungry European elite to visit Hampi after the fall of Vijayanagar Empire[‡]. Who would want to visit fallen temples and buildings under the rule of shrubs and creepers?

---

[*] Ibid.

[†] Ibid.

[‡] Ibid.

Today, all these sites, somehow in their restored state, are for public display and standing here even in present times, one can feel both the extremes this place has witnessed in history.

Strangely, when I think of the Vijayanagar Empire, I picture an oriole. In school, while we learnt about the empire, I was distracted by an oriole perched on a tree outside the window. Our school, set in a rice field far from the city, was a place of simple joys: no uniforms, small-sized classes and hands-on learning featuring activities such as farming, cooking and painting the walls.

I was the shortest in class, nicknamed 'bonsai', and I struggled academically. I heard the dreaded phrase 'Indrajeet More, Madam is calling you' on a daily basis. Yet, my fondest memories are of exploring the fields, spotting spiders, finding caterpillar pods and plucking mulberries—anything but studying or sports. This is why I associate an oriole with the Vijayanagar Empire, a white-throated kingfisher with the Boston Tea Party and cattle ploughing with the Rowlatt Act.

That was a lot of history.

* * *

At Virupaksha Temple, I noticed a family staring at us. Their son seemed to be my age or maybe older. I assumed they were staring at Chang since foreigners get that a lot in our country. But then they patted me on my shoulder and, shockingly, spoke in Marathi, 'Aren't you the guy from YouTube? You went to Gokarna in 3000 rupees, right?'

I nodded in surprise; it was the first time I was recognized, that too just after the first episode, and in a place where I didn't expect to find any Marathi-speaking audience. They clicked a photo with me; I wanted to as well, but in that moment of excitement, I simply forgot. I don't remember now, but I am sure I must have blabbered something silly to them. Chang was amazed at my fan following while I pretended to be cool about it, but deep inside it felt extremely special to have met my audience in person for the first time, outside the digital world of likes and comments.

We spent the afternoon sitting at an Israeli cafe and later decided to continue our walk ahead. The temple road ended at a big monolithic bull diverging to a narrow trail through the shrubs. A short walk and we found ourselves at another temple as big as the earlier one; it was the Shri Achyutaraaya Swamy Temple. The delight on the watchman's face showed how deserted the site was. The three of us sat in different corners, lulled by the silence of the echoing void, imagining how each part of this structure was touched by an artist from that time. Would he have known that this Aihole–Pattadakal* styled architecture would last this long, making people aware of the glory of the great Vijayanagar Empire? How much would it have all cost? Was he a devoted artisan or forced labour? Was it a woman? Did he even believe in the god whose representation he was carving out?

---

* Pradosh, 'Hampi, Pattadakal and Aihole', *Bombay Nomads*, 5 September 2011, https://www.bombaynomads.com/cms/2011/09/hampi-pattadakal-and-aihole.html

It was the golden hour of 6 p.m.—Hampi's evenings are as amazing as the afternoons are ruthless. The warm light of the setting sun fell angularly on the temple walls, partially exposing the carvings. Just like the sunset giving it the best light before going down, this city, which had died ages ago, still has some life surviving in its domes, arches and pillars. Will this life thrive again? Or will it diminish over time due to the growing crowd of people scraping the rest of what is left?

On a macro level, each structure resonates the aftermath of a grave conflict among two powers; for one, it was home and a conquest for the other. Hampi kept burning for six months after the allied Deccan Sultanates* ransacked the whole city.

It didn't take much time for the sky to turn dark. The sun set even before I could wrap my thoughts, and it was time to leave.

Day Two, 18 February 2019

Refusal is arguably the hardest of all the diplomacies. Especially when you make eye contact with a vendor who has made up his mind to sell his product to you. It was out of this same feeling that the homestay owner sold me his room yesterday. It had no Internet connection, no mobile network, zero ventilation and no accessible electric charging points. It was a dungeon. Today, I checked out and got a similar room, but a bit less shady, for the same amount. A small, cute gangway of pale-yellow walls partially covered with creepers led to my room. It was all blue

---

* 'Battle of Talikota', *Jagran Josh*, 9 October 2014.
  https://www.jagranjosh.com/general-knowledge/battle-of-talikota-1565-ad-1412077564-1

from within, with a small bed in the corner adjacent to the window. They had Wi-Fi, but it was as slow as a sloth, and the charging points were far from the bed. But, at least, it had good ventilation and colours, and the owner didn't seem like he'd slit my throat if I refused to stay.

By this point, I had also figured out how to make my Rs 3000 budget work. Transfers were covered as production costs, so only my expenses during the three days counted. Transport costs weren't included in the video, which made some people think the budget was a sham. I split my budget to Rs 1000 a day: Rs 300 for food, Rs 500 for accommodation and Rs 200 for public transport. Despite that, I even managed to save a few hundred. In fact, the petty cash Anusha gave me before every trip was never spent. It piled up to a point that I ended up shooting an episode entirely on that money.

Hippie Island

Dosa had become my go-to breakfast by now. Each time, at a different spot. These dosa stalls were opened only in the morning and shut shop by afternoon. A bald man in a lungi folded upwards and his forehead completely covered in sandalwood paste was busy manning his stall and simultaneously making dosas. He was more innovative than the lady from the previous day. Chocolate dosa, egg dosa and banana dosa were some of the fusion items on the menu. He also accepted Google Pay. Foreigners were liking his 'Indian version of crepes'. Making dosas, taking money, clearing tables, complimenting the ladies, chit-chatting with his daily customers and yelling at those occupying the stools—he pulled off all this and much more single-handedly.

While paying him for the dosa, I inquired about Hippie Island. It was then that a French couple offered to join me as they were heading to the same place. The three of us left for Virupapur Gadde, which lies on the other side of the Tungabhadra River. It is known for its flea markets, continental cafes and for having a more chilled-out atmosphere than Hampi. Since alcohol is banned in Hampi, people find booze and a lot more in Virupapur Gadde across the river. This could be the reason why it is also known as Hippie Island, although it is not really an island.

I had heard about these cute little saucer-shaped coracles that take you across the river, but all we could find was one engine-driven boat seemingly older than the monuments around. For a swimmable distance of five minutes, we waited for half an hour until the boat filled and the boatman completed his nap. We were charged Rs 50 even though we all knew that the standard rates were not more than Rs 20. When the passengers complained about the overpriced rates, he shrugged them off in a higher pitch. The problem wasn't just the pricing; it was the derelict attitude of the boatman as a result of having zero competition in the trade—an excellent example of a problematic monopolistic market.

After all the drama, Hippie Island turned out to be a total bummer. It was a long road with a few hostels and boho cafes on one side and paddy fields on the other. A half-naked person with braided hair riding a scooter would pass by you every three minutes. It was a perfect representation of generic hippie culture that you find all across India's major backpacking destinations. It'd make a great place to hang out for a djembe night, but if you are in Hampi, of all places, you would prefer a more essentially Hampi experience. A white guy waved at me from a bakery, and to my surprise, it was the Russian traveller I had met in Gokarna, whose mother had served us tea at a beach shack. I'd always find him lying in the hammock reading an ISKCON book. The French couple hit it off with the Russian fellow, and they decided to join him for a walk to some monkey temple. Where do these white people make their itineraries from?

I, who had lost all interest in the whole Hippie Island sham, returned to explore the other side of Hampi.

* * *

Although every structure in Hampi was built in different time periods, at this point, it all started to look the same to my naive mind. I wasn't expecting much from Shree Vijaya Vitthala Temple either. Being a UNESCO world heritage site, the temple had to be swarming with tourists. The iconic stone chariot structure had cast a long shadow against the setting sun. It was the only place that provided enough shade for me to stand in with my bare feet. There was no corner left by the people taking selfies. The pillars of the temple being hollow from within were constantly patted by the visitors. I badly wanted to stay there, sitting and sketching the chariot, but the guard didn't allow it. He took his job way too seriously, aggressively drawing away the crowds like a shepherd. He first shooed me away, and later, a girl making a TikTok video.

Walking back to the main town was the least boring thing I did today. This hour-long walk helped settle the feeling of disappointment. It was just me all the way and a few langurs staring at me. Most of the rocks scattered around had chainsaw-like patterns. These patterns were formed due to the systematic breaking of these rocks by tools. Hampi is full of rocks, some like these—shapeless, scattered, discarded. Some carved, put together. Some were gods and some . . . some were just rocks.

The sun was on the horizon until I reached the monolithic bull statue. Looking at the blurred silhouette of the temple at the end of the stretch, I simply couldn't move any further. Sitting on the stairs, I waited for the sun to set. The winds and the music of bells and conches from the Virupaksha Temple echoed in the expanse of the plain. The shadows travelled with the setting sun, cooling the rocks. After a day of hassles and the desperation of trying to fit everything in place, I found a moment that could be fully mine. The place had a rhythm of its own, which I discovered for the first time.

I called Aai (my mom) that night. After describing to her the minutest details of the sunset, all she had to ask was if I had eaten or if I was staying somewhere isolated. It wasn't easy for her at first, but she eventually made peace with my constant travelling. Even with the worry, I'm sure she must be a bit proud of me, which she'll cunningly never show. It was a year ago, on the eve of my first trip to Gokarna, when Aai and I had an argument. Except for a few spurs of rebellion, I was mostly at the receiving end. It went on until she said, 'You can go wherever you want, but make sure you don't come back home.' But, the next morning, there were two envelopes lying on my packed bag. They had train tickets for my trip with all the details about the tour packages written down. 'You're a kid—a haphazard one,' she told me. I don't hold on to a lot of things, but if do, she knows how much it matters. This is what I have taken from her—she left home at a very young age to pursue a career in Kathak and still chooses to do what she loves.

Day Three, 19 February 2019

Mathanga Hill

It was pitch dark when I left for Mathanga Hill at 4.30 a.m. The urge to see the sunrise from up above got me walking in the middle of nowhere. The haunting silence and the absence of any humans or even a streetlight made it even tougher. Equally sceptical of climbing in the dark, I spotted a few hikers ahead at the base. Sharing a torch, our sunrise enthusiasts' club began the ascent.

Mathanga Hill was a scary game of Jenga. One pebble out of the place and the whole pile would collapse. Unlike other monuments, this was an artwork created by the winds. Although the boulders of Hampi seem like they've been mindfully arranged, it is the wind and the annual rain that erode these rocks into such shapes. The light faded in softly till we reached the top. Starting to climb early was a good decision. Virupaksha Temple was clearly visible to the west, while Achyutaraaya Swamy Temple to the east, getting back in colour in the morning sunlight.

A soft speck of orange gradually grew into a vast spread of amber, filling the sky and tracing the ochre yellow of the land. The sun with its warm, scattered rays rose from the horizon of Achyutaraaya Temple. By now, we could also see the Tungabhadra River flowing parallel to both the temples. Her banks were the only green patches, predominantly filled with rice fields and dense banana plantations. The majority of the land was just rocks that were turning warm and would heat up in a couple of hours. Huge and endless. On them, colonies of langurs had their territories well defined. In the epic Ramayana,[*] Hampi (then Kishkindha) was the place where Shri Ram assembled an army of monkeys to rescue his abducted wife, Sita. They made it all the way to Sri Lanka and fought bravely. Although having such a legacy, here they were, quarrelling among each other to procreate with the best female of their troop.

* * *

Driving a vehicle in unfamiliar places is a different kind of fancy. Especially if it is a bicycle! The cheapest option that gives you the correct speed to see passing things without crashing. Every turn you take, you find yourself in a new setting. More

---

[*] Ruchi Pritam, 'On the Ramayana trail—Kishkindha at Hampi', *Pragyata*, 6 February 2018, https://pragyata.com/on-the-ramayana-trail-kishkindha-at-hampi/

than navigating, I am excited by the novelty
of discovering new roads, getting lost or
passing through villages. Given the fact
that I almost always travel by public
transport, having your own vehicle
to roam around feels slightly more
empowering. My last day in Hampi
started on a promising note. I
rented a bicycle for just Rs 80 per
day and decided to ride south to
visit the royal enclosure, the nucleus
of the Vijayanagara Empire. By now, I had stopped counting
the temples and had also forgotten their names. I only wished
that I were an assistant to a historian and could live here for
months. I crossed the brilliant Ugra Narsimha sculpture and
the octagonal bath, taking a few breaks at coconut vendors
doing business under the shade of roadside jamun trees. The
road, though empty, felt alive as the sunlight danced through
the swaying banana trees, as ancient temples peeked from the
hillsides and the hum of my bike harmonized with the cool
breeze running through my hair.

After heavy pedalling, I finally made it to the royal
enclosure. The complex had architectural wonders that only
experts could comprehend. I, however, had to assume things
and rely on information boards that, although looked elaborate,
explained something as obvious as, 'Following is the throne
where the king sat. He carried out his daily proceedings here.'
OF COURSE!

I was standing at the place where Vijayanagara emperor
Krishnadevaraya and his ancestors and predecessors ruled
from. It is a pyramid-shaped structure, at a height of roughly

20 metres. A platoon of an army is carved on its sides. The first few blocks have infantry and cavalry on top, and then the elephants. Warriors wielding spears, swords, bows and arrows are carved exquisitely.

Each place I covered, I would film around for a while, spend a minute or two observing and proceed to the next one like a classic tourist.

A path straight ahead led to the great stepwell called Pushkarini, the most geometrically satisfying piece of architecture present there. This inverted pyramid-shaped structure has multiple steps within its primary flight of stairs. Symmetry so precise, it can easily be a location for a Wes Anderson film. The guard there explained to us the efficient system of channels that fill the well with the water from the Tungabhadra River. Looking at the kind of town planning, it seemed that the Vijayanagara kings focused on building temples and public infrastructure. Gazing at these ruins makes one feel a sense of envy towards those Persian and Portuguese travellers in the fifteenth century who got to experience this city at the zenith of its cultural and economic prosperity.

ARCHEOLOGICAL MAP OF
HAMPI

N

TUNGABHADRA RIVER

HIPPIE ISLAND

HAMPI ROAD

TO HOSAPETE

ROYAL ENCLOSURE

INDEX

1. VIRUPAKSHA TEMPLE
2. HAMPI MAIN MARKET
3. HEMKUT HILLS
4. SAASIVEKAALU GANESHA
5. MONOLITHIC BULL
6. SUGREEVA'S CAVE
7. VIJAYA VITTHALA TEMPLE
8. ACHYUTARAYA TEMPLE
9. MATHANGA HILL
10. UGRANARSIMHA TEMPLE
11. LOTUS MAHAL
12. ELEPHANT'S STABLE
13. KING'S THRONE
14. PUSHKARNI

'Free'

As I returned and unlocked my bike, two people came down pedalling towards me, with one of them waving. It was the French couple from Hippie Island. They were in search of food, so I joined them because I was starving too. Since there was absolutely nobody around, we rode a mile till the Kamlapur crossroad but couldn't find anything there either. It was a scorching hot afternoon, and every single shop had its shutter down.

'Oh wait, there's a banana godown right ahead. We can buy a few bananas from them.' I spotted one while noticing a tempo filled with raw bananas being unloaded. We approached the truck, and Anastasia, the girl among the two, asked in her hesitant English if we could get some. I could still remember her name for all I knew by that name was the muscle-numbing drug. 'Who is named after a drug?' I wondered.

One of them pulled out a machete and cut off one banana from his heap.

'No, there are three of us. We want a few more . . . like a dozen,' I said, in a mix of Hindi, English and exaggerated sign language.

'Wait,' the man said, and he went inside.

There was a major communication issue—two French people who couldn't speak English, an awkward Indian who knew no French and a few locals speaking in Kannada. All of us stood there clueless, waiting for the man. In just a moment, he came out of the godown with a bunch of fresh, ripe bananas, cutting off the overripe ones. The cluster must have had at least twenty to thirty bananas hanging. We were trying to explain to him that we only wanted a few of them, and now we had the whole bunch!

'We don't want to buy that much.'
He only understood the word 'buy', to
which he replied.

'No buy . . . free . . . free. Take.'
And gave it to us. We were given
an entire cluster of bananas for
free! That was like lunch for the
three of us. The curious look on
the faces of the French couple
worked, and it took care of a
meal for us. We responded with
wide smiles, and the French made the
namaste gesture as a way of saying 'thank
you'. (They were yet to travel up north to
learn the term *shukriya* for 'thank you'.)

We sat under a jamun tree, relishing each banana. A family
of langurs gathered around their evolved friends. We clearly
had more than we needed; maybe even the langurs knew it.
The next thing we knew, there were seven of us under the
jamun tree savouring the bananas. After we were done, we let
the langurs finish their share and rode back towards the main
market.

In most touristy areas of India, the locals are more likely
to charge extra money from foreigners. But I have witnessed
many such instances where the locals were extremely generous
and warm to the foreigners travelling with me. The hospitality
in such places is rarely a show of boastfulness and instead a
reflection of humility and genuine fondness to feed people.

This mini adventure cost me a seven-minute delay to reach
my bus stop. If I were in north India, I would have to wait
another fifteen minutes for the bus to arrive, but here, I had

to beg my driver, who didn't give two shits of sympathy to my out-of-breath voice. Bouncing my rucksack and dodging angry pedestrians, I finally got into the bus.

* * *

Hampi was a dream, vibrant with colours, aromas and a blend of melodies. The entire trip felt like a meditation, with every sense fully engaged. The vast rocky plateau, the fresh turmeric-scented water sprayed on the ground in the morning, and the aroma of sandalwood and tuberose in the temple sanctums. The temples, both majestic and intricate, appeared tiny from a distance, blending seamlessly into the endless landscape. Timelines coexist here physically, much like how the fertile plains of Tungabhadra merge with the arid plateau.

Yet, I remember Hampi in fragments, mainly the moments spent alone, walking or observing life around me. Much of what I saw is a blur, as I was in a frenzy to capture everything. I overshot the trip, fearing I might miss something. For the first time, I felt a deep disconnect from my work. I love filming places and people, but here it felt like I was rushing to cover as much as possible, quickly moving from one spot to the next. With only three days, I quickly realized that Hampi isn't suited for such a short visit.

Every city has its pace, a rhythm, and if not travelled at that pace, you barely take away anything. I learnt this here. This trip was a rushed attempt to maximize coverage and squeeze out time to let the place sink in. I realized I needed to define my pace of filming and adjust it to that of the place. Filming is the only medium to have a conversation with a non-living place, and to do that with utmost sincerity, you need to let yourself anticipate less and participate more.

FOUR

JAIPUR

Go for the royal, stay for the crazy.

'*Indra, Jaipur la zaanar ka?*' (Indra, will you go to Jaipur?) Avirat sir asked me on a call that day. It had been two weeks since I returned from Hampi. We hadn't met for a long time. You know how you have a few friends whom you rarely catch up with, but every time you do, you have the most real and candid conversations. Avirat sir was one of those friends. I sometimes even doubted whether he, being a successful businessman, passionate teacher and avid photographer, really enjoyed a teenager's company or was he this nice to everybody else. I used to work as a trek leader in Avirat's travel firm, and it was he who introduced me to wildlife and birding. A hostel brand had invited him to Jaipur for a three-day meetup, but since he was busy, I happily took his spot. As I was travelling anyway, I decided to stay back and shoot an episode in Jaipur. Figuring out the logistics at the eleventh hour was a hassle. I hadn't yet learnt to keep things prepared, and instead became a pro at improvising at the last minute.

During the meetup, I had already roamed around half the city, and I believed backpacking here wouldn't be too tough. It is Jaipur after all—the pink city! One-fourth of the world must have visited this place, and two-thirds must have heard of it as 'Jay-pore'. Unlike Gokarna or Hampi, Jaipur was more favourable in terms of accessibility. Since Zostel was the only hostel located in the old city at that time, it was my first option to crash. I just had to carry my luggage for barely a kilometre from one hostel to another.

Day One, 11 March 2019

It was a busy afternoon on the Hawa Mahal road and surprisingly cold for the month of March. Fortified by walls and intricate heritage gates, with honking vehicles swarming through, the old city is an excellent example of how life has found its order amid the chaos of old and new. All the houses within the compound are painted peach, which collectively appear pink, hence the name 'Pink City'. Except for one big road to Amer, passing via Hawa Mahal, old Jaipur is very congested, with narrow lanes having particularly gastronomical names like Jalebi Chowk, Masale ki Gali, etc. Its detailed architecture quite complemented its local life. Shops of leather bags, antiques and textiles added a lot more colour to those historic buildings and carts of gajak and jalebis did their best to add some flavour to its dusty air. Vendors sold beads, tribal puppets and expensive souvenirs on

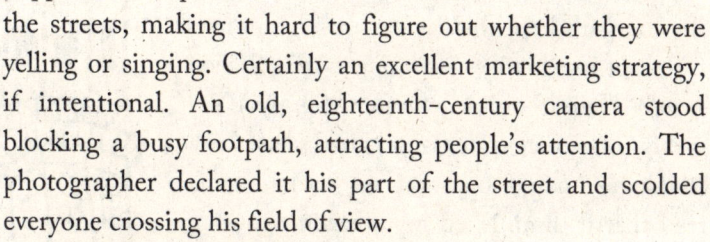

the streets, making it hard to figure out whether they were yelling or singing. Certainly an excellent marketing strategy, if intentional. An old, eighteenth-century camera stood blocking a busy footpath, attracting people's attention. The photographer declared it his part of the street and scolded everyone crossing his field of view.

'Very few companies make film for such cameras. I order mine all the way from France,' he bragged. He took great pride in explaining the functions of his camera to every passerby who stopped and then persuaded them to get their photos clicked for a good Rs 300. Everything about the camera was vintage, except for the photo of Goddess Laxmi tied to it with a rubber band. A camera that old certainly needed the blessings of the goddess of wealth.

All the important monuments are in the city centre. Hawa Mahal, Jantar Mantar, City Palace—everything on the same premises. You can buy one composite ticket for all the places except the City Palace (which is looked after by the Royal Trust of Jaipur). I got an additional student concession on the ticket upon showing my college ID. I realized I'd used my college ID for travelling more than I wore it in my college. I'd agree that more than my philosophy degree, it's my college ID card that's been so useful.

Hawa Mahal was the first monument I visited due to its unavoidable prominence right at the main road. Hawa Mahal or the wind palace* was named for the number of windows it had on all of its five floors. These windows were mainly built for the women of the royal family to watch the festivities happening outside. A solid grill on the edge of the footpath kept the flock of Instagrammers from getting hit by oncoming traffic. If you search '#Jaipur' online, the first thing you see is this. The exact same frame. I had seen Hawa Mahal so many times on my social media feed that it diminished my amazement upon viewing the real thing. This was one of those many experiences diluted by the constant onslaught of visual data on the Internet.

The road perpendicular to the Hawa Mahal road led to Jantar Mantar, an indigenous space observatory. I, being an absolute layman in astronomy, roamed around like a shepherd at a modern art gallery. What amazed me was the tower of Isarlat, a 140-foot-tall victory monument spawned after another civil battle

---

* 'Hawa Mahal', *Rajasthan Tourism*, last updated on 4 May 2024, https://www.tourism.rajasthan.gov.in/hawa-mahal.html#:~:text=The%20five%2Dstorey%20building%20looks,%E2%80%9CPalace%20of%20the%20Winds%E2%80%9D

among the Rajputs.* A mind-spinning flight of spiral stairs
led to the windy top, perfect to capture the whole city in a
timelapse. Right from the main road and the grand City Palace
to the heights of Nahargarh, everything looked like a jigsaw
puzzle, with not a single piece in place yet seemingly complete
as a whole.

City Palace was where I spent most of my time. Being
the private property of the royal family, everything here is
well preserved. Unlike most of the palaces in Rajasthan, this
one hasn't been refurbished into a luxury hotel yet. Most of
the chambers are open to visitors, but the king's and queen's
chambers have a special access that costed pretty much the
entire budget of my trip. The courtyards, spacious and
blooming with flowers, quite evidently display the royal fancy
for strolling.

The darbar (king's court) is a marvel, brimming with
colours. The throne at the centre of this big hall is the same
height as the rest of the chairs, which was a charming shock
to me. These chairs have a distinct foreign design. Maybe
they were a gift from the British, I wondered. On the left of
the throne is a white marble elevation, covered by a dense
net of floral carvings, constructed for the queen to sit and
keep an eye on her husband. Varied patterns on its walls
show the reincarnations that the darbar has undergone over
time. The pillars are Hindu, the windows Islamic, the chairs
colonial and the 'Please do not take selfies' signboards, post-
colonial.

---

* 'Isar Lat', *Tourism of India*, https://www.tourism-of-india.com/isar-lat-or-
swargasuli.html

The Royal Guard

I sat in the courtyard, musing and sketching the beautiful arches and pillars tinted with evening sunlight. An old guard in an elegant black coat, a red turban and a remarkable white moustache caught my attention. He was just a guard, but the way he stood at the entrance made me realize that etiquette was not restricted to class. Unlike your average government caretaker, lousily lounging on his stick and yelling at tourists taking photos, he stood royally and greeted everyone with a light smile. He was as royal as the palace. His demeanour reflected a sense of ownership towards the space. At his age, it was quite evident he's spent a good number of years working here. At one point, he fascinated a group of German uncles by taking off his turban and demonstrating how to wear it. Only in Utopia would anyone do their job this well. As I was leaving, I showed him his sketch that I had drawn a while ago. He flaunted it to his fellow guards. His smile remained one of the souvenirs from this trip.

After spending an eventful day roaming around this city, I could actually experience a part of Rajasthan that goes beyond what Rajasthan tourism sells it as. They have milked *Kesariya Balam* (a folk song) to an altogether 'move on already' level. Talking about moving on, it reminds me of the royal families. The locals here have strong fixations with the royal family. Each of them. And while they talk about it, they make it sound like the prince owes them money from the evening they shared a pyaaz kachori together. In Jaipur though, not everyone is a fan of its royal family, since 1) many Rajput ministers past served in Mughal courts;[*] 2) the princely state of Jaipur accepted East India Company's subsidiary alliance policy[†] and 3) also supported the British in curbing the uprising of 1857.[‡] With this history today, the royal family of Jaipur has their fair share of haters and admirers. But no matter what, I, for one, became an absolute fan of Queen Gayatri Devi while on this trip. She has my heart for being the woman she was. I can go on about her until the last page, but let's just return to our trip. (Please google her later.)

Despite all the internal power struggles, external invasions and politics, the modern generations pay tribute to their ancestors' valour by preserving these monuments like their own family heirlooms.

Day Two, 12 March 2019

Amer and the caretaker lady

'Wake up, dude, we gotta go,' my dorm mate Bruno woke me up. He was a Mexican cinematographer I had met the previous night, and we had decided to visit Amer together.

'Are you going to take a shower?' he asked.

'I don't think so,' I replied sleepily.

'Great. Neither am I. Chop chop,' he rushed.

---

[*] Willy Logan, 'A Not-so-great Great Man: History of Jaipur', *Willy Logan*, 13 September 2016, https://www.willylogan.com/?p=1225

[†] Neha Rajora, 'Cultural Landscapes of Amber, Rajasthan', *researchgate.net*, August, 2013.

[‡] Ibid.

The public bus rattled through dusty roads and dropped us 7 km away at Amer Fort, or Amber Fort, as many people call it, for some inexplicable reason. People are crazy about Amer's main attraction, the elephant ride. They take you up the fort on an elephant to give you that royal Rajput feel, for which you have to  pay some Rs 500–1000. We chose to take the stairs as we were low on budget and too poor-looking for a royal ride. Bruno was in his pyjamas, and my eyes weren't even fully opened.

Seeing a row of elephants marching up the fort, we assumed it was going to be crowded up there. We were right. Flocks of classical European fanny-pack tourists stood blocking every gangway; noisy Indian families rushed everywhere, making sure not a single artefact was left untouched by their frolicking children. Everyone was in awe—some were in awe of the architecture while others were referring in fascination to various Bollywood period films shot at every location here.

Along with Jaigarh and Nahargarh, Amer* too is situated on the heights of the Aravalli hills. The guides say that all three forts are interconnected through secret ways. Once home for the Rajputs, later on, the fort was taken over obviously by the

---

* 'Amer Fort', *tourism.rajasthan.gov.in*, last updated in May 2024, https://www.tourism.rajasthan.gov.in/amber-palace.html#:~:text=One%20of%20the%20top%20tourist,sandstone%2C%20and%20with%20white%20marble

Mughals, as a result of which Amer Fort is a good example of Hindu–Islamic architecture. We were at the harem, where everything was feminine, floral and larger than life. A sweeper woman in the traditional yellow sari smiled at us after random eye contact. She wore a red bindi and bangles of the same colour. Watching all the tourists walking around, she was chatting and giggling with her fellow worker, with a broom in her hand.

'*Aap ki ek tasveer le sakta hu*?' I asked her if I could take a picture of her.

'*Meri? Kyu*?' (Mine? But why?) she asked surprisingly, adding, '*Photo na khicho*', abruptly dismissing. I proceeded to catch up with Bruno.

There was something about her. Not in terms of physical beauty, but something deeper, more intrinsic. It's fascinating how workers at heritage sites are exposed to such diverse cultures. They may not fully participate, but they witness their traditions being observed with curiosity every day. I wonder how that makes them feel. Do they see themselves through this lens of fascination or is their work simply a means to survive? Do they feel distant, as if the significance of their heritage has been diluted by the monotony of routine? The intersection of familiarity and fascination must be a strange place to exist, where something so personal becomes a spectacle for others to consume.

'*Aap ko photu khichni hai na? Aao, ye dekho.*' (You want to click a picture? Come, see this.) The lady with the broom stopped me and led me to a compartment a few stairs below, towards a locked, grilled door. She opened the lock and allowed me to go quickly to have a look. It was a pitch-dark water reservoir.

'*Kya hai yeh*?' (What is it?) I asked. The lady explained to me about the water channels of the fort and how artificial air conditioning was done by circulating wind through cascades full of water all through the structure. It was just a quick sneak peek into a dark room, but still a very warm gesture of hospitality. For that moment, she took so much pride in being my guide, and so did I, for being allowed to see a prohibited place, though just a reservoir.

All the time, it kept me wondering how this monument, or rather a shelter, must have affected the people living in it, that too in a tumultuous age of continuous conflicts. Spaces aren't just walls and roofs; they inspire, impact and quietly evolve us. Although only the royals could afford such grandeur, the fact that they chose this instead of a pale grey block to live in is commendable. I get this exact feeling while roaming across the old parts of every city. Every time I watch the Gothic-style Chhatrapati Shivaji Maharaj Terminus (CSMT) structure in Mumbai while eating vada pav at Aaram across the road, I can't help but think how contrastingly ridiculous Dombivli station, where I alight every day, looks. Walking around the peths of Pune, one can't help but stop and take in the elegant beauty of those quaint wadas. Those houses speak volumes about the people who've lived there. They're worlds apart from the soulless IT hubs on the outskirts.

I don't get the majority of people's fascination towards tall buildings; they look like a 3D printer glitched and keep making a pile of the same design. How have we now become so utility-oriented that we care so less about the aesthetic quotient of any object or piece of infrastructure? Or have the definitions of beauty and aesthetics changed over the course of time? Why do these modern cities look so obnoxious? Just pale blocks of cement and overhead wires we live in. Is it that we no longer afford beauty or do we just not care?

A few years down the road, I might read this and find it naïve. I could be working in one of those glass buildings. Or would I feel the same while looking at the CSMT building from Aaram vada pav across the street. Whatever the case, I'll surely look back on these days as a reminder that while the world shifts, the things that truly resonate stay with us. And maybe that's what keeps us grounded.

* * *

By the time we reached the hostel, everyone was leaving to catch the sunset at Nahargarh. 'Remember the spot where DJ and his friends used to meet in the film *Rang De Basanti*? Yeah, that's where we're headed,' said the hostel volunteer. 'You're right on time! Come with us,' he added. Too excited to care about being tired or not having a shower all day, we joined the group.

Sitting on the fortress and watching the sunset over the Pink City was worth the effort of hiking up to Nahargarh. The orange shade of the sky blended perfectly with the pink of the city. A cricket match was in full swing on a sand dune at the foothills. The distant cheering faded away as it got dark, leaving behind only the whistling of the wind getting colder and colder. None of us knew each other—total strangers brought together by the shared satisfaction of finding a sense of belonging in an unfamiliar place.

Day Three, 13 March 2019

'Hey, Indra, where are you heading?' asked Shyeni, lounging in the common area, on seeing me leave. A flight attendant from Singapore, Shyeni was with us yesterday at Nahargarh. I remember her very well because she was the shortest of all. Her little eyes behind those round brown glasses squinted even more as she smiled widely. She spoke as fast as she moved.

'Hey, Shyeni . . . I am leaving for a walk. Trying out some street food from this list,' I said, showing her the map I got from the reception, and asked, 'Want to join?'

'Wait a moment. I'll just get my purse,' she said, rushing off to get it.

We started off with the India Coffee House,* a chain of cafes from colonial times. Although cafes, these old Indian coffee houses have the ambience of a government office. Noisy fans, shaky chairs and waiters dressed in white uniforms and turbans form the key identity of these places. There, we boosted ourselves with coffee and went ahead to a snack corner for the kachoris.

---

* Karthik Venkatesh, 'A short history of the India Coffee House: Conversation, revolutionary politics and a different way to do business', Firstpost, 13 January 2021, https://www.firstpost.com/art-and-culture/a-short-history-of-the-india-coffee-house-conversation-revolutionary-politics-and-a-different-way-to-do-business-9184321.html

Just like Mumbai has vada pav, Jaipur has pyaaz kachori. If you ask anyone for the best kachori shop, half the people are most likely to suggest Rawat Sweets. We, however, couldn't visit Rawat's and had to settle for the one near India Coffee House. The perfect ratio of pudina (mint) and imli (tamarind) ki chutney was the most remarkable part.

It was the massive lassi after the kachori that made us realize we were full. Shyeni and I shared a ten-inch earthen glass full of lassi at a well-known place called Lassiwala. It is due to this that Jaipur has more than one Lassiwala. As common as its name, the place had no character whatsoever, just like the multiple Lassiwalas across the city—they all look exactly the same! It was only this Lassiwala that had the highest Google ratings. The owner, although not great at marketing, knew how to make damn good lassi. Our lassi moustaches were enough to display our satisfaction.

Wind View Café

It was my last day here. I had covered a considerable part of Jaipur, so I decided to take time and sit sketching at the Wind View Café opposite the Hawa Mahal. I had crossed it plenty of times in the past three days. But today was the first time I observed it in such

detail. Commissioned by Maharaja Pratap Singh and designed by Lal Chand Ustad,* this five-storeyed, terracotta pink building had stood here for hundreds of years, overlooking the ever-changing city of Jaipur.

The gallery at the back of the palace faced the cafe. Its storeys appeared to be of uneven height. It was covered with an eclectic variety of windows: some large, some small, some intricate and some plain. Some of them had tinted glass, while others had wooden flaps. One simply can't help being astounded by the fact such architectural excellence can exist in the most arid of lands.

'That's a beautiful sketch,' commented a lady from the adjacent table, interrupting my train of thought. 'Have you been inside the palace?' she continued.

'Thank you. Yes, I visited it yesterday,' I answered.

'I am planning to visit there tomorrow. I just got done with my work, and I have an extra day to spend. Is it worth the visit?' she inquired.

'Um . . . I don't know. It is as simple on the inside as it is grand from the outside; there are fewer intricacies than you might expect. It has no extraordinary architectural wonders. Yet, it feels like every corner of the palace has a story to tell. It has the appearance of a regular household—only, tailor-made for royalty—simple, elegant and functional. If you're looking for magnificence and splendour, though, it might not interest you,' I rambled, instead of a yes or no answer. Most of it was coming from a silly place of impressing her. I had almost bought

---

* 'Jaipur's Hawa Mahal, an iconic piece of architecture and its history', *Times Travel*, 28 June 2023, https://timesofindia.indiatimes.com/travel/destinations/jaipurs-hawa-mahal-an-iconic-piece-of-architecture-and-its-history/articleshow/101334904.cms

into the romanticism of meeting an older woman at a cafe on a trip. I assume that she enjoyed my long-winded musing since she paid for my chai. It later struck me that we had never introduced ourselves. There is something wonderfully freeing about sharing a piece of our mind with complete strangers. Maybe they go home and wonder, 'What crap was this guy talking about?!' Or maybe not, but such moments feed our curiosity in the most silly ways every time.

Day Four, 14 March 2019

Tatkal

It took us Indians a learning curve to adjust to the railways when it was first introduced by the British. Now, it is one of the biggest public sector industries with an almost cult status. People have online fan clubs for almost every train. Then there are people like me who, despite travelling frequently, have zero idea of how the hell this system works. I was supposed to leave today, but my tickets weren't confirmed yet. Going unreserved is always an option, but at this point, I had grown nauseated of it. Especially while travelling by North Indian railways, a haywire affair.

So, there's this thing called the 'Tatkal quota'. A slot of few seats that only opens twenty-four hours before departure, and only the maestros manage to crack it. There was little scope for me to get a reservation for a train tomorrow, but I decided to stay back in Jaipur for another day and gamble on this opportunity. The slot opens at 11 a.m. sharp on the railways website. I was ready with my form filled out since 10.50 a.m. But how on earth was the Tatkal quota exhausted within nanoseconds of it opening at 11 a.m.? All the seats were booked while I was processing the payment! Establishing a rational society seems simpler than booking a damn Tatkal ticket!

Okay, I failed. What next? Stay back another day and give it another try? It seemed a very stupid choice, as I had only Rs 500 left from my budget. I could have easily gotten some more if I had asked, but I was afraid I might resort to such allowances more often. Besides, on non-righteous grounds, counting the transport and three days of the meetup, I was in Jaipur for a week now and really craving for home. Okay, fuck this, I am travelling unreserved in the same train tomorrow; it's just a twenty-seven-hour journey!

* * *

On an optimistic note, I had a day at my disposal. The first thing I did was go to Wind View Café and complete the sketch I'd left incomplete the previous day. Ah, the satisfaction of a disproportionate sketch! It was just 10 a.m. and I had practically the whole day to kill with nothing more than a 500-rupee note. I remembered meeting a college friend for dinner the previous night and her offer to visit the block printing cottage she worked at as a textile designer. It was in a village called Sanganer, 18 km south of Jaipur. I immediately called Shreya and asked if she was free. She too was bored and happily agreed to show me how the ancient art of block printing is done.

The Cottages of Sanganer

Shreya met me on the highway, right where the bus dropped us. Right there was an eatery, busy with handloom workers, and a filling meal of gatte ki sabzi and roti cost us only Rs 57. You know you are travelling locally when the food rates are this cheap.

'I got these carved yesterday,' Shreya said, showing me a few wooden printing blocks that she had designed. 'Aren't they pretty? These are to be taken for sampling today,' she explained.

Sanganer had no factories or offices per se. All the work was mainly done in the basements of local houses. The printing house we visited was just like any other rural north Indian house—children playing outside with a tyre, a lady drying chillies up on the terrace, firewood stacked up in a corner of the veranda. A separate entrance led us to a dingy room with paint cans and wooden blocks of various designs scattered across. The white fabric pinned to two end-to-end rows of long tables stood out amid the pigment stains. Except for the fabric, of course, every surface in the room was covered in pigment stains. Especially the workers' clothes; there were three of them working on the fabric.

Two workers took a break and attended to us, while one of them continued working. He was operating in a smooth rhythm, dipping the block in pigment and evenly stamping it on the fabric. There was a subtle grace and ease in his action that kept me engaged. One of the workers selected a block from Shreya's collection and started preparing the pigment in a wooden tray as suggested by her. Then he prepared the shade in the tray and placed a net and a soft piece of fabric upon it.

'It is for preventing blocks from collecting excess pigment. So that it doesn't spread,' Shreya explained.

Gently dabbing the block on the fabric in the tray, he placed it on the sheet of cloth, patted hard twice and lifted it after stamping a beautiful maroon floral design. Further, she tried the same design in different colours and then changed the

blocks. She tried stripes, flowers, circles and triangles, finally settling on a specific design. The workers got busy printing it on the vast sheet of cloth.

They kept dipping the block in paint and stamping it onto the sheet until it got filled with the pattern. All three workers worked in harmony. They were following a rhythm; none of them rushed or skipped a beat. This reminded me of the scene in the film *Modern Times*, where Charlie Chaplin goes in a loop of tightening bolts. I continuously hummed a melody in my mind to their beats of printing.

Coming to Sanganer through a dusty road and catching an allergy was absolutely worth it. I wanted to film the whole process, but the locals were not comfortable with the camera, so I had to enjoy it for myself.

* * *

At the hostel, after winning two rounds of chess and losing five, I realized it was too late for dinner. On the empty cold streets, luckily, there was this one place open, running on full capacity. A big tandoor at the entrance, and marinated chicken hung up on skewers looked tempting. The waiters were rapidly taking orders, and the cooks rushed too. I could see no tourists around, only the shopkeepers, drivers, workers and vendors . . . And some adaptable outsiders like us. In no time, I had a plate of tandoori chicken on my table, served with pudina chutney and onion dipped in vinegar. I ate like there was no tomorrow. It wasn't the best tandoori chicken, but it was enough to kill my hunger.

Disaster

Coming back, I crawled inside my sleeping bag and slept as early as possible, in preparation for the hectic journey back home tomorrow. As I was broke, Akash, the hostel manager generously let me crash in the common area. Around 1 a.m., a terrible pain in my upper abdomen shook me awake. Sweaty and suffocated, I unzipped my sleeping bag and got out. The pain grew worse, and I started to feel the uneasiness travel through my chest and up my throat.

Akash and the hostel cook were sleeping on the couches next to me. I got up as quietly as possible, so as to not wake them up, and rushed to the washroom to hurl the contents of my stomach down the drain. I was afraid I'd pull out my intestines with only bones and pale muscles left inside my body.

I collapsed onto the cold floor. 'Son, you have gotten food poisoning,' I said to myself. It was definitely the tandoori chicken! For sure! A 'Delhi belly' is the last thing you want on your solo trip. Usually, it only happens to foreigners. Throwing up took so much of my energy that I couldn't move. The washrooms and the common area were on the far ends of the hostel. Covering that distance was an excruciating task. I gathered the strength to reach into my backpack only to find out that there was no medicine for food poisoning in the first-aid kit! 'How am I supposed to travel tomorrow? That too, without a reserved seat? Will I have to stay back another day? I should have stayed hungry all night rather than eating the damn tandoori chicken!' All I wished was to be at home. But there was no home now; I had to deal with it on my own. I prayed that it would be my last throw-up and that I could go back to sleep in peace, but I ended up making three more trips to the washroom that night. I will never forget that washroom, ever—each and every tile, the measurements of the hand spray, even the Pantone shade of the sink's colour. It was a nightmare!

Day Five, 15 March 2019

Things got under control around 5 a.m. From 5 a.m. to 7 a.m. was the only time I got some sleep. After I woke up, the pain was gone, but I had no energy left. It was going to be a big risk to travel alone in this situation. But then there was no point in staying back either. I managed to get myself together and leave for the railway station.

There was another traveller who had to catch the same train, except she had a confirmed ticket. We decided to share a cab to the railway station. Everything was fine until then, but then something happened in the car. Now, I have a big problem with travelling in a car with the windows shut and the AC on full blast. I felt as ill as I did the previous night. In a panic, I asked the driver to stop the car and got off midway. The other traveller went ahead. I threw up again under a flyover and sat on a bench with everything around me revolving. I couldn't see anything. It took me ten whole minutes to get back to reality. I felt as light as a thin strand of hair on a feather after throwing up. It was mainly because of the car and also because I hadn't eaten any breakfast. I fed myself a cup of chai and a few biscuits (which were the most hygienic food items nearby). I had the choice to go back to the hostel, but I still wanted to catch the train. In fact, more desperately to go home. Putting on my backpack, I started walking towards the station.

Unreserved

Although I was an hour early, the train was at the platform (since it departs from Jaipur itself). It was already full, including the reserved compartments. Not only the seats, but the gangways were occupied too. I tried negotiating with the TC.

'You see these people?' he pointed at a bunch of folks standing, looking at him with puppy faces. 'They all want a seat. You see the crowd? Impossible!' He brushed off my plea like a ruthless zilla officer.

Seeing a huge load on my back, out of nowhere a guy showed up and offered to share his seat with me. '*Dono bhai saath jayenge,*' (The two bros will travel together) he said cheerfully. All the way, he kept telling me about his endeavours in search of work in Mumbai and celeb-spotting in his free time. He got off somewhere at midnight, and a family showed up

there later. I continued my journey to Mumbai sitting on the corner of a berth and fortunately not throwing up again.

* * *

I was supposed to stay in Jaipur for not more than three days. But after spending a week there, I can certainly say that the energy of the city is contagious. What makes Jaipur the best city to visit is the spectrum of madness. One can find contrasting qualities of royalty and crazy here. Among the people, there is a sense of pride, irrespective of class. They are enthusiastic to get to know you and also share about themselves. They can be reserved most of the time but are also conveniently trendy about several things. I kid you not, I had an autorickshaw driver greet me with, '*Khamma ghani*, bro.' I say this having only explored the touristy part of the city, but to venture into the core life of Jaipur would certainly be an adventure to document, I would imagine.

Jaipur, just like its markets, is a flavourful ride. This trip remains a key highlight of all my travels, due to its fair share of happy and sad accidents. All the time, weirdly, I could relate more to the foreign tourists than Indian ones. I couldn't cross roads, eat spicy food, was easily excited to see the local puppet dance, used the word 'local' several times and even got food poisoning! It was a tough trip behind the zestful video. Of course, the anxiety of shooting every experience remained, but more than that was the satisfaction of not pretending or trying to make it happen. I had made peace with the fact that this anxiety will continue for a few more travels. At least, until I found a balance between documenting and gathering experiences.

FIVE

RISHIKESH

You won't find it if you look for it.

I had planned Rishikesh only because it was easier to loop in with my trek to Chopta. Exactly a day prior to this trip, I was hiking in the snowy peaks of Tungnath, Uttarakhand. It was my first-ever Himalayan trek with a lively group of nine fellow travellers. We returned to Haridwar the previous

night, and the next morning, the group
left for Dehradun to board their train
to Mumbai, dropping me somewhere
on the highway intersecting with
Rishikesh. From here onwards, I
had to continue my trip solo.

With two bulky backpacks weighing me
down, I waited on the Haridwar highway for
a lift up to Rishikesh. I had asked my friend
to take one of my backpacks home, but
expectedly, he forgot. The down jacket that
saved me over the last ten days was now
the heaviest of my luggage. The gruelling
eight-hour bus ride from freezing cold to scorching heat
only amplified my exhaustion. Sleep-deprived and famished,
all I yearned for was to take off my wet socks and rest my
weary feet.

These discomforts, though bearable during the trek, now
seemed magnified in the absence of familiar faces and the
contrasting environment. I couldn't help but feel a sense of
hollowness, a mental numbness within, hindering my ability
to function optimally. It took a moment of self-convincing to
gather the necessary motivation for what lay ahead.

Unsettling the dust, an army truck rattled past and stopped
a few metres ahead. One of the cadets offered his hand to
pull me up the convoy. It dropped me at the city's outskirts,
and then a biker offered me a ride up to Tapovan. Unwilling
to travel alone, my mind kept returning to the memories of
Chopta, particularly those of *her*.

Day One, 19 May 2019

Rishikesh, with its remarkable mythological significance, has served as the resting place for pilgrims on their Char Dham Yatra for thousands of years. Today, it is famous among backpackers and mainstream tourists as the yoga capital* of the world. Especially its northern region, Tapovan, where the rapids of the Ganga meanders forming a slip-off slope. (No surprise, it is called the Goa Beach.) That is where all the yoga ashrams are, from the most primitive one to a seven-star luxury retreat. Everyone comes to Rishikesh seeking spiritual enlightenment. They serve one for every wallet here. Well, given the short duration of my trip and perpetual fixation towards superficiality, I highly doubted attaining one.

It was already mid-May, and we wanted to put out a new episode in the next ten days. Hence, Rishikesh seemed a more feasible option. The call was driven primarily by the need for convenience. But there was another much sillier reason behind choosing Rishikesh. I, having been recently exposed to 1970s rock music, geeked out on the trivia that the Beatles had come here in 1969 to learn meditation. Now, although I wasn't even born back then and don't know exactly why I would reminisce about the nostalgia of the Beatles coming to India, I still chose to ride on that wave. Trust me, it was just a phase.

My first encounter after coming to Rishikesh was with the Beatles themselves. As I wandered through the congested lanes along the riverbank, a stroke of luck led me to a Beatles-themed cafe tucked away amid the bustling crowd. While

---

* 'Rishikesh', uttarakhandtourism.gov.in, https://uttarakhandtourism.gov.in/destination/rishikesh#:~:text=Rishikesh%20is%20commonly%20referred%20to,to%20learn%20yoga%20and%20meditation

finding accommodation was important, my growling stomach reminded me of my true priority—food. Having journeyed on an empty stomach since morning, my hunger had reached its peak. I opened the menu and realized it was an obvious tourist trap: Led Zeppelin Pizza, John Lemonade, George Hamburger and Pesto McCartney Pasta. That, some photo frames of the band and the *Sgt. Pepper's Lonely Hearts Club Band* album on repeat, was the extent of their cafe's Beatles theme. Unsure of what these dishes would taste like, I stuck to familiar flavours, ordering a bowl of Parmesan Alfredo Pasta. Trying hard to ignore the pretentiousness of the cafe ambience, I looked outside at the curve of the rapidly flowing Ganga. A set of foreigners basked at the shore reading, while some others practised yoga asanas. I took the first bite of my pasta and was convinced about why they tried so hard to sell their below-average food. It did the job though, as the cafe was almost full. It attracted the kind of travellers that John Lennon described in his song 'Imagine', me included.

Tapovan

Walking is probably the only feasible option in Tapovan because the lanes are too narrow and crowded for vehicles to easily pass through. However, even walking can get a bit tiresome due to the steeply inclined roads already jammed by hordes of selfie-clicking families. Especially the Laxman Jhula, which is an old and frighteningly shaky suspension bridge

connecting both the banks. It is so narrow that if an adamant cow decides to sit in the middle, the whole city comes to a standstill.

At 4 p.m., I hastily dumped my luggage at a decent hostel nearby and set out to take a stroll across the bazaar. I promised myself not to rush, as this was going to be my day to unwind. But hurrying was inevitable because I was at the wrong place to try and slow down.

I could barely see anything for more than three seconds as someone would cross my path and the next scenario would be completely different. Like the time when I got stuck in a whirlpool of people and ended up in the middle where a bald monk was dancing, cheerfully chanting 'Hare Krishna' and simultaneously strumming his guitar. Every dodge in the crowd revealed a different visual.

A long, congested stretch with souvenir shops, a money exchange agency, a cafe and a tattoo studio repeating in the same order ran alongside the riverbank. Walls were filled with posters selling yoga sessions and massage services. Reiki, zen, mindfulness, Ashtanga yoga—you name it, they had it. The majority of the shops sold gems and other precious stones. Shopkeepers claimed to sell you the purest gems and Rudraksha beads to make your life better.

'Oye, come! See, gems! I give you the most authentic Rudraksha. A better life, good life. Wealth and good sex life,' they yelled.

'My friend, try this ring, and you do sex like bull!' I overheard a shopkeeper telling an intrigued foreigner. Every other absolute stranger will walk up to you and very convincingly address you as 'my friend'.

Exactly opposite this was the other side of the river. The markets here displayed a calm and rather less desperate approach to doing business. I had a lot to talk about, yet, at the same time, didn't feel like engaging in any conversation. They sold comparatively niche things here: harem pants, yoga mats, singing bowls, bamboo toothbrushes and an abundance of books on Indian topics that fascinated 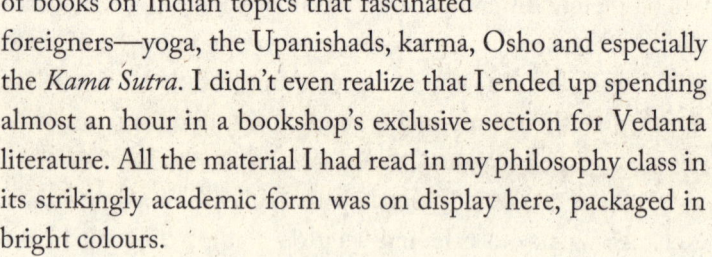 foreigners—yoga, the Upanishads, karma, Osho and especially the *Kama Sutra*. I didn't even realize that I ended up spending almost an hour in a bookshop's exclusive section for Vedanta literature. All the material I had read in my philosophy class in its strikingly academic form was on display here, packaged in bright colours.

I ended my long, aimless walk at a little shanty that was a Tibetan cafe. Sitting there all by myself, I felt as though I'd been doing this for years. Like a mundane routine. I've been on many solo trips before, some much longer than others. But I have never once felt lonely on any of those trips. On this one, however, I felt strangely left out. It was ironic to feel like an outlander in this supposed spiritual homeland that seemed to welcome and nurture everyone else.

Subconsciously, I kind of knew the reason behind this Shakespearean melancholia. It wasn't just the fatigue of trekking in Chopta but rather a longing that intensified it. It's surprising how you can know someone for years, yet, in a different setting, they reveal an entirely new side. That's exactly what happened with Vedika, my high school senior, who joined our trek unexpectedly. Suddenly, every memory of Chopta was intertwined with her presence.

In school, we barely crossed paths. My most vivid memory of her was during an annual gathering when she performed a solo dance to ABBA's 'Thank You for the Music'. She was centre stage in a flowing white gown, moving with such grace, while I, along with others not chosen for any performances, stood behind her in black, holding shimmery musical note cutouts.

She'd seen an Instagram story I posted and decided to join the trek. Not that we spoke a lot there. However, among the entire group, the moments I spent with her stood out the most. There was no instant romantic spark or butterflies in the stomach, but an unspoken connection began to form. Our conversations carried a quiet ease. We both saw snow for the first time, but the childlike wonder in her eyes made the experience even more magical. Without her, I might not have noticed half the things I did on that trek.

I've never really embraced the idea of a travel romance. Mostly because I rarely meet solo travellers my age, and since you might not meet again, there isn't much to look forward to. (I realized its perks much later.) But here, the possibility of seeing her again back home made everything feel different, almost inevitable.

On the last day, while the group had gone out to birdwatch for Himalayan monals, we decided to spend our evening on the campsite. Burying our hands in our down jackets, we went for a stroll down the meadow towards a thick growth of deodar. The crisp sounds of pine cones cracking beneath our feet guided us in our direction. A gigantic root next to a stream became our bench, where we sat until it got dark. Playing each other's favourite songs segued from cautious talking to a long, shared silence. Watching her lay down on the earth, spreading her curly hair amid the foliage of rhododendrons, I asked myself, 'Do you want to address it?' And on that very instance, I dismissed the idea and let the moment unfold itself. This was one of the rarest moments of getting to feel familiarity in another person's presence.

The next day on the bus, as the mountains started to disappear in the sky, we had a talk.

'Was it for the mountains?' she asked.

'I really hope not . . . I really wish to see you again in the city,' I expressed.

'I am not the one going to Rishikesh,' she smirked, and coyly added, 'I shall wait for you.'

This was all kind of corny and new to me. The next morning, after Vedika left, I turned to my heavy luggage and realized how utterly lonely it would be to not see her for at least another five days. My time spent with her was exactly everything I had yearned for. I have heard that first love is outrageous, mad and whimsical, but all I felt was a sense of familiarity and being grounded.

Without even having enough time to process it, I was on my way to Rishikesh. A restless urge to hold her hand surged within me as I walked through the lanes of Tapovan. My palms remained cold in the pockets of my down jacket. As the day passed, it became increasingly evident that this wasn't just a fleeting encounter; I had never experienced such feelings before. Increasingly, I could feel a cold hollowness within, and it got heavier to walk.

The absurdity of experiencing love and longing at the same time.

Day Two, 20 May 2019

The hostel I was staying at was more lifeless than a post-lunch break government office. Travellers lounged in the common area, the lethargic receptionist sank in his chair pretending to be busy, bookshelves were shabby, Jenga blocks spread all across a rough carrom board with its strikers missing and the activity board looked more like an investigation wall from a crime drama. A less boring accommodation had to be found.

Surfing through the maps, I found one just a stone's throw away from the riverfront. It boasted a charming courtyard that doubled as an open-air cafe. Hari, a seemingly twenty-year-old local lad with an infinite amount of curiosity, checked me in. 'How did your parents let you travel this far?' 'How much do you earn?' 'Where all have you been?' His questions kept bombarding me. He referred to all the foreigners as 'Bro' and all the Indian travellers as 'Bhaiji'. I never saw him addressing any girls, though. Besides, there were barely any female travellers in that hostel.

The dorm room upstairs was a proper architectural malfunction—a Picasso painting brought to life in three dimensions. Very unlike its photos online, there was just one big floor sporting a weird combination of warm colours. A couple cuddled on one of the unorganized beds. My assigned bed sat inconveniently in the middle of the room, strategically devoid of any charging points. Next to it was a corner that served as a dumping ground for lost and found items: T-shirts, deodorants, tobacco packets, rolling papers, yoga mats, undies, bras, sunscreen and ample copies of *Shantaram* and *Lonely Planet* guides. I might as well have found an abandoned toddler if I'd dug deeper. The mess, however, gave the hostel its character—a

no-nonsense backpacker vibe.
It wasn't looking to please
anyone—no fake travel
quotes, no grungy bulbs
on rope hanging down a
wooden log, no 'Hi sir,
we are having a curated
street food tour for Rs 2800'

or 'Scan this QR code to access our in-house menu'. AND it
only cost Rs 250 per day!

'White water river rafting'

I was running dreadfully late, and the sun seemed determined
to scorch me at 10 a.m., as if it had mistaken itself for a blazing
midday inferno. Today's agenda included the highly sought-
after white water river rafting adventure, followed by the iconic
Ganga aarti. River rafting is such a big deal in Rishikesh that
one simply can't say, 'I went to Rishikesh but couldn't find
rafting anywhere.' No matter which road you're on, you will see
a jeep carrying rafts and participants (either dry or drenched)
passing by every two minutes.

As I signed myself in, I found myself thrust into an
interesting dynamic—a lone stranger among a group of five
towering, fat friends, seemingly in their early thirties hailing
from Delhi, or maybe Haryana, I'm not sure. They were, to say
the least, loud. Imagine frolicking teenagers, but bigger. And
with beards.

We were transported a few kilometres on the outskirts,
where the river was shallow enough to get our raft afloat. One
of the guys flaunting flashy rings and chains of gold took upon

himself the task of being the backbencher of the club. He heckled the instructor while he was briefing us on the safety rules. The very nature of these people is the reason why I look at group trips with a tinge of scepticism. The band of hot dogs, in their confining life jackets and wobbly helmets, was prepared to face the rapids. On our instructor's commands, we advanced our pedals in synchronization!

'Team, pedal forward on my count! One . . . and two!' he yelled from behind.

The raft gained speed after sliding down from an elevation and drifted according to the rapidly flowing river through massive porous rocks. The group suddenly went silent after we hit our first rapid in a quick jerk. Soon after the first rapid, we hit the second and third one too. I, rowing at the front, was the first one to face the splashes. Within seconds, our raft started spinning on a swift rapid, making all our attempts to set it in a direction futile.

The group, no matter how scared, was having a blast. I was rowing, but not a hint of adrenaline coursed through me. Their enjoyment was starting to irritate me. All I wanted was to rip off the life jacket, dive into the river and swim downstream to bask silently on a sun-soaked rock. Instead, the sun's rays so pierced my skin that I was barely able to breathe in that life vest. Every moment, I couldn't shake the feeling that I was in the wrong place.

Further ahead, at a rocky patch, our raft halted with several others. The spot was overly crowded. Rafts were parked just like the taxis outside Dadar railway station in Mumbai. Amid this frenzy, a little shop became the epicentre of all activity. A massive crowd practised the mandatory ritual of devouring Maggi noodles and chai. Cigarette butts filled up the pores of the rocks. Women yelled at their kids at the highest frequencies. Selfie sticks were pulled out, and people with their soggy limbs sticking out of their neon orange life jackets queued to jump off rocks. Everyone passionately played their part to ruin whatever tranquillity was left. It was no longer a natural ecosystem; it had become our very own amusement park. I chose to take a nap in the raft while the others in my group joined the ruckus. A crowd of high-testosterone Delhi tourists was certainly not my idea of a serene escape. Yet, there I was, right in the midst of it all, desperately seeking escape.

I feel travelling and vacation are two different things. Both are valid but sometimes, we find ourselves in situations we never anticipated, surrounded by individuals whose energy clashes with our own. It is quite necessary to be aware of the kind of choices we make in our travels, otherwise we end up ruining it for those who have come with clear distinctions of the two.

* * *

It took me a bowl of thukpa and an hour at a quieter cafe to wash away my weariness. Thukpa and momo have become my comfort food now. My second day of the trip was almost spent, and even today, the notion of being in Rishikesh seemed elusive and distant. It honestly didn't feel like I was in Rishikesh at all.

I attended the evening Ganga aarti in the sheer absence of my senses. I could hear the reverberating sounds of the melodies. The lamps swung by the priests faded with the distant lights of the Laxman Jhula, appearing as specks of yellow circles growing bigger. I found myself back home, cosy in bed or at the office, immersed in ruthless editing. I was simultaneously collecting rhododendrons in the valleys of Chopta and roasting marshmallows by a campfire. Throughout the day I fought my urge to text Vedika, although I wasn't sure what I should share with her. I wished she was there with me. I wondered how she would be feeling about this. Would she be missing me? Would it be too much for me to tell her how I feel?

It was a novel feeling, and I lacked the tools to deal with it, for nobody has really talked about the loneliness that comes with travelling. Everything felt so out of touch that I doubted my very desire to travel.

Day Three, 21 May 2019

Hey Jude

On my last day, I decided to cover just the Beatles Ashram. Being economically feasible, it was the only thing left to visit.

In 1968, two of the Beatles, George Harrison and John Lennon, had visited Rishikesh.[*] They stayed at an ashram called Chaurasi Kutia to learn Transcendental Meditation (TM) from Maharishi Mahesh Yogi. Later, Ringo Starr and Paul McCartney joined them too, and the place became less Chaurasi Kutia and more a sensational Beatles Ashram.

Shivering in the cold, I left for the Beatles Ashram at 7 a.m. All the shops were closed and only yoga sadhaks walked barefoot on the empty streets. Gradually, the shops started disappearing, dusty trails replaced concrete roads and the trees grew dense. On the other side of Laxman Jhula, 3 km in the woods, I was in the Rajaji National Park territory. The trail grew narrower, ending up at a big, closed gate with 'Chaurasi Ashram' painted on it and a board that read 'opens at 10 a.m.'.

I was two hours early! I should have checked the timings before leaving. Unwilling to wait for another two hours, I decided to gamble on some cheap adventure. So, this big, bold gate, hysterically, had an equally poor fence. Walking a few metres ahead in the shrubs, I somehow managed to sneak in through a shattered opening. Honestly, it felt great! I remembered Werner Herzog, a legendary German documentary filmmaker. He was once asked what technical skills film students should be taught, and he replied, 'It should mostly be lockpicking and forging shooting permits.' The thrill of jumping a fence and the joy of saving Rs 150 easily surpassed yesterday's rafting experience.

Although an ashram, the place had all the vanity for its Western practitioners. Once a big buzz in the media,

[*] David Chiu, 'The Beatles in India', *Rolling Stone*, 14 February 2021, https://www.rollingstone.com/feature/the-beatles-in-india-16-things-you-didnt-know-203601/

Chaurasi Kutia was now in shambles. Creepers cracked open through the walls, doors were broken and window panes were shattered. It looked like an ambitious private project rundown by environmental activists.

The only thing keeping the Beatles Ashram interesting was the graffiti. The ruins of the ashram were home to some intensely bizarre murals. Psychedelic motifs and lyrics of popular Beatles songs were used in prominence. Trails covered in foliage wandered through domes and arches flashing vibrant typography. The shattered state of the ashram did not even remotely radiate spirituality, but an eerie hypnotic enigma could be sensed in its air. The wall art, although already seen on Instagram posts from all possible angles, gave the place a pop culture charm. An art form easily dismissed as vandalism in public spaces had repurposed the entire establishment, giving it a new identity. A rare occurrence of unfiltered beauty in chaos. More like an archival photo used for typography practice. The graffiti on those rustic walls had signatures of their artists; would they have known they'd co-created the piece with time itself?

The place was a testament to the enduring power of art and its ability to transcend generations. Despite that, I curbed my urge to click any pictures immediately. I'd already seen so much of the Beatles Ashram on social media that there was barely any intrigue left for this place. What social media does to travelling (or rather any sublime human experience) is basically what porn does to sex.

As I circuited the place, it got crowded in no time, and I took it as my cue to leave.

* * *

I had spent one third of my day at the Beatles Ashram. The walk, as magical as it was in the morning, was dehydrating while returning. I had half a day left for my thirteen-day Uttarakhand trip to end.

I was parched, sleep-deprived, my feet were sore, and I could barely turn my neck to the left. It felt like I had been living in Rishikesh for years. I had never wanted to go home this badly.

'Why didn't I come here before?' I said to myself as I checked into Moustache Hostel. It had everything I'd wanted—a good cafe, cosy beds and happening company. A group of foreigners sat chatting at the desk and heckled the receptionist; a dog came running, fiddled around my feet and then chased me all the way to my dorm. Interestingly, all the bunkbeds had curtains for privacy. It was good in a way, but it also made the dorm look like a low-key brothel (I have only seen brothels in movies). After settling in, I joined other travellers on the terrace. Although there were tables and chairs out on the lawn, everyone preferred laying on the grass itself. Mellow acoustics filled the ambience. An Irish traveller cut a watermelon for all of us; he introduced himself as a falconer, or someone who trains falcons for hunting.

'But hunt what?' one of us asked.

'Anything, bro . . . snakes, pests . . . other birds,' he replied, adding, 'I mainly train them. And sometimes take them to guard farms and vineyards.'

Nobody remembered his name; we all called him the falconer.

Finally, it was just four of us and everyone else had slowly left. Cigarettes were lit, and subsequently, I too got up to find my own corner. The sun had set, leaving its soft haze on the horizon. From the terrace, the bustling city and the distant aarti seemed so tiny in contrast to the tranquil Ganga.

It felt like I hadn't visited Rishikesh at all. In fact, I didn't even know what about this trip would stay with me, except maybe the yearning. I couldn't resonate with the feelings most people experience here. Looking back now, I can see things more objectively, but during my entire time there, I felt guilty for not feeling spiritual enough.

I constantly moved from cafe to cafe, exchanged seats and hopped accommodations, but the unsettling feeling of not finding joy kept gnawing at me. It made me question whether I truly enjoyed my work. Despite my best efforts to focus on filming, even that felt uninspiring. The shoot was so dull and dry that I couldn't even watch the entire video. The last three days were an odd mix of rush, haste, boredom and hollowness.

All I wanted was to finish my trip, wrap up my work, and race back to Vedika. I kept daydreaming about taking her back to the mountains, where it all began. It felt naive, maybe even a bit irrational, but my feelings for her deepened with each passing day. As I sat with those emotions, I realized that this was the first time I had felt such intensly for someone. If we hadn't parted ways, I might not have realized this. We could have spent two more days together on the train, met up the next day and carried on as if nothing had shifted. But the time apart revealed something deeper. It wasn't just the allure of the mountains. We truly liked each other, and there was something

worth exploring between us. Those three days
of unexpected distance finally gave way
to a quiet certainty that evening. A
belief in the present and a hope for
whatever lay ahead.

That night was the quietest
time I found in the entire trip. I
could see people cheering, traffic
booming and the Ganga aarti at
its crescendo, but I couldn't hear
anything. All I could feel was the
crisp air caressing my dry, dusty skin. The chaos of Rishikesh
from that distance appeared to have finally gone into sync.

As soon as I landed in Mumbai, I received a text from
Vedika. She had been called back to her college and had to
spend almost a week in a remote village for a medical camp. Six
more days of dreadful waiting.

SIX

DHARAMSHALA

Lofty peaks and rosy cheeks

On 7 October 1950, Chinese forces surged into the city of
Lhasa, the capital of Tibet.* The high-altitude region that
remained closed for foreigners for several years was destroyed
by the People's Liberation Army of China. Tibet was no longer
a free country; it was made a part of the People's Republic of
China. The peaceful Buddhist country of Tibet turned into a
burning centre of discontent. Monasteries were demolished,
scriptures were destroyed and several monks set themselves
ablaze on the streets. The religious and political leader of Tibet,
the 14th Dalai Lama, had to flee to India.

In 1959, His Holiness the 14th Dalai Lama, along with
80,000 Tibetan refugees, came to India. The then prime
minister of India, Jawahar Lal Nehru, offered him political
asylum and provided support in setting up refugee colonies.†
The office of the Government of Tibet in Exile was set up in
the high altitude region of Dharamshala, Himachal Pradesh,
giving means of livelihood to the Tibetan refugees. Today,
Dharamshala is also known as Little Lhasa.

My trip to Dharamshala happened out of this intense
urge to explore the mountains again after Uttarakhand, but
this time alone. Unlike Rishikesh, I was extremely pumped up
and highly certain about this trip. It was going to be my first
time travelling solo in the mountains, and I could possibly get
to camp as well. All the research was done beforehand, and a
rough, flexible itinerary was made. Three days are not enough

---

* Jamyang Norbu, 'Tibet in India: A people's history of the Tibetan resistance',
  Frontline, 22 July 2023, https://frontline.thehindu.com/books/tibet-in-india-a-
  peoples-history-of-the-tibetan-resistance-book-excerpt-echoes-from-forgotten-
  mountains-by-jamyang-norbu/article67094048.ece
† Ibid.

for a trip in the mountains, but for a working person who cannot afford a long holiday, this was a perfect plan.

Disaster

It was the beginning of June, and as usual, the trains were fully booked. Braving the unbearable Indian summer heat and unhygienic railway compartments, I survived the thirty-plus-hour journey from Mumbai to Chandigarh in a cramped general bogey. Yes, after all that happened in Jaipur, I still had the nerve to travel without a reserved seat.

On the same day, I had to catch a bus late at night from Chandigarh. It was going to take another sleepless night in a bus to reach Dharamshala. Till then, I had seven hours to spend in Chandigarh. I was continuously sneezing, my eyes were watery and irritated and my nose had turned red; I had caught a dust allergy on the journey. Crashing in a hotel room seemed like a wise decision, rather than spending seven hours at the bus stand and making my dust allergy worse. I had many things planned, including a long trek in the coming three days, and falling ill was the last thing I wanted, so I preferred to be safe.

I found a cheap room for Rs 500 somewhere, though not very close to the bus stand. It was super shady, like the ones they show in *Crime Patrol* (a popular Indian TV show based on real-life crimes) after the victim's sex tape is leaked all over the Internet. The room was bright pink, and the walls cracked. There was the usual Medimix soap placed on the washbasin, a photo frame of Kajol and Shah Rukh Khan in a tulip field hung asymmetrically and the towel provided had a yellow spot on it.

But at least it had a working AC and a cosy bed—not really cosy, but at least a bed. I was more than happy. Nearby, I could see just one shop at a corner selling chole puri. The cook was sweating profusely, and the oil he was frying the puris in was darker than its vessel. I chose not to use my backpacker instinct here and settled for ordering a Subway sandwich for lunch. I have been judged for saying Subway is my go-to meal in any place while travelling.

I was so tired that I don't remember when I fell asleep. I guess it was soon after lunch, around 3 p.m. Having absolutely no track of time, I woke up due to the constant ringing of my phone. I had seven missed calls from an unknown number. When I called back, an irritated voice yelled,

'*Bhai, kithe ho? Bus aa gayi si.*' (Bro, where are you? The bus has arrived.) It was the bus driver. I checked the time and it sent chills down my spine. It was exactly 1 a.m.! I had slept for around ten hours! Everything he was saying on the call was so hard to process, due to my waking up in shock, still being sleepy and panicking. I pleaded with him to wait for me, but he had made up his mind. Seven missed calls had hurt his ego, and he left after cutting my call with, '*Sirji, ab toh gedi na rukegi.*' (This bus won't wait any longer.) And the bus left without me.

The whole point of resting before an overnight journey was lost. I had missed my bus, and I was sitting in the hotel room in panic, with my hands and feet cold. After a quick breakdown, I checked for the next bus, which was straight after twenty-four hours. I was stuck in Chandigarh for another day.

Frustrated, the whole night I was awake; I had already spent all day sleeping. There is nothing worse than knowing you've missed your bus and not being able to do anything about it, except sit staring at your phone. It all happened due to the hectic rail journey. Extending the stay, food and booking a new bus ticket cost Rs 2000. It cost Rs 800 for the bus ticket, Rs 700 for the stay and Rs 500 for food. I spent my own money; the incident was too embarrassing to let anyone know. I spent the next day in my room, watching downloaded sitcoms the whole time.

After the previous night's incident, I waited at the bus stand for an hour prior. The bus arrived and I left for McLeod Ganj. Never thought catching a bus would make me feel so accomplished. It felt as if I had already completed the trip. It took me three days to reach McLeod Ganj!

Day One, 6 June 2019

I spent my night in the backseat of a maniac-driven bus, struggling to sleep without spraining my neck. It dropped me at Dharamshala bus stop, and a shared cab further took me to McLeod Ganj. I almost got down on my knees and kissed the earth for finally making it after all the chaos. McLeod Ganj is the upper region of Dharamshala and is comparatively less touristy. It is a town surrounded by little villages like Bhagsu and Dharamkot.

The temperature drastically dropped as the altitude increased. Walking my way to the main square of McLeod Ganj, I could see army jeeps passing by, monks walking along and many other backpackers just like me. There were stalls selling tea, Maggi noodles and momo at every 100 metres. There was the beautiful valley on one side and thick growth of oak, pine and deodar on the other side of the misty road. A stretch of local handicrafts shops run by Tibetan refugees ran from the Namgyal Monastery to McLeod's main taxi stand, further continuing towards Bhagsu and Dharamkot. My hostel, The Triangle Folks, was at the end of the market, in Bhagsu village. From the busy taxi stand, a narrow lane went upwards, ending at a bright three-storey building with patches of cold blue. The reception was in the courtyard, full of flower pots. The sun had covered most of the plants and was still travelling.

'Hey, I have a booking . . .' I said to a boy sleeping on a bench in the shaded part of the courtyard.

'It's just 8.30 a.m.; you are early, my friend. Check in is at 2 p.m.,' the boy replied, squinting his eyes. The sun had reached his feet. He conveniently moved his bench and bought some more time for his slumber.

'Umm . . . Okay, I am leaving my luggage here. I'll be back by 2 p.m.,' I said. Taking out my fleece and camera, I left my backpack at the reception and headed for a walk. I didn't want to waste the beautiful morning.

While at a cafe for a cup of coffee and pancakes, my phone beeped.

I had a notification: Aayush replied to your story. '*McLeod madhe ahes ka re*?' (Are you in McLeod?) Aayush was a friend from my college. He happened to be in Dharamshala, volunteering at a Buddhist school as an English teacher.

'What is your plan for the day?' he asked.

'No plans . . . I might cover the nearby area,' I answered.

'Well, let's head to the monastery,' he suggested. We quickly made plans and decided to catch up at the taxi stand.

We had worked together in our college theatre production 'Laila on the Rocks' two year ago, but we hadn't interacted much back then. In fact, I could barely remember his real name—we all called him 'idli'. Nobody knew why. He wasn't even a south Indian. In our theatre circle, there were quite a few people whose real names no one knew. We all referred to them by the names of the characters they had played: Jesus, Kasav (tortoise), Shah Rukh, Dafli.

The market had opened by now. Little wooden Tibetan shops sold incense sticks, essential oils, Tibetan flags and singing bowls. Many important offices of the Government of Tibet in Exile, museums and monasteries are around that area. In the centre is the Namgyal Monastery, where His Holiness the Dalai Lama lives. We were thoroughly checked and let in.

We were now among hundreds of monks in red robes sitting in the corridor and chanting *Om mani padme hum* on their handy prayer wheel. The hum of their chanting and the aroma of spicy incense filled the void of the monastery. The golden Buddha statue in the inner sanctum overlooked all those monks through his half open eyes and fully awakened soul. It was indeed a rare occurrence of silence among a huge number of people. Unlike the old and slow monks in the sanctum, the ones outside the monastery were very young; toddlers, in fact. They were short, chubby and running everywhere, holding up their robes. They greeted everyone with their adorable smiles and showed no shyness while posing for pictures.

Visiting the St John in the Wilderness Church right after a monastery was a big mood shift. As the name suggests, the church is inside thick woods. Built in stone and wood, the interior has beautiful vintage lamps, spreading a subtle glow in the room. We were teleported to a hamlet in the Scottish Highlands. But the flocks of tourists, however, kept bringing us back. Seeing a camera on me, everyone assumed I was a photographer and asked me to click pictures of them on their smartphones.

'*Beta, hamari ek photo loge?*' (Son, could you click our picture?) a group of chattering Delhi aunties asked. One of them handed me her phone saying, 'Click in HD mode haan, beta.' I tried fitting them all in one frame. However, they stood blocking the church in the background and made me click dozens of photos in different poses, landscape mode, portrait mode, etc., including the mandatory peace sign.

It was an absolutely touristy day. With a very neutral point of view, I shot all the activities. By this point, I had become bold enough to record myself in public. I no longer felt conscious of people around me while vlogging. Of course, they will look at you and maybe judge as well, but you don't know them anyway and probably won't meet them again—this thought made me more comfortable in front of the camera, unlike the initial

St. John in the Wilderness

days, when I would be extremely awkward on getting unwanted attention.

It was evening, and I still hadn't checked in. My backpack was lying at the reception. Finally, after returning to the hostel, I got my bunk bed. Crashing on the bed of an empty, fresh-smelling dorm was the moment of utter satisfaction. After four days of hectic travel, I had a soothing hot shower. The room was all white and smelt like lemon. It was summer, and yet there was no need for an air conditioner. Temperature in the evening got down to 13°C. I was in the bed, feeling warm and cosy. Not missing anything or anyone. It was a reward for all the madness I had gone through in the last four days. These little luxuries on a backpacking trip make it all worth it.

Day Two, 7 June 2019

'So, what plans for the day?' asked Amruta. She was a doctor working in Chhattisgarh whom I met at the hostel last night. We both sat in the common area basking in morning sunlight, eating buttery parathas for breakfast.

'I'm planning to hike Triund,' I said, tearing my paratha to release the steam inside.

'This early?' she asked. Triund is a peak adjoining McLeod Ganj and a popular camping spot.

'I am hiking solo; I want to reach the top before it gets dark,' I replied.

'It doesn't take that long. If you take the Gallu Devi Temple route, you won't be hiking alone,' she informed, adding, 'Do you want to join me for a meditation session before leaving? I am going to this nearby place called Tushita Centre. They have a community meditation session every morning.'

'I am on a budget.' I knew these things are exorbitant.

'It's free,' she said, smiling.

We were seven minutes late, and the meditation hall was full. Looking at the footwear outside the hall, I could guess there were more than 100 people inside. The rest of the people were sitting on a lawn outside the meditation hall, in the woods. There must have been sixty to seventy of them. I could barely spot an Indian among them—all foreigners with their sippers and mosquito repellents. All the heads turned to look at us when we entered, and they kept looking as we awkwardly sought some empty spaces. We quickly took off our shoes and sat among the group. There was a loudspeaker amplifying the instructions of the teacher inside the hall. He sounded German from his accent. Closing our eyes, we followed what he said. That was the moment I willingly let myself obey a white man.

We both felt slightly out of place, not because we were barely meditating, but because the presence of some seemingly serious meditators around intimidated us. I was glad not to be sitting inside the hall among hundreds of people, or else I would have missed out on the sweet sounds of the wind running through the thick trunks of pine trees, the callings of forest birds and the pecking of a woodpecker.

Slowly and quietly, I took out my GoPro and tried to take a shot—a short pan of the whole lawn. Quickly switching on the camera, I recorded the shot, and as I pressed the red button to stop, 'beep beep beep,' went the camera before shutting, catching everyone's attention. Suddenly, sixty to seventy people were looking back at me, this time with annoyance. I quickly put the camera in my bag and shut my eyes. Embarrassed, I left in no time after the session ended.

Tushita Centre was just a small part of this big day. The main task was to trek all the way up to the Triund peak, pitch my tent there and camp for the night.

9350 ft above sea level

Triund is a peak 6 km to the north of Bhagsu village. It's a popular trek in Dharamshala. Although there are campsites at the top, I decided to carry my own tent. My reasons were pretty valid. 1) The campsites up there are too commercial and unnecessarily expensive; 2) I wanted to avoid the crowd as much as possible; and 3) I wanted to carry my own load and pitch my own tent to experience the freedom of camping solo.

Stocking up on six protein bars and three chocolate bars, I started my journey all pepped up. I hitchhiked from my hostel to Gallu Devi Temple, the starting point of the trail. There are two routes to Triund, and the one that goes from Gallu Devi Temple is the easier one. To my disappointment, I saw a long line of equally excited crowds at the registration desk. There were only two cops lethargically dealing with the entire crowd. They checked everyone's ID and let them go after making them sign in a register. I waited and waited, and waited.

'Do you have a booking up there?' asked a guy in a yellow hoodie. He didn't seem like a tourist.

'Booking for what?' I replied.

'Are you going to stay for the night?'

'Yes.'

'Then you are supposed to pre-book your stay at a campsite.'

'It's okay, I have my own tent,' I quickly answered.

'No, it is not allowed. You can only stay if you have a booking. The campsites have their tents, and food is included too. Only Rs 650.'

'Who are you? The agent?'

'No, I am a friend . . . not agent . . .' he said, trying to persuade me. I scanned him from bottom to top. His loose harem pants, like the ones Akshay Kumar wore in *Bhool Bhulaiyaa*, contrasted sharply with his bright yellow hoodie. He kept rolling up his sleeves throughout the conversation, but they kept slipping down his skinny forearms.

'I think I am good,' I said, trying to get rid of him. The line was moving slowly.

'It's better if you book now; else the cops will send you back,' he warned me. He could barely stand still as we talked. His impatience showed in the way he kept shifting his weight from one leg to the other.

'Well, in that case, I will book at a campsite when I reach. Okay?'

'See for yourself. I warned you already . . .' He finally left irritated.

It was finally my turn, and I completed all the formalities. The cops did see the tent attached to my backpack, but they let me pass. Their silence validated that the guy in the yellow hoodie was trying to scam me.

It takes two hours to reach the top, but since I was carrying a 30-litre backpack with a 2-kg tent on it, my pace was comparatively slow. The trail was rocky and had a gradual climb. Leaning forward, I climbed with a steady pace. I wasn't out of breath yet, but the tent I had buckled up in my backpack was falling off from one side. After every twenty minutes, I had to take off my backpack, tighten the buckle and put it on again.

Putting my backpack on and off was more tiring than the actual trek. But still, it was better than the crowd I was trekking with. Groups of college picnics were all over the place. There's always this one fellow in every group who carries a Bluetooth speaker and dedicatedly plays Punjabi hip hop, therefore ruining the silent sounds of the mountains. You wouldn't want to listen to Bollywood songs while trekking in the quiet mountains on a cold evening. Do these self-proclaimed connoisseurs of hip hop get paid for their service at the end of the trek?

Barely a kilometre into the trek, and I could hear people cribbing about signing up for it.

'Why are you making us climb mountains? It's a holiday, dude! We could've stayed in the hotel room instead!' The guy who took the initiative to get his friends on this trek was blamed. Poor fellow must've regretted it so much. People were hiking in flip-flops, denim jeans and leather jackets. Just when I thought I'd seen enough for the day, a lady wearing a sari passed by panting. Who wears saris on treks? Perhaps it sounds normal to you, but for a guy in proper hiking boots, quick-dry clothes and 7 kg of weight on his back, it was a moment to have. It might come across as a bit judgemental, but it's really tough to ignore all the yelling and littering along the way.

It took me three-and-a-half hours to reach the top. There was still light on the top. Triund, a flat ridge stretching almost a kilometre, further continuing to a snow line of mountains. Dharamshala was on the east of the ridge. HPCA Stadium,* one of India's highest cricket stadiums, could prominently be seen from the top. On the west was the magnificent range of the Dhauladhar mountains. This is the best part about mountains—

---

* Popular local trivia.

getting to experience both the humility of the valleys and the dominance of the top. People were busy searching for their respective campsites all over the ridge. Some were arguing with the campsite guys for not having charging points; a few boys had sneaked in liquor; a group of chattering girls were busy deciding how to pose for their perfect selfie; uncles and aunties had given up on everything, and they sat panting, waiting for their porters. It was chaos up on the mountain. All the mountains from the surrounding area were probably feeling sorry for the poor Triund.

Making my way from the hustling campsites, I found a considerable flat land of tender grass a few hundred metres away. A big patch of rocks became the fortress of my campsite. From this place, all the other campsites looked very tiny. Their noise couldn't reach here. Working out my sore calf muscles and shoulders, I pitched my tent and within a few minutes, my campsite was ready!

I was tired but not exhausted. I have no words to describe the pleasure of taking off my shoes and rubbing my feet on wet grass. I sat on the rock until it got dark, gazing at the clean white Dhauladhars. Among these magnificent mountains, I found myself very tiny—tiny, yet not insignificant. And the mountains magnificent yet not intimidating. Huge yet calm, just like an aged sage. Carrying my own tent all the way up here was absolutely worth it. Nothing felt so liberating as making a strange land my home. It was empowering but also very humbling. How much shifting have these powerful mountains gone through to form this beautiful, folded structure? I wondered. I was still in the Shivalik ranges; what would it be like in the trans Himalayas?

The Dhauladhars looked steady and static, but they were constantly moving from within. Once a vast void of ocean is now a beautiful landmass, endowed with rich resources that flourished many civilizations. After such a long time, it no longer felt like just a shoot for a travel series, but something much more than that. I wish I was a poet to describe this beauty. I wish I was a painter; I could paint each cut on a rock. I wish I was a philosopher to find a deeper meaning of this form of nature. But I am none of these. All I could do was sit, gaze and feel my long breaths making my heart lighter so that it could soar above the mystical Dhauladhars.

* * *

Day Three, 8 June 2019

Do you have permission?

It was freezing midnight when I heard the sound of footsteps coming near my tent.

'*O bhai, bahar ao,*' (Hey brother, come out) asserted a husky voice.

There were two men standing outside my tent; one had a beard stubble. They seemed like locals.

'Whose tent is this?' asked the one in a brown sweater. It was pitch dark, so I switched on my flashlight. They looked serious.

'Mine,' I answered.

'Do you have permission to camp here?' The same guy questioned me.

'I didn't know about the permission.'

'This is forest land; we are from the department.' They surely didn't look like department men.

'Then, how come these other tents are allowed? If I required permission, why wasn't I stopped at the registration desk? The policeman clearly knew I was carrying a tent,' I argued.

'Listen, boy, if you don't have the required, permission you must pay the fine . . . 1000 rupees,' the other guy raised his voice.

'I don't have that much money.'

'Then start descending,' he said bluntly.

'I can't do that either; it's 12.30 a.m.,' I refused, but this time calmly. I was travelling solo and certainly did not want to get into any trouble in the middle of the mountains. My seventeen-year-old self would have made a scene there and then have gotten into some trouble. But this time I kept cool.

'How much money do you have?'

'Not much; how much do you want?'

'Give 500,' said the brown sweater guy. For sure, they weren't forest officers.

'I have 200.'

'Works.'

'Here you go,' I paid them two bills of Rs 100.

'Thanks, friend. Where are you from?' Their tone had changed.

'Mumbai,' I replied unenthusiastically, going back into my tent.

'You've come all the way from Mumbai alone? You got balls, bro! Take care of yourself.' I ignored it and went back into my sleeping bag.

A blissful morning

The night was unbearably cold. My sleeping bag was too thin for this temperature. I wore all the t-shirts I had under my fleece and was still shivering. The whole night, I kept rolling down the slope on my left and pushed myself up the other side of the tent. As I woke up, I couldn't feel any sensation in my left hand since I was sleeping over it all night. It was so numb that I wouldn't even feel a bit if it got chopped off. It took me some time to get the blood flow back in my arm. The tips of my nose and ears had frozen. I sat in my tent zoned out for a couple of minutes staring at nothing until I was fully awake.

It all felt fully worth it after realizing what was awaiting outside. I zipped open the side of the tent facing the lofty peaks of the majestic Dhauladhar mountains. The white ice on the peaks was given a bright yellow wash by the rising sun. Swifts and swallows soared from peak to peak. Terrace farms occupied the foothills, and the valleys were covered by a rich growth of coniferous trees. Ranges of serene mountains faded into the violet haze, much like in Caspar Friedrich's painting 'Wanderer Above the Sea of Fog'. The endless expanse of mountain ranges, dipped in tints of blue and violet, seemed to dissolve into the horizon. As the birds occasionally perched on treetops, the imagery was so still it almost appeared like a painting. Nothing moved, not even the clouds. Only the crisp cold winds, caressing the grass, caused a gentle rustle.

It was a sight that will remain fresh in my memories for years. My tent was pitched in the shadow of a huge rock. I walked a few steps, getting out of the cold shadow in the warm, wet grassy patch of sunlight. Taking off my fleece, I sat there basking for a while, brushing my teeth. There is nothing more beautiful than the luxury of sitting on wet grass carefree. Well, in cities you never know if it's really dew or a dog's piss. The sight was so breathtaking, I could hardly blink, for I did not wish to miss out on anything for even a second.

'Would the locals here still find this sight beautiful? Would they too be as amazed as me looking at these valleys? Or would the terrain be just another hardship in their lives? We run from our city lives into nature the moment we get a long weekend. Where do these people go on their long weekends? Do they aspire to come to the cities? Or do they even feel the need for these little escapes?' My mind naively wandered into this vast void. I wondered whether our minds are more tangible than we think. Sitting in a closed room, I imagine the mind to be a small sphere. But in that open space, I felt its boundaries had expanded, making it limitless.

The Descent

Before leaving, I had Maggi noodles for breakfast at the top for a proper Rs 70. In McLeod Ganj, you get it for Rs 40, but as the altitude increases so does the price. Having steaming hot Maggi noodles in the Himalayas is a ritual. All the packing and the breakfast warmed me up and energized me to start my descent. I was in no mood to trek from yesterday's route and face the overwhelming crowd again. I had heard of another trail that passes via Bhagsunag waterfalls but wasn't quite sure about it.

'*Bhai, Bhagsu falls ka rasta kahaan se hai?*' (Which is the way to Bhagsu falls?) I inquired with the shop owner.

'Bhaiji, keep walking straight, following the ridge; you will see yellow arrows painted on the stones; that'll lead you to Bhagsunag,' he replied.

I started following the Triund ridge. Walking through patches of rocks and grass, rocks and grass. After a kilometre or two, patches of grass started disappearing, and the ridge became narrower and steeper. Stepping on the stones to stay sturdy, I was climbing down the mountain now, following the yellow arrows painted on the rocks. I was all alone on that route; there wasn't even a single goat. The sky was clear and blue, ending at the far-reaching mountain ranges. There were colourful settlements in the valleys. Although I had to look down while walking all the time, watching out for loose rocks, I took short breaks to enjoy the surroundings and my solace.

There was a black kite soaring very close to me. It was chased away by the ravens and was returning somewhere. It hovered some ten to fifteen feet over me; it must've found someone familiar, travelling solo just like her. It was a kite for sure. It's easy to tell if the bird soaring above you is an eagle or a kite. If its tail resembles a Japanese fan, it is an eagle, but this one had a fork-shaped tail, so it was a kite. A black kite. This was one of the initial facts I learnt after I started attending bird walks. At first, I thought it must've spotted a hare or something in the rocks, but it wasn't the case. The kite was just soaring above me, taking quick dives after two to three rounds. We both covered half the way. Till the rocks shrank to stones and further shrank to gravel, and the arrows were no longer clear. There used to be an arrow mark after every 50 metres. Then, gradually, an unclear arrow appeared every 300 metres until I could barely see any signs. There was just one stone further ahead, fully painted in yellow, that didn't help me navigate in any way.

I kept walking instinctively, tracking the foot trail. Midway, I crossed a demolished house that was now just a pile of rock slabs structured into walls. I hoped to find a person there, but it was empty. It had been three hours, and I'd not spotted a single mobile living entity except the kite. Although the town was pretty visible, I couldn't find a well-demarcated route leading to the town. A kilometre ahead from the stonehouse, I spotted two to three mountain goats grazing on a small pasture. 'If there is livestock, there should be somebody to look after it,' I wondered. Descending down to the pasture, I saw smoke coming out of a chimney, and after rushing in anticipation, I spotted a house. I sighed. It was a rustic wooden Himachali house that appeared quite brittle standing on an elevated platform. A tethered cow outside mooed at me as I entered the premises.

'Namaste, where are the Bhagsunag waterfalls? Can you please tell me?' I called out. A lady came out of the kitchen, wearing a shabby-looking man's shirt in contrast with the red floral scarf wrapped around her head. She seemed like she had just completed the first chore of her day.

'Where is Bhagsunag waterfalls?' I repeated as she looked at me.

'Bhagsunag,' I emphasized, as she was not able to understand me. She pointed towards a pathway that led inside a thick canopy of deodar trees.

'Shukriya,' I smiled.

'*Koi baat nahi.*' She smiled back. Her voice was similar to my mother's.

* * *

After walking for another half an hour, I could finally hear the waterfall. It was on the other side of a cliff covered with dense forest.

It was a long trek; I could've easily gotten down from the Gallu Devi Temple route, but the scenery here was priceless and worth the physical stress. I had climbed for four hours with a heavy bag yesterday; I couldn't sleep well, and then this rough descent. I was extremely exhausted, out of breath and sweaty enough that it left white salt lines on my black t-shirt. My eyelids were drooping out of fatigue, and my calf muscles weren't in good shape either.

It was the last leg of a long trek. My water bottle was empty by now. Parched, I walked impatiently towards the Bhagsunag waterfalls. My sore muscles struggled to bear the weight of my backpack. I heaved a sigh of relief on finally hearing the waterfall in the distance. I desperately wanted to take off my shoes and dip my feet in its cold water. In anticipation of a much-needed pit stop, I walked even faster with all my might.

And what do I see when I reach the majestic Bhagsunag waterfalls? A milky white flow of mountain water cascading down from the heights of gigantic black rocks, forming fresh, clear pools with colourful pebbles visible. The sound of the water falling echoed as it was covered by a dense deciduous forest . . . and then there was the species of Indian uncles in underpants occupying the whole territory with their jiggling bellies. Their hairy bodies danced in the flow of the cold water. They had managed to completely take over the tranquillity of the surroundings with their hooting.

My feet stopped at the very first sight of that ruckus. My shoulders fell in disappointment, sinking with the heavy weight of my backpack. I swallowed my idea of filling up my water bottle and dangling my feet in the stream and continued my walk in sheer dejection. This wasn't the end I had expected after an intense trekking experience.

While crossing the stream through slippery pebbles, one of the men yelled from the crowd, embarrassing their wives.

'Hey boy, here!' A guy and his friend were sitting on a rock near the pool, drenched. They must have taken a break from their dance party.

'If you're going that way, right there is Shiva Cafe . . .' He pointed at a crowded cafe upstairs.

'Ask if the order of two plates of Maggi and a farmhouse pizza is ready. If not, ask the guy to hurry up,' he 'instructed' me; it wasn't a request.

What!? Who does that? Who asks random strangers to get an update on their pizza?

'Sure, I got you.' I don't know why I said that. But seeing the pile of shoes outside the cafe, I changed my mind and continued my walk.

* * *

Walking for three hours straight with just 500 ml of water, I finally made it to the Bhagsunag taxi stand. I had a bus to catch at 7 p.m. from Dharamshala. But before that, the last task of the trip had to be ticked off—shopping! I usually don't shop on any of my travels, but if I ever do, I rarely buy anything for myself. I'm not particularly into souvenirs. I used to believe I despised materialism, but I realized I just keep misplacing things.

I purchased a Kullu shawl for my mother and two bottles of rhododendron wine. One for Anusha, our creative producer, and one for me (I made a promise to open it only on a special occasion but ended up finishing it with Vedika in her car the other week—still a special occasion). They did not provide any samples, but it had rhododendron written on it, which sounded exotic. These flowers are found only in parts of Himachal and Uttarakhand. I wrapped them in my fleece and safely placed them in the upper section of my backpack, making it heavier than before.

An overnight journey got me to Kashmiri Gate, New Delhi, at 8 a.m., and from there I had to catch a flight back to Mumbai. The joy of reaching home the same day was off the top. I used to enjoy train journeys during my honeymoon phase of travelling, but now it felt draining and lonely. The railway smell became even more nauseating. However, I'm sure I'll start complaining about air travel as well after a while. I'll probably want to travel by ship then and eventually grow out of it too and look for a new mode of transport.

The seat belt signs were off. The airplane grew silent. Watching the sunset from the window, I remembered the one I saw yesterday from Triund Peak. After a night at Triund and then on this hectic journey, I had acid reflux, dark circles and muscle pain and was fatigued. Each part of my body was sore. The high of my last trek still hadn't shaken off. In the last couple of hours, I'd put my body through a lot. I didn't even realize it, but none of this could be possible without a single organ in place. The airplane seat felt like a lover's hug, and I could finally take off my shoes and stretch my toes. It was a moment of being aware and also grateful for having an able body to support all my dreams and take me to heights and lengths. On this realization, I let out a natural sigh of long breath.

Landing at Mumbai airport, I waited for my luggage at the conveyor belt. I could see my backpack approaching, but it was drenched and reeked of wine as I took it. The disaster I was afraid of had happened in the cargo. At Mumbai airport, I was left with a wholesome trip minus one of those bottles of exclusive Himachali rhododendron wine. My fleece, underpants, shirts, books and the Kullu shawl reeked of wine for one whole day. Ugh! I want to end this chapter on some highly deep and motivational note, but some things are just meant to be anti-climatic.

SEVEN

AUROVILLE AND PUDUCHERRY

If you ask someone, 'Where are you from?' and they reply,
'From the universe,' you're in Auroville.

I still can't remember how this plan was made, but every time I met Savani, one conversation was always on the table: 'Let's please go on a trip together.'

Savani is my first friend from South Bombay. We met at one of BhaDiPa's open mic events, where she kept talking about Girgaon. Fifty per cent of what Savani sounds like is just giggles. We share piles of cringeworthy content, unnecessary trivia and politically incorrect jokes on a daily basis. As Anusha says, our 'camaraderie' is what got us hosting food videos together.

This was on the day when Savani called me. 'So, I have an idea. *Dil Chahta Hai* is turning eighteen this year. Let's do a group trip episode and package it as an ode to the film,' she said. 'We can upload it around the 10th of August, because it's Friendship Day!' She had clearly thought this through.

'I am so on board! But I doubt this will be approved,' I said. One of the reasons I travel solo is because it's feasible for production to send a one-person team; the cost directly doubles if another person is added.

'Ask Anusha! I don't even mind self-funding my trip. I just need a vacation.'

'So where? Goa?' I asked.

'Let's do Pondy!' (I am sure she must've come across a photo of an aesthetic window in Pondicherry, now known as its original precolonial name Puducherry, on Instagram.) And as we had hoped, Anusha did agree to this collaboration. Later, another friend Sushant joined too, and we booked our tickets that night itself.

I know both Savani and Sushant through BhaDiPa itself. The three of us joined the company at the same time. Sushant and I met for the first time on our very first jam session for Marathi stand-up comedy. His set was a riot that night. He lived in Thane, so I had company till halfway. We both ran to catch that last train. The entire commute, we talked about college theatre groups. I was a junior in my college theatre circuit while he was just out of it. He is this shameless dude who will go up to any random person and literally ask for anything, and the person will probably end up giving it, too. Sushant had a wicked sense of humour, and that is what really bonded us.

We mostly got together for work, and for a long time, we kept cribbing about not being able to do a group trip. Finally, the three of us were free on the same dates. This was going to be a new experience—our lite version of *Dil Chahta Hai*!

Day One, 23 July 2019

The easiest and most preferred way to reach Puducherry is via Chennai. We landed there a day prior to the shoot. Sulai, my only friend in Chennai, let us crash at his place in exchange for Chitale's bhakarwadi, the classic Maharashtrian snack. I had been following Sulai on Instagram for a while, mainly because he was one of the very few people actively shooting on GoPro at that time. Sulai's apartment was near the shore. We chilled on his terrace in the breezy midnight, learning about his obsession with Casio watches and Hot Wheels cars. He had recently started collecting them. By now, I'm sure he must have their entire collections.

Catching an early morning bus to Puducherry, we got down 12 km before, at a little town called Auroville.

I have heard a lot about Auroville from other fellow backpackers while travelling. In 1968, Mirra Alfassa,[*] popularly known as Mother, a spiritual collaborator of the great philosopher Sri Aurobindo, came up with the concept of a universal community. Thousands of people from 124 nations

[*] SNS, 'The Fascinating Story of the "City of Dawn", Auroville', *Statesman*, 22 January 2022, https://www.thestatesman.com/travel/fascinating-story-city-dawn-auroville-1503040512.html#google_vignette

and twenty-three Indian states gathered around a banyan tree and inaugurated this land as an experiment in humanity. They had brought soil from their respective homelands and started this settlement based on the teachings of Sri Aurobindo. Today, this settlement is spread across 20 square kilometres across this banyan tree. The whole idea behind Auroville was to establish an ideal, self-sufficient community of individuals irrespective of gender, age, race, nationality or profession and promote unity and sustainable living. Although the idea sounds a bit utopian, I am sure even that place wouldn't be devoid of conflict. This was our main topic of debate during the journey. Savani being a lawyer, I being a philosophy student and, well, Sushant just being fond of talking, this was inevitable.

Auroville had a surprisingly unique design. It is a circular town, with the Matrimandir being its nucleus. It is the golden ball that you see when you search for Auroville online. There stands proud a hundred plus-year-old banyan tree near the Matrimandir that is technically the nucleus. Yes, we did try to swing on its aerial roots. It was the only tree standing in the barren plateau. This space is now taken by strategically built pavilions. Every community has their own pavilion, such as the African Pavilion, Tibetan Pavilion, etc. Each pavilion frequently hosts traditional gatherings, potlucks and festivals. In the same orbit, a community solar kitchen prepares food from their own local produce. The outermost orbit, consisting of the rest 60 per cent of the land, is covered by forest and agriculture, both cultivated and conserved by the Aurovillians. Knowing this, I keep wondering how tough it would have been to get everyone on the same page.

Interesting workshops take place every other week in the pavilions. Outsiders are allowed too, but they have to pay in thousands. A big board at the visitors' centre displayed notices of these workshops and various other sessions like yoga, kalaripayattu, massage, etc. There was a three-week workshop about building tree houses! Tree houses fascinated us, but the fees quickly brought us back to reality. None of us wanted to pay Rs 40,000 just to learn to build a treehouse. Well, considering the rents in Mumbai, 40,000 seems a fair deal, but then finding a tree is an even tougher task.

I have largely spent time individually with Savani and Sushant. Being with them together made me realize that the three of us have no sense of direction whatsoever. We just aimlessly walk until one of us either takes charge or we serendipitously spot a place. This entire trip was a series of aimless walks ending up at pretty monuments. This is exactly

MATRI MANDIR, AUROVILLE

how we made it to Matrimandir. We saw it through the fence, some 50 metres away. This big ball of golden plates! Their concave shapes reflected sunlight, making it appear shiny. It stood out in contrast to well-groomed lawns in the expanse.

Sushant and I really wanted to see it from within, and Savani, being Savani, was cool with anything. We'd heard that it looks like a crystal and that you can see a thin beam of sunlight streaming down from a hole above. It sounded like the perfect place to meditate in peace. Unfortunately, all the visitors' slots for both days were booked, so we didn't get to see it. In my opinion, this one thing leaves the chapter incomplete, because when we told our friends back home that we couldn't make it inside, we were roasted for almost two weeks.

The town was empty; we didn't see ANY cars, but a foreigner would pass by on a bicycle every twenty minutes. One could see a stark difference between the visitors and the residents. The residents have grown accustomed to visitors, like national park animals. We clearly looked like visitors, which was a good thing because no one really bothered us. No hawkers, salesmen or noisy shops. Contrary to what I was told, Auroville seemed quite lethargic that day. Most of the roads were empty too. Heck, some of them weren't even actual roads; they were just small pathways in the woods!

Time travel

Having eaten a simple lunch, we checked into our hostel. It lies between the green belt and the main centre of Auroville. Just like the town, our hostel too was quiet and lifeless. It was quite primitive. There were eight Keeth Houses made up of bamboo and coconut in two rows of four each. Below the huts, there were benches overflowing with things such as hula hoops, juggling balls, Dapo stars, a karaoke set, a dusty chess board, Monopoly, weirdly painted empty bottles of beer and a lot of other stuff. A wall full of psychedelic art surrounded the huts. No wonder the hostel was called 'The Time Traveller' hostel. The place looked like a ransacked village from a Vietnam War documentary. There was just one dog, a rebellious one, and he was the only energetic animal around, apparently with no one to play with. Well, we had no complaints! It was a unanimous decision to book an exotic hut to stay in.

The attitude of the hostel manager mirrored the vibe of the hostel. He showed up only after we called him thrice. Skinny, curly hair, a loose tank top and shorts—he looked like the poster boy for indolence.

'Hey, bro; you're the Mumbai guy, right?'

'Yes . . . the Mumbai guy.'

'Right there, that's your shack. Make yourself at home. Those are the washrooms; the light bulb's broken in the second one; gotta replace it. Careful with the dog; he has his own mood swings. That little hut is the kitchen; wash the plates and stuff after you use them. Yup, that's it; have fun!' he drawled and turned to leave. He had done his job.

'Hey, wait, why is this hostel called The Time Traveller? It doesn't have a sci-fi theme as such . . .' asked Sushant, inquisitively. He had no idea he would regret asking this.

'Why does everyone want to go to a futuristic place when it comes to time travel? There are many answers and many lessons to take from the past too,' he turned around and said.

'The whole concept behind this hostel is to give you a primitive experience, which will connect you to the earth, dude. Back in the day, man was so connected to nature—to his roots.' He had found three twenty-first-century humans to recite his sermon to.

'Now you see this bullshit corruption and politics and technology around. This illusion of development, of nations . . . I tell you, man. The cities and toxic industries we live around . . . It's all leading us to fucking nowhere. We have lost our touch with nature, bro . . . that's the whole point.' He summed up his speech vaguely, checked us in and went back to his hut.

We had a whole shack to ourselves; that too, only for Rs 900 per day. It was pretty sturdy and had a unique look.

Climbing up the ladder brought us to a bamboo door. Inside the shack, there was just one switch board and a yellow dim bulb that enhanced the feel of the brown rustic room. It smelt like bamboo inside. I was a bit sceptical about Savani and Sushant liking it or not, but they did. Savani was the only girl in our trio, so we were worried  whether she'd find it comfortable. But the best thing about Savani is that she is super adaptable to everything. She fits in anywhere, in no time. She is the most patient and accepting person I have ever seen; I still wonder how she is a lawyer.

* * *

On our first day itself, we'd figured that Auroville is not a two-day-visit place. It can be best experienced by living here at least for a week or two. However, we stuck to our roles of being absolute tourists and making the most of it. Savani and Sushant were actually on a vacation, while I had to constantly remind myself to film. The time I usually reserve to take B-rolls or record my reactions was replaced by mindless heckling and splitting bills. Although vlogging had become a part of my muscle memory, a random conversation would easily carry me away. So much so that we spent the latter part of the day in our shack without even realizing it was already dark. Now I get why people on group trips are always running late.

At 8 p.m., when we were at our peak of hunger, we learnt that all the shops and cafes in Auroville shut by 7 p.m. They were closed when we came in the morning, obviously due to it being too early. They were shut in the afternoon, which is understandable because it's too hot in the afternoon and there's no one outside. And they are closed at night! When are the shops here open? Aren't people here interested in earning money?

Luckily, I had around eight packets of instant ramen in my bag, so we ended up slurping ramen in the kitchen. Sulai gave it to me when we were leaving from Chennai. He had gotten it from Saudi Arabia. I don't know the connection between Sulai, Saudi Arabia and instant ramen, but it was our saviour at the time.

Day Two, 24 July 2019

When it comes to food, the three of us are arguably no-nonsense eaters, and the best part was that none of us really mind experimenting with local food. Last night, out of a major fear of missing out, we saved a few good cafes on maps and decided to go cafe hopping today. All we needed were wheels; it was certainly impossible to walk in such hot weather.

'I am not opening the shop today, but you guys can come by 10 a.m. and call me. I'll come down and give you the scooter,' said the scooter rental guy on call in his south Indian accent and cut it before we could reply.

Why are people here so business-phobic? The Mumbaikar in me got yet another culture shock. Finally, after reaching the shop at 10 a.m., we called him. He showed up after an eternity, we signed a few papers, and finally got our scooter.

Since we were low on budget and it was easy to get lost here, travelling triple-seat was a feasible idea. Plus, we planned on sharing one dish in each cafe so that we could try them all and save more money.

Auroville Bakery was our first stop. It had an elegant black metal signboard hanging on a tall pole visible from a distance with 'Auroville Bakery' and a rolling pin engraved in white. A big pile of wood lay outside the shop, which meant they probably had a wood oven! We felt the magic as we opened the door—a mixed aroma of freshly baked bread, exotic cheese, dark chocolate, sweet milk, cinnamon, cardamom and various tempting bonne bouche rushed in and filled our senses.

Most of the people coming in were regulars, familiar with their orders and spending little time beyond greeting those they knew. Photos of Mirra Alfassa (the Mother) and Sri Aurobindo were prominently displayed at the counter. The women working behind it, presumably locals, moved gracefully in their vibrantly coloured saris, with fresh jasmine gajras tucked in their hair. It was a refreshing sight—watching women in traditional Indian attire serve croissants and sourdoughs with warm smiles. The counter overflowed with an assortment of baked goods: flaky croissants, glossy bagels, crispy baguettes, nutty sourdough, hot pies and colourful tarts.

While we were stuck in the dilemma of what to buy, a lady

donning an apron and gloves came to the counter with a tray full of freshly baked croissants and emptied it in a basket near the bagels. That made it clear!

'One chocolate croissant, one cheese and one plain,' I ordered without a second thought. If I were asked to describe the taste in one word, I would simply say, 'divine'. It was THE BEST croissant I have had so far. Big, well baked, not too sweet, flaky layers on the outside, soft as cheese on the inside. It was so satisfying just to look at the chocolate and cheese oozing out after every bite. Even the plain croissant tasted great. It wasn't chewy at all, quickly melting in my mouth. Utterly satisfied, we headed to our next stop with our now highly raised expectations.

'Beans and Bagels' was a fancy cafe. Their entire menu sounded like the credits of a French film. Like a clueless fellow at a ticket counter, I bugged the lady, asking her silly questions like, 'What does Cinnamon Cacao Butter have in it?' 'What is El Bulli?' and so on. She answered them all, but not before correcting my pronunciation.

Mike Wilson, a Chicago-born chef, first came to India on a backpacking trip. His brother's unfortunate bike accident led them to stay in Auroville for a few extra weeks, and that's where he met his wife, a French Tamilian who taught at an equestrian school. They later left for France, where he had his first 'real bread' and fell in love with the craft. A visit to her parents inspired him to start baking his own bread in India, of all places! And that's how 'Beans and Bagels' came into being.

We spent the next hour just roaming around Auroville; we weren't in search of anything. Closing our maps and riding purely on instinct through random lanes and bumpy paths in the woods. We had figured out our own way to explore

Auroville. You can't really make a list and go around ticking things off. On this ride, we ended up doing subsequent things as well—finding a Fiat vertically planted in the ground, mock driving a 1960s caravan bus, keeping count of dream catchers and peace signs along the way, visiting a sound garden and halting for coconut water in between.

Whatever we documented, if arranged in a particular way, could make a crazy music video.

Past food

As exotic as our brunch was, our dinner was right at the other end of the spectrum. We spotted a place called Maiyam *Past* Food on the maps. Unlike all the fancy places we visited today, it was exactly what we'd imagined, but in fact more. It had a beautiful Tamilian vibe and a menu full of traditional food. The tables were low enough to sit on the ground with legs folded. An intricately carved wooden Ganpati sat at the centre of the room. A large shelf next to the Ganpati was filled with jars of south Indian spices, enriching the room with their aromas. The place had a very calm and cosy ambience, transporting you to simpler times. We were their only customers and were welcomed with smiles.

'We don't have a menu. We prepare different dishes every day,' said the owner after we asked him for the menu.

'Today, we have the rice platter . . . and we are preparing puttu right now,' he continued.

'Alright. Get us three portions of everything', Savani placed the order. We were a bit sceptical about the rice platter. What would it be like? We had expected something more. Something like a proper meal; perhaps some sambar, rasam, veggies—the usual stuff.

In no time, a lady got us three earthen plates filled with varieties of rice preparations. There was sambar rice, curd rice and tamarind rice, along with sauteed okra and two kinds of chutney. The first bite itself was so tender and comforting. We have no idea what these chutneys were made of, but I am certain I could eat that for the rest of my life.

Then came the 'puttu', which we were having for the first time. Puttu is a common rice-based breakfast dish across south India, but here it was served as a dessert. They had added ragi to it too and served it with grated jaggery and coconut milk. It looked more tempting than it sounds. Savani did the honours and had the first bite. She layered a scoop of the puttu with some jaggery and coconut milk and ate it. Sushant and I were staring at her face, waiting for the verdict. Her eyes opened wide in awe. I got that on video.

I don't remember the last time I had seen so many colours on one plate. Living in cities, we are so habituated to sticking to the same set of vegetables. I had forgotten that  even rice has tastes and textures. Quick cash and mass demand have narrowed down the varieties of vegetables a land can grow. There are several such vegetables I remember eating in my childhood that have vanished from the markets. If it's not about the ingredient, what else matters in food?

Maiyam's food was not just a dinner but an artistic experience. For the first time, I was moved after having 'tasted' something. Despite the ingredients being familiar and not some exotic novelty. I'm not exaggerating, but what I had at Maiyam Past Food was not just mechanically prepared to make business. These people had prepared their ancestral dishes with immense compassion and love that made our dinner stunningly delicious. With every bite, it felt like coming home after a tiring day.

* * *

Day Three, 25 July 2019

Our last two days in Auroville felt like two years, and we still couldn't make the most of it. We realized that Auroville is a place where you come alone for at least a week or two, spend your time volunteering at a farm or some cafe, attend meditation sessions or simultaneously work on your dream art project. The place is a bit too calm and solemn for a vacation with your friends, and considering our enthusiasm levels, we thought Pondy could be a more appropriate place to match them.

Puducherry is a union territory that was once a French colony.* The French left, but this town still has the essence of France in its houses, cafes, shops, churches and people, which

---

* Britannica, 'Puducherry', *Britannica Encyclopedia*, 5 May 2024, https://www. britannica.com/place/Puducherry-India

is why it is also known as Little France. Ever since I watched the film *Life of Pi*, Pondy had been on my wish list.

We left for Puducherry early in the morning, asking the auto guy to halt at Auroville Bakery for our last breakfast. We packed a regular croissant, one cheese, one chocolate, one lemon tart and a slice of a tomato pizza. The auto wala overcharged us for halting at the bakery but it was worth it.

The White Town

White Town, once a French colony, is a quaint neighbourhood of heritage buildings, wide boulevards running under the shade of gulmohar trees and a breezy promenade. The rest of Puducherry has a majority of Tamilian houses and a small Muslim settlement. All three settlements are closely knit and yet seem to be different worlds on either side of the road. Our BnB was in a picturesque alley of White Town. Hidden in the shade of bahavas (cassia), it is a white building with blue windows and a peach-coloured board with 'A La Villa Creole' embossed on it. A narrow flight of wooden stairs led to the reception desk (more of a household study table). Next to it was a balcony full of flowery creepers, converted into a cafe where a European couple was about to checkout. It gave a view of the La Bourdonnais street under the carpet of yellow cassia flowers and the smell of freshly brewed coffee.

From the top floor, we could see not just White Town but also the ocean through the round wooden windows of our vintage yellow room. Little soaps and shampoo bottles arranged on the clean linen were the first thing Savani and I spotted after checking in. After spending two nights in a highly primitive accommodation, we were here in a fancy French house. It was indeed time travel, moving from ancient huts into the colonial era.

The pace of Pondy is that of a bicycle. You could spot more bicycles than mopeds here. It is best to cover the town's long roads without missing out on a pretty letterbox or a street lamp. The three of us were given ladies' bicycles; mine was blue, Sushant took the turquoise one and Savani was left with the pink, and she complied. With no specific route in mind, we let ourselves go wherever we pleased.

Our bikes rolled from the thick shade of the gulmohar, chasing sunbeams in between. Every house was unique in its own way. Wooden doors, carved letterboxes, verandas filled with white and pink bougainvillaea, slender iron street lamps. The aromas of hot coffee and pizzas fresh out of the oven from nearby cafes filled the air. It reminded me of the movie *Before Sunrise*, and I made a mental note to watch the other two movies from that trilogy once I got back home.

* * *

Valaiyapattiyar

Peddling, we crossed H.M. Kassim Salai, and the little French settlement drastically changed into a bustling Tamilian metropolitan area. By this time, Savani had given up and was walking with her bicycle. We slow-peddled to match her pace.

Valaiyapattiyar was the best thing that happened to us on this trip. Again, we found it during an aimless walk! It was less a restaurant and more a heritage house converted into a simplistic hotel with a relatively cheap menu. They had placed tables and chairs in the courtyard surrounded by huge pillars, a classic Tamilian architectural motif. The menu and the owners' zest to tell us about every dish gave us the confidence to experiment. They had prawns, mutton, quail, ducks and a great variety of fish. On recommendation, we ordered prawns and roast chicken and were given a few curries to taste—an orange one, a green one and a red one! I found a prawn in the red one and the green one was just a carnival of coconut. The prawns were juicy, tender and loaded with rich south Indian spices. Pepper and curry leaves were added generously! Normally, the three of us would hardly ever find a place like that.

Apparently, both my friends had very little appetite. Therefore, we had times when finishing a meal was on me (which I happily did) and also times when, despite the food being delicious, we couldn't finish it off. The regret of not being able to taste everything in this area is inexplicable.

* * *

We knew we just had one day to roam around Pondy and yet after stuffing ourselves with so much food, we decided to crash back in our room and indulge in the most Maharashtrian way possible: a *vamkukshi* (afternoon nap). Afternoons are the worst part of the day. It is when productivity hits a dip. I am sure none of the scientists have ever invented anything in the afternoons. Poets, writers and musicians have interpreted mornings, evenings and nights in so many ways, but it's the damn afternoon you will rarely find any artistic expression for.

On our evening ride, we covered two bookshops, drank three cups of coffee each, quickly walked around the Immaculate Conception Cathedral.

Little things like these made this a memorable trip. I would think of these moments and giggle on my own during commutes. I remember my editor cluelessly looking at me as I smiled at each part of the video that reminded me of the madness happening behind the scenes. It was also then that I realized the three of us speak terrible Hindi.

We had prepared ourselves for a sleepover at Chennai airport for the night because 1) Our flight was next day early in the morning; 2) We didn't want to spend any more money on accommodation; and 3) It was thrilling—the three of us are fans of Tom Hanks in *Terminal*. It was only at a Subway outlet at the airport that we encountered a stranger to indulge in mutual disappointment for airlines, but other than that, it was just us all night entertaining ourselves by analysing Deepika Padukone's career from *Om Shanti Om* to *Yeh Jawaani Hai Deewani*. We didn't even realize our flight had been delayed by three hours. We were the only people laughing among all the agitated passengers in the waiting area.

It was when the flight took off that we slept, and woke up all groggy as it landed. It was raining cats and dogs in Mumbai. The three of us parted ways.

I'll be honest, Savani and Sushant are the kind of friends I doubt sometimes. A voice in me is always critical, wondering if we really have a bond or are they generally this nice to everyone. They both somehow repeatedly prove me wrong. Friendship is

one of the best ways to show love; it's not as passionate as a romantic relationship nor as forceful as any blood relation; it's that sweet spot of organic fondness for each other's being. I got to experience the fun of friendship much later while growing up, but it always lights up my face when I hear a familiar name and reply, 'Oh, we're friends!'

Given a choice, I would choose to travel solo, but I think I now get the motivation behind travelling with friends. It's not for the place that you travel but to make the place a milestone for your friendship. If it's for the people you share a similar wavelength with, nothing can be merrier than that.

I sometimes worry that we might grow apart, that all of this could one day become just a memory. But instead of letting that fear take over, I'm choosing to let it grow organically. I want to grow from this experience and work on making our relationship stronger, so that no matter what happens, we've made the most of our time together.

EIGHT

VARANASI

Riverbank of time

The last episode shot up the views. The social media team was talking numbers that flew right above my head. Appreciation messages came in on a daily basis, as people shared experiences from the first solo trip that they planned after watching my videos. I was figuring out how not to be awkward after running into a fan at a cafe. These moments were special, but I mostly tried to not give in to them because one day this series would end and something else would start from scratch. It was a borrowed fandom. Of course, with its share of criticisms too. Constant travelling and working on edits helped me stay away from these shenanigans.

Meanwhile, we updated ourselves as well: the office was renovated; there were two editors and a proper social media team now. I was reminded that I was promoted from an intern to creative director. The series had a set format now, and so did our approach to working on it. After Chinmay, our content head, left, Sagarika took over all the programming. It was Sagarika, or Rika as I called her, who performed a wide range of tasks that included noting everyone's dates, giving feedback on ideas, maintaining a content calendar (giving her the moniker 'Calender Girl'), sending videos for subtitling, getting approvals, giving life advice and sharing memes, as well as her type-C charger and headphones. There were some jobs that no one else could do as perfectly as Rika. Her being particular about things also turned out to be annoying at times, and we'd have our moments of petty fights too. She roamed around the office, beating her coffee all the time. No one has seen her drink it, though.

Earlier, Anusha would directly transfer the production money to me before every trip. But now that things were streamlined, it was Poorva who dealt with production and money matters. Poorva spoke very little and often gave death stares during conversations, which is why I was scared of talking to her. She managed to be two extremes at the same time: a sweet, pampering grandma, who gave warm hugs, as well as a grumpy, leather jacket rider jack. She was unpredictable. I was so envious of the two of them who could perfectly do all those jobs that I sucked at. With such a lively team and so many other projects running parallelly, BhaDiPa's office had become a powerhouse of ideas, always willing to listen and be open for feedback while coming up with economical ways to execute them.

Due to my semester exams, I couldn't travel anywhere, so we didn't have anything to put out for that month. We would either have to figure out something in the next three days or skip an episode.

'It could be Varanasi!' I suggested. I had saved Varanasi for such a time. Last year in October, having spent a good thirty days there, volunteering at a backpackers' hostel, I knew the place in and out. No matter how much I hesitate from making such strong statements, those were the best thirty days I'd lived. I celebrated Diwali for the first time away from home with a group of strangers. We lit lamps everywhere in the hostel, tried making rangoli, got henna on our hands, the foreigners too pulled off colourful saris and kurtas, and we stayed up all night on the rooftop cafe playing cards and gobbling on sweets. Exploring Varanasi for a month, I was familiar with its lanes, boatmen, a few monks, the temple opening and closing timings—everything. I could even tell all the rituals they did before starting the Ganga aarti.

The sudden plan excited me, as I would be able to relive all those sweet memories. But little did I know that since it was September, the retreating monsoons would have filled the banks of the Ganga, submerging all the ghats.

Day One, 4 September 2019

Aai wasn't home, so I had full freedom to be disorganized. She would have kicked my ass and made me pack my bag a day prior. I could never do that. How can you pack your bag, leaving out your toothbrush for the next morning? How is it a packed bag then? Also, I'd take hours to pack, but having a time constraint of say, an hour or thirty minutes, it'd take me less than fifteen minutes to get ready, along with the thrill. It sounds weird to many, but it honestly does make so much sense. In my defence, I've never left anything behind in that hurry.

For my mother, there is a very thin line between excitement and panic. She most often goes on to panic. She panics when she receives an OTP; she panics when you win a lottery. She would panic even if I had booked my tickets a month ago. It's very annoying, but on days like these, when she isn't home, everything suddenly appears to be tough. The home doesn't feel familiar at all.

I woke up at 3 a.m.—three hours before the flight. Nevertheless, I made it in time. It was a drastic temperature change on landing after a two-hour journey. While Mumbai was clogged by the monsoon, Varanasi was dry as a desert. I was adjusting to flying more frequently than earlier. For a guy who used to spend thirty to thirty-five hours on trains, it almost felt like teleporting. The airport being far away from the city, the scene outside was no less than a railway station. Cabbies rushed to get my backpack and directed me to their cabs with their self-determined rates. But as soon as I showed my wallet, they flipped and ran for other bags to grab on. Not even a single guy looked back.

Seeing me walking out, the cop at the gates, very generously, using his authority, got me a ride till the main road.

'*Arrey, aap student ho; aap se thodi itne paise lenge*,' (You're a student; you shouldn't be overcharged) he said cheerfully.

From the main junction, tripping on Bhojpuri songs, a shared auto dropped me at Luxa Road for only Rs 45. Getting there was even more hectic than the journey from Mumbai to Varanasi. I was staying at Zostel again, the place where I volunteered last year.

'Arrey, Babu!' Anuj bhai sprung out of his chair. He always called me Babu, which I found very embarrassing. Anuj bhai ran Zostel Varanasi, and he knew his job very well. He was this 25-year-old obedient, hardcore, vegetarian Brahmin who knew every verse from the scriptures. His father had taught him all of it, as being a priest was his backup plan just like any Brahmin in this city. He was shorter than me and faster too. Anuj bhai could pull off any task but talk to women.

'Did you get married?' Of all the greeting etiquette, this was the first thing I asked him.

'Arrey, nahi Babu, my mother is searching a good bride for me.'

'Isn't it your job?'

'No, I'll be happy with whoever my mother selects,' said the mama's boy. I wondered if he really meant it or was just pulling my leg.

'Did you have lunch?' he asked.

'Yes, I did. I had some litti chokha on the way,' I said. Litti chokha is a traditional dish: litti are stuffed wheat balls baked on coal, and chokha is an assortment of vegetables cooked in mustard oil. The pungent sting of the mustard oil had left its lasting impact down my throat as well as in my brain.

Well-fed, well-rested and thoroughly cleaned, I left for the iconic evening Ganga aarti, in the company of two American travellers, Jeremy and Nate. We started off with chai worth Rs 6 at a small stall. In most of northern India, tea is served in brittle, single-use terracotta cups called kulhads, made of soft clay from the silt of the river.

'They are biodegradable, cheaper and hygienic than the metal or glass ones,' the cheerful chaiwala informed us. He didn't overcharge us despite seeing two white enthu travellers. 'If you are white, you must be rich,' is the common belief of Varanasi vendors.

The way to Dashashwamedh Ghat is through Godowlia Chowk, arguably the busiest junction of the city. If you follow any road around the ghats, you are likely to end up here. The place is all time full of pedestrians, hawkers, cycle rickshaws rattling around, moped drivers ramming into people, a cow having her me time right in the middle of the road, clueless cops randomly yelling at people sticking to their barricades and everyone honking as though it's their moral duty. The streets of Varanasi are some of the most unpredictable places on Earth. You never know when you're going to land on a pile of cow dung, get run over by a vehicle or be the aim of somebody's stale dinner from the previous night.

The famous Ganga aarti, or what the tourists call 'fire ceremony', is performed on all the eighty-eight ghats of Varanasi, but the grandest of them all takes place on

Dashashwamedh Ghat. If you don't know what a ghat is, I'll try my best to explain. It's a platform on the river bank with stairs for devotees to go into the river for a bath or to perform religious rituals. Hinduism mainly being an agrarian religion,* many of its rituals are nothing but forms of paying gratitude to various natural resources. The Ganga aarti is yet another ancient Vedic tradition of paying tribute to the holy river that had irrigated the nearby lands for ages. The practice is as old as the river and the ghats alongside.

We were an hour early for the ceremony. Children made their way through the tightly packed crowd, selling flowers and candles. It was like standing in the crowd at a concert; the slightest of the body moment would have been felt by the other person. 'Definitely not a great place to have a boner,' I imagined. 'How could one possibly even get one here?' I counter imagined.

The stage for the Ganga aarti was submerged. To my disappointment, they had moved the stage to the terrace of a sari shop nearby. Far from us, but at least a bit closer to God. There were chairs on the terrace, but for that golden seat, sir, you had to pay. I couldn't shoot anything from that distance. Out of disappointment and boredom, we left early. Although the three of us shared an equal zest for adventure, our day was being spent in an extremely lame way. I was documenting everything just for the sake of it.

---

* Lydia Thomas Kissa and Aristidis Matsoukis, 'A Study of the Role of Hinduism on Agriculture in Relation to Climate Change: The Case of India', *Researchgate*, December 2019

Shivji Ka Prasad

Our desperate attempts to salvage our day led us to a lassi shop in Godowlia Chowk.

'Bhaisaab, three strong bhang lassi!' Nate confidently ordered, in his Captain Russel-sounding Hindi. The glass full of white lassi turned dark green after he mixed bhang (edible cannabis) in it. Bhang—yet another attraction of Varanasi. There were government-certified shops preparing bhang and selling it for as cheap as Rs 5 per chunk.

The lassiwala encouraged us by saying, 'Shivji ke nagri me aye ho; Shivji ka prasad samajh kar pee jao.' (You're in the city of Shiva; consider it Shiva's blessing and drink up.) A huge poster of Lord Shiva smoking a chillum caught our attention. It is said that when Lord Shiva drank the poison that came out of churning the ocean, he was given bhang to cool him down.

The three of us chugged it in one go, paid the lassiwala and walked back to the hostel feeling all sober. We had our dinner and played Jenga at the cafeteria, but still couldn't feel anything. We thought we were scammed, but the moment I got up to keep the plates, I tripped and everything around me wobbled. A coloured brush had been dipped in a bowl of still water. I had lost my sense of feeling, but I could see. I could see without blinking. I could see more than I was looking at, in fact.

'Jeremy, do you feel anything?' I asked.

'My head is heavy,' he replied.

'Nate?'

'Yeah . . . a light buzz. I can see you guys are super high, though. I am enjoying it. Jeremy, your eyes are fucking red, dude. You guys are stupid; it's hilarious watching you high,' Nate heckled us.

Somehow, we made it to the dorm, helping each other balance in the pitch dark. I fell on my bed with my head heavy, throat dry and mind rushing on multiple levels. No one had told me bhang makes you hallucinate. Laying on my bed in the haunting darkness, I kept staring at a light bulb through a blue glass window, terrified that I'd die as soon as the light goes off. Just like how it is in O. Henry's short story 'The Last Leaf'. With that thought in mind, I sobbed like a toddler. Teardrops ran down my eyes, wetting the pillow. A part of me also wanted to drink water and get up to pee, but I chose to stick to the most dramatic role. Subsequently, all the darkness started to merge into the thin speck of light. I was blabbering something too, which annoyed and woke up a Spanish girl sleeping next to my bed.

'I know you're going through something, but can you please keep it low?' she said in a sympathetic tone. I giggled as I got back into reality and heard another giggle from another bed in the dark. It was surely Nate, for only he knew what we'd done. I realized that the lassi guy wasn't kidding when he said, '*Shivji ka prasad hai beta, pee lo*.'

* * *

Day Two, 5 September 2019

I woke up with a heavy head after sleeping for eons. Jeremy and Nate were still dead on their bunk beds. Due to yesterday's aarti fiasco, boat rides and long walks across the ghats were out of option. Sitting at the cafeteria with a cup of strong coffee and the map laid open, I started to figure out what else could be covered in the shoot.

The Silk Route

There is a Muslim neighbourhood called Lallapura known for its household looms that have been manufacturing the world-famous Banarasi silk saris since the medieval era. Although I know nothing about saris, the process of weaving is a trip to watch. Moreover, such small household businesses not only contribute to the local economy but also retain their cultural identity. Such occupations definitely deserve to be acknowledged. Shooting this lesser-known part of Varanasi would be fun, I wondered.

The bylanes of Lallapura being too tiny, the cycle rickshaw dropped me a few blocks away. I could hear the rattling of power looms even before I had reached. Along the empty lanes were noisy basements full of artisans running their looms. Although many of them were replaced by power looms, some old craftsmen chose to stick to the traditional methods. The last time I was here, one

of the vendors showed me around and explained the whole process of how they turn arthropod excreta into a brilliant work of art.

'These silk saris are so thin, you can actually fit them into a matchbox,' he repeated every other minute. A Bangladeshi girl actually went ahead and bought one for the crazy amount of Rs 70,000! That is nuts! Seventy thousand rupees for a sari? It was more shocking when she said that the saris they sell here are not even half the price of those in fancy stores. I could produce a movie with that much money. 'Producing movies' or 'buying camera gear' has become my default measure of comparing costs. But looking at the working conditions of the craftsmen, it seemed that their share in the profit was equal to that of the silkworms. The basements were shabby and the machines not oiled properly, but, ironically, the fabric was vibrant and shiny. Colourful threads of red, yellow, green, orange and so on were woven into a fine sheet textile designed with gold called zari. Although a treat for the eyes, it is disturbing to imagine that the drapes around the tall and skinny mannequins in shimmering stores come from places such as this.

As I stepped into one of the busy workshops, everyone stopped their work and looked at me standing at the door. I was blocking their light, I realized.

'*Andar aa sakta hu*?' (Can I come in?) I asked hesitantly.

'*Ha bhai, bilkul, darwaza khula hai*,' (Sure, you can; the door is wide open) said someone, and everyone resumed their work. I took out my camera and started filming the process. It grabbed the attention of many. There were four labourers, each handling two looms at a time. Wearing checkered lungis and *banian*s (vests), chewing paan and changing the sequence of threads every time. The machine passed the thread from a wooden stencil and weaved it in a symmetrical pattern. These cards were handmade, and each set had a unique design. A worker took interest in explaining his job to me, but apart from the sound of the power looms, anything else was barely audible. Living in that chaos, the locals of Lallapura had grown deaf to that noise.

* * *

It was way past my lunch time, the time when a meal seems too heavy, but you don't want to stay hungry either. This turned out to be the best time to indulge in some chaat. Although chaat is primarily consumed in northern India, the taste of this street food varies from region to region. I tagged along with some hostel mates for a chaat conquest to Deena Chaat Bhandar, the best of its kind. I used to visit here every other day during my last trip. Several consecutive rounds of chole chaat, papdi chaat, aloo chaat and katori chaat took our taste buds on a roller-coaster ride of sweet, savoury, spicy and tangy flavours and lulled to satisfaction at the first bite of hot and tender gulab jamun. Aatish, a traveller from Hyderabad who also turned out to be a viewer of Budget Backpacking, generously paid for us.

A boat ride to individuality

If you ask me to close my eyes and imagine my last Varanasi trip, the first image to appear would be of the morning boat rides across the Ganga. Floating in solace, rowing through the mist. Watching the rising sun warm up the activities at the ghats. It would be a big disappointment to take this yearning back home this time.

'Babu, you can visit Assi Ghat. There is less water at Assi; I have seen some boats functioning there a few days ago. You might as well get to watch the aarti clearly,' Anuj bhai said, sinking in his shaky chair. He looked even shorter behind the reception desk.

'You want to go to Assi Ghat? You want to attend the Ganga aarti? Boat ride? Huh?' he asked two German ladies who had come to him for recommendations. It was funny when he waved his hands in a circular motion to explain the word 'aarti'.

'*Babu, inko bhi leke jao saath me,*' (Buddy, take them along with you) he said as though I was still a volunteer. Stephen, a hazel-eyed French film-maker of Sri Lankan origin, tagged along with the three of us (the two German girls and I).

Fortunately, a boatman at Assi agreed to take us on a ride for only Rs 500 for one hour. It was a surprising rate considering the scarcity. While the German girls were carpe diem-ing, Stephen and I were anxiously setting up our cameras. The sun had set by the time we were done. We gave up on filming and laid back to have our individual moments. The chaos on the ghats dwindled away, leaving only the sound of rowing and the oars rubbing the edges. Floating candles and flowers sent from the ghats carried the wishes of many. Clueless of where to go and what to do with the wishes. Or have they been heard already?

The rowing had stopped. I was back in the Ganga. In Rishikesh, it was cold, young, wild, pure and swift. Here, though still a bit cold, it was calm, magnificent, old and polluted. One side of the river was shimmering and lively, with thousands of people coming in search of something every day, while the other side was a dark and lifeless landmass of sand. It's so interesting to see how this divide not just affects the land but also the belief system of the people settling here. But what stands out the most is how our perspectives shift as we switch roles, whether we're participants or mere observers. The crowd I was part of a while ago looks entirely different from here. No matter how connected I feel to it, this moment of solitude brings a sense of individuality that is enough to avoid being lost in that crowd. Perhaps that's the true gift of travel.

Day Three, 6 September 2019

My last shoot day started at the Ram Bhandar with a soulful breakfast of kachori chaat and crispy fresh jalebis. The shop had been renovated; the hand-painted board with Ram Bhandar scrawled across it in Devnagari script was replaced by a glossy acrylic sheet with the title printed in bold, red English letters. The modern avatar of Ram Bhandar in the still rustic Thatheri Bazar lane looked as though my grandma just dyed her hair blue.

However, the taste hadn't changed a bit. The ratio of chickpea curry, pudina (mint) and imli (tamarind) ki chutney was perfect. The jalebis were hot and crispy and not too sweet. If you're reading this book to plan a trip, 'The Ram Bhandar' is a place you shouldn't miss. Again, there are multiple Ram Bhandars, so make sure you go to the one that has its title embossed on an acrylic board, bold red with a PNG cut-out of a *mukut*, or crown, on top.

The Burning Ghat

Among all the eighty-eight ghats, only two are used for cremation—Manikarnika Ghat and Harishchandra Ghat. They say the dead cremated in these two places attain moksha,[*] or direct liberation. This belief fuels an endless line of pyres, with an average of 100 bodies cremated daily. At Manikarnika, the fire is said to have been ignited by Shiva himself, a flame that has never been extinguished. The same sacred flame is used to cremate the dead.

A lane narrow enough to fit four people and a fifth fellow on their shoulders led to the riverfront. Huge stacks of wood started to appear after a few metres. People stood congested on the small portion of Manikarnika Ghat; everything else was submerged. The workers carried out their activities swiftly through the family members of the dead standing still. I sat at a teastall watching two bodies being cremated side by side. Usually, there are more, but now they could only fit two.

---

[*] 'Manikarnika Ghat', Tour My India, https://www.tourmyindia.com/states/uttarpradesh/manikarnika-ghat-varanasi.html#:~:text=Manikarnika%20Ghat%20is%20one%20of,Scindia%20Ghat%20and%20Dashashwamedh%20Ghat

The task of cremation and keeping the sacred fire alive falls to the Dom community, who have performed this duty for generations. They work in harsh, almost inhuman conditions, seemingly immune to the emotional weight of their labour. It's hard to fathom what drives them to endure the burning heat day after day. They are called the chosen ones of Shiva, yet their lives are marked by oppression, devoid of basic necessities and overshadowed by death. The Dom community, so central to Varanasi's rituals, remains invisible in the broader life of the city.

During my last trip to Varanasi, a friend and I were determined to visit the underground temple of Masaannath at Manikarnika Ghat. The only path there crossed through the cremation site. We had to sprint through eight burning pyres under the intense heat to make it in time for the iconic night aarti. As we approached the temple, two men stopped us. 'You can't go inside,' one of them called out. 'You might have been touched by a Dom. Go take a bath and then come,' he continued. 'Or come tomorrow,' added the other. It was the first time someone had made such a distinction so clear.

We turned toward the cremation site. The Doms continued their work, lifting bodies onto the pyres we had just rushed past. A wave of disbelief, anger and disappointment rendered me speechless, standing cold amid the flickering flames and the men who wanted us to leave. Doms, the chosen ones, although helped people attain salvation, live in the shadow of the very fire they tend.

No matter what time of the day you visit Manikarnika Ghat, it feels the same. Be it the night of my last trip or the morning of this one.

'Nobody is allowed to cry here. It is a sacred journey of the soul towards eternity. It should be celebrated and not wept upon. Women are emotional and can't handle the sight, so they are kept away,' said the tea stall owner after asking him why I couldn't see any women here. I'm sure there's a more logical explanation, but in Varanasi, especially on the ghats, everyone has their own rationale for these rituals. Like the time I overheard a local explaining to an American why pregnant women aren't cremated: 'The foetus inside a woman's womb is suspended in a vacuum, which can explode if set on fire.' He had said that with conviction.

One of the two corpses was taking too long to catch fire. Three Doms were busy struggling to adjust the wood with their long bamboo sticks. The corpse was too tall for the pile of wood. I could see his foot hanging out of the wooden logs. It swelled up as the body burned, until a point where it could actually fall off. It had now turned pale and ugly. The Dom

poked it with his stick and pushed it inside. The flame engulfed it in no time.

In moments like these, all talk of morality, goodness, cruelty or values fades away. We are reminded that beneath it all, we are just flesh and bones, bound to a cycle with no absolute truth. At Manikarnika Ghat, you come face to face with the grimmest realities, both external and internal. I don't know if the dead truly attain salvation here, but those who leave this place take with them answers to some of their most unsettling doubts.

* * *

Bylanes of Varanasi

It was the last day, and our last attempt to catch the Ganga aarti brought Stephen and I to Assi Ghat again. This time we went walking all the way through the maze of small alleys running along the riverfront. That part is the oldest of all and the most romanticized in Bollywood films and literature. As told by a local, the region being prone to foreign invasions, it was easy to run and hide in such narrow and complex lanes, or galis. Although this part of the city is devoid of traffic, the cows are everywhere. It is impossible for even a single traveller to not spot a cow blocking the way in his entire trip. Just like their jumbled network of overhead wires, these lanes are tough to navigate, even for Google Maps. So, ultimately, the only source of knowing the directions are the nonchalant locals. With their mouths packed with paan, they will just slightly nod their heads and have you guess the direction.

Stephen had his camera, and I had mine; we took our time shooting everything that caught our fancy. Shops of books, perfumes, Madhubani paintings, the smell of laung lata (local sweet) spreading across the neighbourhood, lassiwalas churning lassi in big pots, a snake charmer kid running with a cobra in a loose basket, vendors heckling each other and quickly getting back to business as soon as a tourist walks in, self-proclaimed Aghoris sharing their chillums with a bunch of foreigners. The best way to explore Varanasi is to simply get lost in these bylanes. They will always lead you to a surprise.

* * *

The first thing we did on reaching Assi was go to Vatika Cafe. If you've watched the film *Masaan*, this is the place that Deepak (Vicky Kaushal) takes Shalu (Shweta Tripathi) to on their first date. This place serves heavenly apple pies. I know, having an apple pie in a place like Varanasi sounds strange, but they genuinely bake it well. Perfect edges with a warm and tender filling of juicy apples and honey with a hint of cinnamon inside. Last time, an English backpacker and I had come here. We loved it so much that we took a whole tray for the entire hostel. I could come to Varanasi a million times only for Vatika's apple pie.

We kept ourselves busy at a handicraft store nearby until it was time for the ceremony. Stephen was searching for a poster of Shiva performing the Tandava, the aggressive dance he is known for. Unaware of the exact word, Stephen kept on explaining, 'I don't want him meditating. Show me a more badass Shiva,' to the shop owner.

Meanwhile, Surabhi, an Instagram friend, showed up. She was a student at Banaras Hindu University (BHU) and lived nearby. The three of us grabbed convenient seats and sat for the Ganga aarti. The preparations before the ceremony are as beautiful as the main gig. Watching the platforms being cleaned, lamps lighting up and flowers arranged sets you up for the treat ahead. Unlike at Dashashwamedh Ghat, pre-recorded chants were played here. Nevertheless, the rituals were the same all throughout. Starting on a high-tempo *Shiva Tandava Stotram*, followed by the melodious Ganga aarti and ending with soothing shlokas. Watching young priests in silk drapery waving the burling lamps in each direction in perfect sync is a sight to behold. These rituals have been the same every single day for several generations, but every time you watch them, it fills you with peace.

Assi Ghat

After the aarti, Stephen and Surabhi left. I stayed back until the ghat was empty again. A few BHU students were strolling after dinner, discussing politics; an old foreigner sang Johnny Cash playing his old guitar. He wore a cute panda cap with a mic tied to it; the nimbu chaiwala was wrapping up his business. The bottom of his long kettle 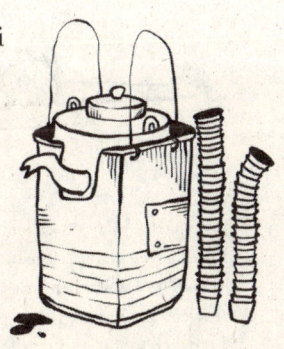 had a compartment for burning coal (Varanasi folk have many such jugaads for a lot of their daily needs); self-proclaimed masseuses roamed around taking people's hands and giving them a demo of their skill. They were actually good at it. Their clients laid on the stairs and got their backs fixed; two kids dressed up as Shiva and Vishnu ran around begging for money.

Varanasi has something for everyone. Some find it in temples; others elsewhere. It was here that Tulsidas composed his legendary works,[*] Adi Shankaracharya propagated the concept of *Advaita Vedanta*,[†] King Harishchandra himself cremated the dead[‡] and Kabir found the bliss of solitude.[§] The ghats of Varanasi have been the perfect catalyst for various cultural evolutions, home for great artists and have flourished several schools of Indian philosophy. Inspiration, livelihood, knowledge and faith—the ghats of Varanasi have been home to everyone seeking these.

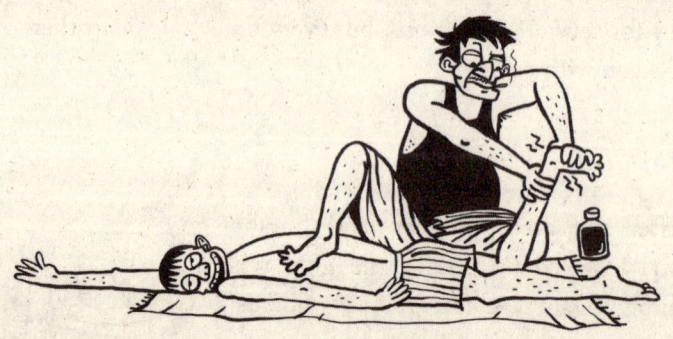

---

[*] Samyuktha Vijay, 'Awakening Devotion: The Life and Works of Tulsidas'

[†] Renuka Narayanan, 'Kashi: In step with history', *The Hindu*, 13 November 2021, https://www.thehindu.com/features/magazine/Kashi-In-step-with-history/article59835333.ece

[‡] 'Harishchandra Ghat', Kashivishwanath.in, https://kashivishwanath.in/harishchandra-ghat-history/

[§] Anuradha Goyal, 'Finding Kabir—The poet and saint in Kashi', India Tales, 7 January 2013, https://www.inditales.com/kabir-in-kashi/

The Varanasi I experienced on my last trip was very different from the one this time. I shouldn't really compare a month-long stay to a three-day getaway, but, in physical terms, this city is changing a lot. The narrow lanes are being made wider. The government's programme to create a gigantic corridor for the Kashi Vishwanath Temple and revamp Dashashwamedh Ghat is in full swing. I actually found myself on a clearing full of demolished houses after passing by Manikarnika Ghat. During the demolition, several other ancient temples were discovered hidden in the close clutter of houses. The ghats, with whatever was left on the land, were the same, as were the people on it. With all their smiles, judgements, beliefs, fears and faiths.

Although the city is changing in many ways, change, however, is not Varanasi's favourite thing. No matter how poetic the city's character is, it has the face of deep-rooted patriarchy and casteism. I remember talking to a ten-year-old kid at a shop, and the first thing he asked me was:

'*Kaun jaat ho?*' (Which caste do you belong to?) It was a shock for me to see such a young kid discussing caste.

'*Matlab?*' (What do you mean?) I asked, still not expecting what he meant.

'*Arrey jaati . . . jaati . . . Jaise hum Brahmin hai, ye bhai Yadav hai . . . tum kaun ho?*' (Just like I am a Brahmin, this fellow is a Yadav, what is your caste?) He explained.

I wanted to hear more from the boy, but seeing me a bit stunned, the elders chased him away.

Religion is a big part of this place. For me, although I belong to the same faith, I cannot relate to a lot of its ritualistic practices. At twenty, religion is still a big word for me. Here, however, the aarti sounds the same as the oars unsettling the water. The aroma and first sip of nimbu chai are as soothing as the bell chimes from a distant temple.

For this reason, I feel Varanasi is each one's personal trip and not necessarily the same every time. The city treats you according to what you bring with you. It is unsettling and overwhelming yet calming to the core. It is up to one to choose to get lost in the lanes of chaos, centre yourself at the ghats or just observe from the other shore of objectivity.

NINE

NORTH GOA

Any time of the day in Goa is afternoon.

Travelling with a backpack is no less than a duo trip, as it occupies as much space as an obese toddler. Every time I'm at a cafe or in a bus, I have to spend a few minutes adjusting it. Of all my anxieties, losing my bag from my sight is the biggest one. I would rather sit uncomfortably than keep my bag in the overhead compartment of a bus and risk getting down without it. Yes, that has happened before.

A happy accident

As I boarded the bus and was busy struggling to fit my bag in the front of my seat, a German guy came looking for his seat and stopped next to mine.

'Yeah, 11!' he said, dumping his backpack, which was heavier than mine. Now, we both were struggling with fitting them beneath our seats.

'Hey, man! Heading to Goa?' He figured, obviously. 'North or South?' he asked.

'North Goa,' I replied.

'Oh great, I am sure you'll love it,' he added zestfully, as if he had an ancestral home there.

'Oh, have you been there before?' I asked.

'Thrice,' he boasted, adding, 'this is my second time in India.'

'Second time? That's interesting; so what was it that brought you here again?' I was curious.

'It was an accident,' he smirked.

'An accident?'

'Yeah, dude, it's a funny story . . .' and he started. Co-passengers like him make long journeys fun.

'When I first came to ze India . . .' he said in his German accent, vaguely pronouncing 'the' as 'ze'.

'I fell in love with ze place. I go back to Germany, and a few months after that I have a road accident. Ze bike hit me . . . I broke my leg. But all the treatment costs were taken care of by my insurance company, and ze guy who hit me also gave me money. So, I thought I could make a second trip to ze India with that money,' his brown eyes grew wider as he narrated the whole story.

'When I go back, I wish one more bike hit me and ze guy gives me more money and I come again here,' he finished.

He could have gone anywhere else . . . or chosen to do anything else with that money. Like buying the latest iPhone, repairing his house, opening a cafe or hiring strippers. Him choosing backpacking AND choosing India again, reassured me that life choices are purely to be made according to one's fundamental beliefs. They are highly subjective yet equally valid and often come from instinct. The German guy had visited eight states so far. What he sees must be so different from what I would see, I wondered in glee.

* * *

Goa, especially North Goa, is what I consider a tourism hazard. In 1510, the Portuguese* invaded Goa; in 1969, the hippies took over[†] and now it's the tourists. I hate it for being so touristy. The first time I had come here, I was ten, and I remember very well that we spent only ten minutes at Calangute Beach and swore to never come here again. This was the main reason I was avoiding shooting an episode there. We knew this episode would have great shareability despite there being a thousand more such videos on the Internet. I have been to Goa several times for freelance work, but shooting a 'travel video' was never a priority. The Internet is already filled with videos like 'Secret beach in Arambol', 'HIDDEN RAVE

---

[*] Britannica, 'History of Goa', *Britannica Encyclopedia*, 5 May 2024, https://www.britannica.com/place/Goa/History

[†] Andrew Pereira, 'The hippie who got Goa the globe', *Times of India*, 22 November 2015, https://timesofindia.indiatimes.com/city/goa/the-hippie-who-got-goa-the-globe/articleshow/49875431.cms

PARTY', 'Cheapest BOOZE in Goa', 'This NUDE BEACH is a must visit', 'Where to find HOT RUSSIANS in Goa' and 'Goa TRANCE party vlog watch full video HD'.

Tourism is perceived as Goa's sole identity; it doesn't need any more promotion for that. Everybody rushes to Goa and does the exact same things, things that could not be further from the true essence of this place. I am talking about all those locations that Rohit Shetty has shot his *Golmaal* franchise in, especially in North Goa. But there is one thing I can keep returning to Goa for—the food. Oh my god, the food. I figured I'd be able to have six fish thalis during my three-day trip; it was that easy.

Day One, 18 October 2019

One egg roll, a chicken puff and two prawns rissois with a cup of tea at Cafe S.F. Xavier, followed by a short walk across the ever-lively Mapusa market, started off my day. Mapusa bus stand is the main junction for buses connecting every part of North Goa. Every bus that leaves from Mapusa has at least one Goan aunty with a Princess Diana haircut and a 'Catholic' dress, who has heavily shopped for ingredients for an upcoming feast. She always gets the front seat, and every bus conductor knows her name. She has issues with people with big backpacks and often gives them a piece of her mind in Konkani. But once you befriend these 'beasts', they will be the warmest to you. Last year, on a trip, the owner of my hostel, Gracy Aunty, who was a bitch to everyone, had helped me score some feni (the popular regional spirit primarily distilled from cashews) after I complimented her plants.

On my way to Anjuna, I changed my mind and got off midway at Vagator. I had heard Vagator was quieter and had better cafes than Anjuna. Also, I'd never been to Vagator. Due to the off-season, most of the hostels were under renovation and were preparing for the New Year crash. I walked in and booked myself a bunk bed at the Folklore Hostel. It was a traditional Konkani house converted into a backpacker hostel. It had all the modern amenities, yet its old-school charm was carefully retained.

Settling down, I received a text: 'Where are you in Goa?' It was my friend Malay's reply to my Instagram story about prawn rissois.

'Vagator! You're in Goa too?' I replied.

'Perfect! Our band is performing in Vagator itself. What plans?'

'No plans!'

'Send me your location.'

The first time I met Malay was while we were shooting a vox pop video for BhaDiPa. He was our sound recordist and had been there for many shoots since then. Both of us are known to only wear Decathlon clothes on shoots, or pretty much everywhere. I have never seen the fellow in any other clothes. Malay was always the hardest person to spot on a set. You had to whisper 'Mallu' in some actor's lapel mic, and he would arise from some mysterious corner. He had this secret place on every set that nobody knew about, where he would sit with his sound box thingy and listen to everything the actors said, even after their shot. One could only spot him when the actors had to change mics or during lunch break, often excitedly rushing over his new vegan diet. Whenever someone in the crew talked during the shot, you could hear him yell, 'Guys, silence ya! What is this, ya!'

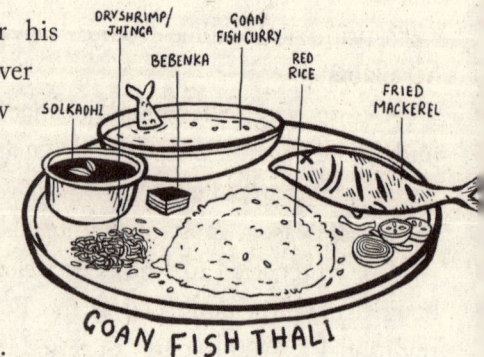

DRY SHRIMP/ JHINGA
GOAN FISH CURRY
BEBENKA
RED RICE
FRIED MACKEREL
SOLKADHI

GOAN FISH THALI

We met for lunch at Vinayak Restaurant. It was my first time there . . .

After that, every time I visited Goa, Vinayak's utterly satisfying fish curry became a mandate. We rode to Chapora Fort, but being thrown off by herds of tourists swarming all over the place, we decided to settle down at a shack for beer at Vagator Beach (not that it was any less bad). I hadn't even touched the camera. It started to rain outside soon before we decided to leave. We stayed back and ordered two more pints. The drizzle turned into a heavy downpour that lasted for almost an hour. People on the beach rushed into the shack, and the space was messy, cramped and wet in no time. Every single person was either sweaty, salty or so wet that even their wives wouldn't go near them. It was definitely not a good day for the waiters. Done with regretting not leaving early, we chose to drive in the heavy rain, managing enough not to skid but landing up being drenched.

North Goa was exactly how I had imagined: trios of drunk men in tank tops, driving recklessly; girl squads jamming the road, debating exactly which turn they missed; foreigners wearing beige crochet; but most prominently, the newlywed north Indians. That's the classic type! You will see men in loud, floral, printed shirts with bamboo hats and the women in an eccentric ensemble of spaghetti tops and denim shorts with hands contrastingly covered in a plethora of red bangles. I probably shouldn't be judging them, but it blows my mind that every time I come to Goa, I get to see these exact stereotypes. I have a feeling that these people are extras hired by the Goa Tourism Department to show they are never out of tourists. THEY ALL LOOK THE SAME! Like people in GTA cities.

The incessant growth in tourism and commercialization has developed a new identity for Goa. Or at least for the northern part. During the 1970s, Goa experienced a massive influx of Westerners, mainly after the socio–political disturbance due to the Vietnam War.[†] They called themselves hippies. Since then, these little Konkani villages have changed a lot. The elements from different cultures have come together and given Goa its quirk.

The mainland of Goa is covered by the forests of the Western Ghats and coal mines. Nobody really talks about it; as a result, it has come under the threat of rampant coal mining. The coastline is full of paddy fields and small Konkani settlements. But they also reflect the Portuguese influence through their churches, bakeries and festivals. Cities like Old Goa or Panaji show these colonial

[*] Britannica, 'Hippie Subculture', *Britannica Encyclopedia*, https://timesofindia. indiatimes.com/city/goa/the-hippie-who-got-goa-the-globe/articleshow/49875431. cms

[†] Ned Cogswell, 'The History Of The Hippie Cultural Movement', *Culture Trip*, 13 December 2023, https://theculturetrip.com/north-america/usa/california/articles/ the-history-of-the-hippie-cultural-movement

traces more prominently. Most of the beach shacks are run by people of other states. You will find artisans from Rajasthan and Uttar Pradesh setting up their shops in Arambol's flea market. Daily markets not only have traditional spices but also sell lines of chorizos (Goan spicy smoked pork sausages), an important element of Goan Catholic cuisine. Idols of Jesus and Mother Mary are worshipped with garlands and candles or lamps, just like any Hindu deity. The majority of the Goan population, which is Hindu, has preserved its indigenous identity, celebrating vibrant and unique festivals like Shimgo and Narkasur Vadh. Just like the surnames and the Konkani language, these festivals are similar to those celebrated in the Konkan region of Maharashtra. This intercultural confluence can also be seen in the subtle Portuguese additions to the regional dialects, such as locals referring to each other as *patrao* (boss) and *amigo* (friend), making it a unique linguistic coalescence. This union of multiple cultures has blessed Goa with a novel atmosphere, and that is what draws me here every time, in spite of the mainstream tourist crowd.

Day Two, 19 October 2019

Last night, a hostel friend and I returned late after attending Malay's gig. We then spent a few more hours on the veranda listening to songs from Bob Dylan to Baba Sehgal (we were very sober). Before leaving, Malay and I made plans to rise early and drive up north to Arambol. Ideally, we had to be back by lunch, but by the time I woke up, it was already 11 a.m.! My phone didn't ring either, which meant Malay too was asleep. After a lot of back and forth, we finally left in the scorching heat, and the sun hit our backs badly!

Crossing the Chapora River, we halted on the highway for some omelette and poi (local bread) and continued further towards Morjim. Hopping beaches from Ashwem to Mandrem, we reached Arambol. We were told that Arambol is not as commercial as other places and that only foreigners and hippies go there. We'd heard stories of full moon raves happening on Arambol and were expecting something similar, but at 1 p.m. when the heat would barely let us breathe. Disappointingly, Arambol turned out no different than Anjuna. It became such a hype among desi tourists that everybody invaded Arambol, and now there were more Indians than foreigners.

No sooner had we gotten to the beach, a skinny fellow with a stubble and fluorescent flip-flops incessantly chased us, insisting that we sit at his beach shack. After we refused, he upped his persuasion by offering us massages and booze. We got rid of him after he added, '*Sirji, aapko jo chahiye sab milega,*' (Sir, you'll get everything you want) probably hinting to some shady business. His persistence and rising temperature couldn't let us bear Arambol anymore. The only time we actually had fun was riding through tall palms, spotting brahminy kites and white-throated kingfishers. Marshland and vast rice fields on either side of the roads make driving here a treat. One can spot a plethora of wetland birds, egrets, herons, storks, kingfishers and ibises. On days when nobody is kayaking in the backwaters of Arambol, flocks of stints, stilts and sandpipers swing around the entire place.

Licence?

All this time, we were roaming around on Malay's scooter, but in the evening, when we parted ways, I thought of renting one myself. Renting a moped in Goa isn't a tough task, as far as you own a driving licence. In this scenario, I was likely in danger since my licence hadn't arrived and my RTO receipt wouldn't work in Goa. I wouldn't mind spending my evening at a cafe and making sketches, but that wouldn't give me any content for my video, so I decided to take a gamble and rent a moped for the evening.

'Don't do it, man; they'll stop you for sure. Look at you; you don't even look twenty,' said my gut feeling.

'I know, I know; I'll pay the fine . . . I really need to shoot something,' I reasoned with myself.

With this dilemma, I left for Arpora, a little town near Calangute and Baga, famous for its Saturday Night Market. Nervously driving, I could see the cops standing ahead of me. There was just a single road to Arpora. No escape. I slowed down my moped and gradually stopped some 100 metres before the cops. Seeing them stopping all the tourist vehicles and checking IDs, I quickly made a U turn and drove back for another 100 metres. This happened thrice before I made up my mind to confidently drive past the cops. I raced my scooter, acting all cool. The 'rules' of the great Indian traffic culture suggest ignoring the cops as much as possible, and I abided by them with utmost passion. This fake look of 'normalcy' quickly fell off my face as one of them waved at me to stop. My hands involuntarily pulled the breaks, and my butthole clenched at the same time.

'Licence,' he said. Without looking into his eyes, I took out my phone and showed him my learning licence. He looked at the licence and then looked at me.

'*Hey naahi chaalnar*,' (This won't work) he said in Marathi, assuming from my surname. I acted dumb while he explained to me how I'd end up in jail. There were several other people too, mostly couples. The guys were super embarrassed and making calls on their phone.

'See, this is a tourist vehicle, so even if you pay the fine, I have to confiscate the scooter.' I kept looking at him cluelessly as he spoke. 'Okay, you do one thing . . . How much money do you have?' He finally made himself clear. I opened my wallet in front of him, which had only three bills of Rs 100.

'Okay, give 300 and go,' he said in utter disappointment, and he took all of it. 'And if someone stops you ahead, just tell them you've been checked,' he continued. The Goan traffic police don't care if you're carrying a bomb; you just need to have legit papers and a helmet. If not, you'll have to contribute to their passive income. I was really lucky to get away by paying only Rs 300, while the current rates were around Rs 800–1600. What surprised me even more was when he said, 'If they stop you ahead, just tell them you've been checked.' It was that easy to get away with all of this!

'Thank you, sir,' I said with a smile and left. All this while two notes of Rs 500 remained untouched in my back pocket. Thanks, but no thanks to Warren Buffett diversification saved my ass.

These are the moments when you are grateful for travelling alone—you don't feel that embarrassed in a place where nobody knows you. I mean, if I were with a date, we would have never seen each other again. I crossed five more check posts saying, 'I've been checked at the prior one.'

After all this drama, I made it to Arpora. When I asked for the night market, a shopkeeper pointed at an empty, muddy ground. It turns out the market didn't set up due to the rains. I broke the law and bribed an enforcement agent just to see an empty ground next to a big hoarding of some cement brand! The model on the hoarding grinned at me for how utterly wasteful my day was.

* * *

Day Three, 20 October 2019

When Goa was colonized by the Portuguese, a deadly epidemic of plague* spread across the administrative area currently known as Old Goa. The population depleted drastically; many died and many fled. The capital was then shifted to Panaji.

---

* Poonam Binayak, 'A Guide to Fontainhas, Goa's Latin', *Culture Trip*, 22 December 2022, Quarterhttps://theculturetrip.com/asia/india/articles/a-guide-to-fontainhas-goas-latin-quarter

The elite fidalgos (Portuguese noblemen), bureaucrats, doctors and teachers bought cheap land around Altinho Hill and established a beautiful settlement, Fontainhas. Today, in the heart of modern Panaji, time comes to a standstill in the charm of the Altinho Hill and the colourful vintage houses of Fontainhas.

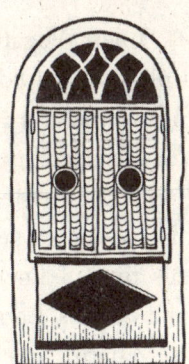

It was Murli and Maria who first introduced me to this place. During my trip to Varanasi in 2018, I met Maria's brother at a hostel. After returning home, he connected me with Maria and her partner, Murli, who had started their own venture conducting heritage walks in Goa. That same year, I had the opportunity to photograph their heritage walks. If it weren't for them, I might have only scratched the surface of Goa's heritage.

With them, I had my first bite of serradura, my first ros omelette and my first sip of feni. After our shoots, we would sit with Chico, a charming old Goan uncle who played Konkani and Portuguese songs on his guitar and shared stories from his youth. Or we'd walk alongside Alirio, who was born and raised in these quarters. We would make pit stops at stairs or on other people's balcãos to rest while he reminisced about how the area looked in earlier days. He'd talk about the time when the roads didn't have streetlights, making them ideal spots for couples to steal moments of love, or how he serenaded his wife before their marriage.

Although my time with Murli and Maria was brief, it was always filled with learning something new. I rarely leave Goa without seeing them every time I come here.

I left Vagator early, made a pit stop at Old Goa and then met Maria and Murli in Panaji. We decided to stroll around Fontainhas—the same old drill that we never get bored of. By this time, I knew almost every lane of this Latin quarter. But the charm of those brightly  coloured houses, tiled roofs, lazy cats, arched seashell windows and azulejo-styled name plates would keep drawing me here.

It's hard to believe such a neighbourhood exists right in the middle of the busiest city in Goa. Although the houses are arguably well maintained, the majority of the people living there are old. They don't have to catch trains, report to their bosses or pay rent, I thought. I mistook them for not having anything to worry about until I met 'him'.

The Violin Man

It was afternoon, the time when Goans enjoy their siesta. The scorching sun and the rice we had for lunch made us too lethargic to walk any further, so we sat on the stairs of a big white chapel, doing nothing. That was when three of us heard a soft violin loop. I can never forget those notes, since it was the only sound audible and everything else was quiet.

'It's the same guy we saw at the bakery,' said Maria. While on our walk, we had halted at a bakery. I remembered seeing a white-haired man in ironed trousers and a striped shirt walk in. I vividly remember him, as it was just us and him at the bakery.

'He does that every day, wearing the same clothes. No one knows why; no one even dares to ask. He's quite temperamental,' she continued.

Among those freshly painted bungalows stood a pale, cracked house. The same old man, but in raggedy shorts and a threadbare inner vest played his untuned violin at his window. The same note over and over.

Curiously, I approached the house and stood near the window, listening to his music. I smiled at him as he noticed me; he smiled back.

'Are you from here?' he inquired.

'No, sir,' I replied.

'Where then?'

'Mumbai.'

He glanced at me and continued with his music. I silently walked away.

The fact that he let me stay for more than a minute and, moreover, engaged in small talk, astounded Maria. 'No one ever gets to do that,' she said. The more she spoke about him, the more I was intrigued by him and his thing with the violin. Until then, I had never known anyone who played the violin, especially on a non-occasional moment.

Late in the evening, I set out to take some extra B-rolls of the area. The shoot was finished, but I was still looking for something else worth capturing. While passing through the same lane, I heard the violin again. It was the same person, in the same clothes, in the same spot, playing the same loop. We exchanged a light smile again, and I silently stood there, listening to him play.

'Nice camera,' he said, stopping me as I was about to leave.

'Oh yes, thank you. Would you mind if I shoot you playing?'

He nodded in a bit of grumpy denial.

Abruptly, he stopped playing and disappeared into his house. I froze, unsure if I'd crossed some invisible line. The silence hung heavy, and just as I decided to leave quietly, he reappeared, holding a photo frame. His hands trembled as he held it out to me, a silent offering. I, who had almost given up on learning anything about him, was taken aback by his sudden eagerness. In the frame, a couple smiled with a baby in their arms—his son or daughter, I assumed.

'It's nice,' I said, trying to fill the uncomfortable void.

'Come in; I will show you more!' he insisted.

From no angle did he seem like the guy Maria had described. Temperamental? He just invited me to his house. Here I got to see him clearly; his house too. It was cracked, dusty and disorganized. Old frames of collage art delicately hung on the walls.

'Do you live here alone?' I asked.

'Yes. But my brother from Germany has come here for a few days,' he said, his voice barely above a whisper, each word a struggle.

'And who is in the photograph?' I asked hesitantly.

He didn't answer, just stared at the frame in my hands, his silence speaking volumes. There was something heavy, something unspeakable, that he kept locked away. His eyes, once defensive, now seemed lost, as if he was searching for a way to let me in but didn't know how. I could feel his hesitation, his desperate attempt to protect whatever was left of his pride.

'You do this every day?' I asked, pointing at his violin.

'Yes.'

'How long?'

'Since I was seven.'

'Seven! And why do you play the same tune?'

'This one is my favourite; I keep practising it.'

When there was nothing else to say, I took his leave. I did not want to disturb him any further. He too waved me off happily (which was probably very rare). Maria couldn't believe any of it. I never did find out who was in  that photo frame or what the tune meant to him. But as I walked away, I realized that maybe it wasn't about finding answers.

The more I thought about it, the more I understood that his life was like that looped melody—repetitive and worn down—but somehow still going. He probably kept playing the same tune, not just because it was his favourite, but maybe because it was the only piece of himself he could still control. In those few minutes, I saw a man wrestling with time, trying to hold on to a past that was slipping away, and for a brief moment, he let me glimpse that struggle.

I left with more questions than I had answers, but I also left with a sense of quiet respect for the battle he fought every day, the battle of staying connected to a world that had long moved on without him. And, in a way, I think we both knew that sometimes, just being heard is enough.

* * *

In a way, I was happy I didn't record the violin man. I have a stronger and more flavourful memory of his appearance and our conversation than any photo. Mainly because of not having to worry about documenting everything.

Not just this one, but all of my Goa trips have been about people. I am so thankful to have vicariously explored Goa first through Sir Mario Miranda's cartoons and not through travel blogs or articles. My father introduced me to him when I was eight and had recently gotten my first cartridge pen. I always strive to see Goa the way he sees it, and maybe that's why some pockets of this place will always remain timeless for me. His depiction of Goan markets, families, tourists and villages remains strong for me to juxtapose with real-life experience while travelling here. All the kinds of people I came across in these trips, I have met them before in Miranda's comics—all of them. Even the violin man, or the Mapusa market Catholic aunty, travellers, vendors, shopkeepers, cats, windows. Laidback, happy, hopeful, jubilant and often annoyed people. His musings on the simple daily life inspire me to point my camera in those directions. Weirdly, documenting people living their daily lives fascinates me. But putting them down in lines or words is a more fun task. This way, I'm sure, the violin man you imagine would be different from one of mine, and as someone else reads this book, a new violin man would be born.

Places keep changing every other day. Documenting them in pictures, drawings, videos or words is the only way to communicate with future generations. It's the same as our mothers taping our school annual days or first day at swimming class. Watching a place grow is what makes one feel more belonging to it.

TEN

SHILLONG

Your grandmother's homemade jar of pickle.

It was a regular day at the office except, for a change, our brand manager Swanand had brought prawns for lunch—he hates seafood! Saurabh, who handled social media, was pulling his leg. While Swanand tried hard to salvage his comebacks with a few of the catchphrases he used on a daily basis. Every time

Swanand learnt a new word, he'd use it wildly out of context until he got bored of it. Like when he tried baba ganoush, the Lebanese dish, during a trip. He added an 'i' to the end and turned it into 'baba ganoushi', using it as a superlative for just about anything. If I asked, 'Hey, Swanand, did you like the recent edit we made?' he'd instantly reply, 'baba ganoushi!' This went on for almost four-and-a-half months.

Coming back to that day, while I was sneaking a huge chunk of prawn from Swanand's tiffin, our phones beeped. Anusha had sent a link to the office WhatsApp group.

'Check the link I have shared in the group,' Anusha paced out of her cabin.

'There is a cherry blossom festival happening in Shillong,' I read.

'It's currently going on,' I replied.

'I think you should go,' replied Anusha, looking at me.

'For the festival? Now?' I asked, surprised.

'Yeah! It would be cool,' she said. I first thought she was joking, as the festival had already begun and would end the following week. It was too last-minute to travel to a place that far. It turns out it was an actual plan.

'It most likely won't be a part of the Budget Backpacking series; we'll have to come up with a new format for that. You shoot the whole thing, and then let's figure out the structure with the editor later?' said Anusha, as if she had already planned it.

'But then what about the next episode?' I asked.

'You can visit Kolkata while returning. So that it will be two videos in one trip,' she explained, emphasizing the word 'Kolkata', her special place of interest. She is most excited when telling stories of her film school days at the Satyajit Ray Film and Television Institute, Kolkata.

In the same discussion, I also requested Anusha if I could take a DSLR camera to shoot this time. The limitations of filming on GoPro had started showing up while shooting. It had a terrible battery life, poor sound quality and it would freeze and shut down during a shot. Moreover, GoPro's major shortcomings, according to me, were that all of its frames would look the same—grainy, pale, flat and round. It seemed like watching a travel video through a door's peephole. It had very little scope to play around with focus, framing, zoom and light. Mutually agreeing on this, we started looking for economical camera leads. The tickets were booked at the end of the day itself.

My fascination for the north-east of India had grown since my solo trip to Assam in 2018 for Rongali Bihu, the Assamese New Year. Traditionally, that is the time the harvesting season begins and the youth in every village perform the iconic Bihu dance. It is a flirtatious give-and-take between boys drumming the beat on their khol as the girls dance arching their backs, indicating an allure of courtship. They also wear red to signify fertility. I have been actively following North-eastern culture and cuisine for a while now. It has become one of the topics I usually geek out on to new people. When I was twelve, my mother took me to an event of North-eastern folk dances. That was the day when I was surprised to be exposed to this side of India. I remember I was in such awe that I went around backstage shaking hands with every girl and got my cheeks pulled.

What draws me the most to this region is its intriguing mystery. There is very little information about this part of the country. The continuation of the Himalayan range, aka Purvanchal, and the great divide of the mighty Brahmaputra

River have made mobility in this terrain excruciatingly difficult. This geographical inaccessibility is one of the reasons the tribes of the North-East are so distinct from each other. Every valley has a tribe with their own unique lifestyles and rituals. If delved into in detail, these tribes have some amazing social structures, family values and alternative lifestyles. The amount of cultural diversity found in such a small area of land makes the North-East even more interesting.

It's also a bitter fact that even today the eight states of north-east India aren't represented enough. Many people, mainly due to their physical appearance, assume them to be foreigners. Although Shillong is quite a popular tourist destination, my attempt would be to capture the most authentic of its corners. This trip was my personal attempt to understand the North-East a little more and document its rawness.

Day One, 14 November 2019

Here's a tip—North-eastern cuisine is an acquired taste, so it's better to start off with known flavours before getting all experimental. I landed at the Guwahati airport at 10 a.m. My first meal here was roasted duck with a potent bamboo pickle at a modest Manipuri restaurant in Paltan Bazaar. Duck meat is naturally oily, and this dish had an extra dash of mustard oil. Chewing it was a good workout for my jaws. There were only two other things on my plate that could potentially fix my dish—boiled spinach and a scoop of spicy bamboo pickle. Nevertheless, with the owner's hopeful gaze fixed upon me, I soldiered through every bite. The pungent aftertaste clung to me as I made my way from Guwahati, Assam, to Shillong, Meghalaya.

In the shared cab I took, we had quite the crew. A spirited Khasi woman, an introverted fashion designer from Kerala and a Nepali girl returning to her family after completing her education. Our driver was a man of few words, but his driving skills spoke volumes. He manoeuvred the roads as though we were being chased by a gangster, leaving us gripping our seats throughout.

As we crossed the state border, a gust of chilly wind reminded us that we were entering new territory. The highway stretched before us, free from those obnoxious billboards that usually plague our eyes. Instead, we were treated to the sight of lush green bamboo and pineapple plantations covering the mountains like a cosy blanket.

Our excitement grew as we drove past the pink patches of cherry blossom trees further ahead. Many local women had set up small wooden shops along the highway, selling items such as tender bamboo shoots, jars of honey, fresh pineapples, hot chillies, finely chopped bamboo and a lot of dried fish pickles. I noted down everything they were selling when we made a pitstop at the petrol pump and also bought a big, fresh pineapple to savour through the ride.

The non-existent homestay

Thanks to our driver, it took us less than three hours to reach Police Bazaar, the busiest spot in Shillong. The combination of lack of sleep, my off-time heavy lunch and the driver's fast-paced journey kicked in my acid reflux. So, no matter how eager I was to give in to the newness of this lively city, all I longed for was to settle into my accommodation, probably get pampered by some chai and, most importantly, take the first dump of my day.

But I still had to travel 4 km further to reach my homestay. Walking on the steep, hilly roads of Shillong with a heavy backpack was getting too tiresome. This time, there was the additional weight of a mirrorless camera and its lenses. It wasn't even 6 p.m. yet, and the sky was already dark, like it is at 8 p.m. An hour later, I reached 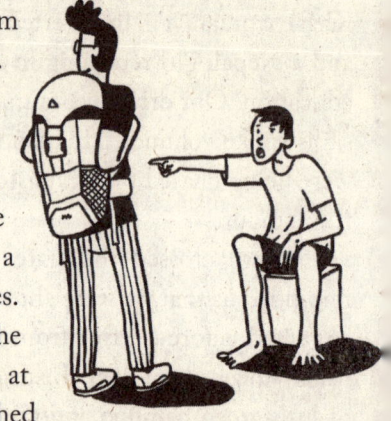 a place away from the city, in an area that seemed devoid of residences, had very few people and shops and had extremely poor connectivity. I walked everywhere around the location but still couldn't find my homestay; none of the locals had even heard its name before.

Finding a slightly better range of mobile network, I called the homestay.

'Hello, I have reached the location but can't find your property?' I finished in one breath.

'Where are you?' asked a distorted voice.

'I don't know . . . I am near the golf links, about 4 km from the Police Bazaar. There are no signs here.'

'No. Not near the golf links . . . the property is 12 km further ahead.'

'WHAT! Twelve?' I exclaimed, shaken by the unexpected reply. It felt like I had just realized that my exam question paper had an extra page during the last ten minutes before the bell rings.

'Yes, go back to the Police Bazaar and get a cab,' the person said.

The call got cut, and I sat near a shop trying to process what the helicopter just happened. I was at an absolutely wrong location, in a lonely place, when it was already dark. How much worse does it have to get? All I could do was walk back, trying to calm my anxious brain and think of a solution.

I explained everything to Poorva, the production manager. She too was baffled. My worst-case scenario was checking into some other hotel in the city. 'No big deal,' I tried to calm myself.

After a while, Poorva texted. She had sent me the location of the Youth Hostel Association's branch in Shillong. The International Youth Hostel Association provides cheap accommodation for trekkers and adventure groups and has their hostels in many parts of India. However, we were doubtful of its existence due to it not having online booking options and the fact that no one was answering our calls.

Having walked for another 550 metres, I heaved a big sigh of relief to see the hostel doors open, right before entering a deserted lobby and an abandoned reception desk. After calling out several times, a guy in a black jacket and brown muffler came running downstairs.

'I want to make a booking; is it available?' I asked with high hopes.

'Are you alone?' asked the guy.

'Yes.'

'Where are you from?'

'Mumbai.'

'Mumbai? How old are you?'

'Twenty.'

'*Ghar pe bata ke aaye ho na?*' (Does your family know you're here?) he asked in an interrogating tone.

'Yes, they do,' I replied.

'Okay, fill this out and give me your ID. It will be Rs 150 per night.' That was the cheapest accommodation I've ever stayed in! 'No bargaining!' he said, adding, 'we don't have rooms; only shared dorms,' and passed me a bulky register.

After a lengthy orientation for my two-night stay at that place, he directed me to a huge empty hall consisting of ten to fifteen beds. There were green curtains and off-white walls; it was basic but clean. It had the ambience of an army cantonment room. This was nothing like the hostels I've been to before, but I couldn't afford to crib. I occupied the bed right next to the *only* charging point in the room and went to take a quick shower. When I returned, the empty dorm was now filled with enthusiastic middle-aged people, loudly chattering about the trek they came from. The poor charging point near my bed now had seven phones and three power banks plugged in along with a broken yet resilient mosquito repellent machine.

I sat on my bed staring at the cluster of those wires with my mind numb. The uncles wouldn't stop bragging at some young boys about how extensively they had trekked in their lifetime and how our generation is doomed due to technology. The dorm was absolute chaos. I was physically and mentally exhausted. At that late hour, everything else was closed. The mishap had anyway killed my hunger. The next day was a shoot day for me; I was sleep deprived and had barely eaten. The cold and the chaos in the room added to my fatigue. I was too tired to even get irritated, so the most natural and spontaneous reflex I could use was to laugh at the whole thing. Such moments remind me of the people I grew up with who knew how to laugh. There have been several such times when finding humour in any situation has salvaged my day from being entirely ruined. The absurdity of the moment was so hilarious that I couldn't help but laugh it off and bury myself in the quilt.

* * *

Day Two, 15 November 2019

Today was the shoot day—a long one. My equipment was fully charged, but here I was struggling to get myself out of the cosy bed into the brutal cold morning. My body jittered as soon as my feet touched the floor. I didn't dare to take a shower and left after changing out of my pyjamas into my hiking trousers. Amid the misty roads, the sunlight fell only on a few patches between two buildings. I halted there, basked for a while and resumed walking after getting enough warmth to calm the grinding of my teeth.

School kids were my co-pedestrians. They walked in bundles of six to eight; this and their agility to overtake slow walkers like me kept them warm. They were much tidier than I was, with their ironed uniforms and shiny boots complementing their youthful comradeship. I was adjusting to seeing people on the roads wearing long overcoats like it was London. My father's generation is probably the last one to have owned and worn sweaters in Mumbai, I figured.

From my observations of the previous day and this walk, I can confirm that the stereotype of North-easterners having great fashion sense actually turns out to be true. I have seen people pull off a decent diversity of clothes ranging from high-ankle boots, stockings and turtlenecks to actual blazers without making it seem extra. The last time I wore a blazer was for a school play; that too, a rented one. I, with my hand in my fleece pocket that still reeked of yesterday's cab ride, felt like an obsolete news reporter at a death metal concert.

Before going to the main venue of the festival, I visited Ward's Lake right next to my hostel. Surrounded by a fine-cut lawn covered with flowers fallen from the nearby trees, Ward's Lake was the centre of attraction for its newly arrived guests—the cherry blossoms. On the banks, the cherry blossoms stood out from the rest of the trees, shedding their papery pink flowers on the still surface of the lake. Quacking geese and pedal boats passed, dissolving the buoyant petals down. A splendid white wooden arched bridge crossed the lake towards the other side of the town. The crowd was as young and charming as a cherry blossom itself. Everybody wanted a picture with the trees—a rare phenomenon to watch. As the crowd increased, flowers falling on the ground got trampled and many were picked up by people; some were even plucking them straight from the trees. Indeed, the cherry blossoms would look prettier on their Instagram feeds than on the trees.

The set-up of the main venue of the 'Cherry Blossom Festival 2019' wasn't remotely connected to cherry blossoms. A giant billboard displaying all the sponsors stood in the middle of the dusty ground. Connected to an empty stage were pop-up stalls of Assamese and Manipuri handicrafts, Khasi fabrics, homemade wines, life insurance policies, pesticides, refrigerators, coaching classes and chiropractors. I roamed around looking for anything cherry blossom-esque. The only thing I found was a pendant at a handicraft stall, which had a 3mm petal of the cherry blossom flower encased in resin. 'Festival of Irrelevance' would have been a more apt title for that event. Looking at my bulky camera, everyone assumed I was a news reporter and forced me to take a bite of them zestfully talking about their business ventures. This alone took up 30 per cent of my footage, which I was sure would never make it on the edit timeline. The entire time I felt like I had gatecrashed a wedding.

As the evening drew near, hordes of people started gathering for a K-pop event. In no time, the dead ground turned into a raging concert. Sudden cheering and hooting caught my attention—it was for the Korean singer Jang Hanbyul, who showed up pretty late. Making my way from the madly enthusiastic crowd, I struggled framing the Korean guy who was fluttering all around the stage. Being short-heighted, I had to stand on my toes, raise my hands up and shoot without being able to look at the screen.

The amount of people and their energies created so much heat that I was boiling inside my fleece. To make matters worse, a girl next to me stabbed her heels on my stressed feet, yelling 'OPPAA OPPAA' right in my ear and perhaps even crying out of excitement. Getting your toe stubbed and not being able to bend down and touch it is one of the worst pains. At this point, I had to obviously give up on shooting, and since I couldn't even watch the performer properly, I turned to watching tall people in the audience. They'd gone nuts. That was probably my first and only encounter with Korean pop music. It makes me feel really old every time I narrate this incident to my K-pop fan friends.

I can normally function anywhere but in crowded places and loud noises. I have severe repulsion towards both of these, which makes me the weakest Mumbaikar. Out of this fear, I have never been to any clubs (not that I could afford clubbing at that age), I can't make quick decisions on directions on noisy streets and I always have a tough time commuting on Mumbai local trains during peak hours. There have been times, precisely thrice, when I've had a panic attack and fainted while standing in the doorway of a jam-packed train. When my eyes opened, I found myself seated in the same train clutching a stranger's water bottle while everyone around is looking at me like they just witnessed a miraculous resurrection.

A mix of odours consisting of sweat, leather and fruity perfumes suffocated me enough to make me struggle my way out of the crowd. Overwhelmed, I elbowed myself to an open space and started to pack my camera. It was at a higher risk. Sticking to the handy GoPro, I headed to the food counter. That was the only thing that mattered now. The food section primarily featured Naga and Khasi cuisine. It was there that I tried the unforgettable doh snam for the first time.

Doh snam

'If you want to have authentic Shillong food, you should go for that,' a volunteer told me, pointing at a large boiling pot with foot-long sausages simmering in it.

'This is doh snam. Pork sausage. You eat pork?' he asked, and I nodded. The lady at the stall took one sausage out of the pot, diced it into small pieces and attempted to make it look presentable by sprinkling a few chopped onions and chillies.

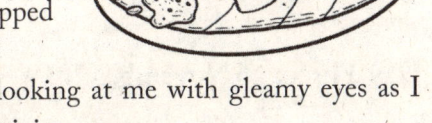

The volunteer kept looking at me with gleamy eyes as I took one big piece of that juicy sausage.

'Good?' he asked.

'Good,' I affirmed. It was soft, chewy and had a nice meaty flavour that even overpowered the chillies. A preparation of very few, yet distinct flavours. 'What is in it?' I asked further.

'Doh snam is a local Khasi dish. The filling is basically chopped pig innards. Cooked in its blood and stuffed in a long, thin bag of intestine.'

The last bite of doh snam stopped midway from the plate to my mouth. I exchanged an awkward smile with the volunteer and finished the entire thing. My endeavour to explore the local cuisine was very well taken care of.

* * *

It was a wrap for me. An eventful day was ending but it felt like something was missing. I kept my camera rolling in anticipation of one moment that would make me go back to my room and watch my footage. But it never happened. Having accepted that filming non-fiction comes with its own uncertainties, I found joy in the feeling of having spent an entire day with myself. I barely talked, but I smiled more often and observed more than any other day. I had anticipated a grand festival, but it was a massive disappointment. However, if I ever were to go back to this day, I would shoot things differently. I would shoot the moments that actually went unnoticed: basking in the sun, overcoats, floating cherry blossoms, waddling ducks and simmering doh snam.

Day Three, 16 November 2019

I was so busy covering the festival that I didn't even realize how the trip ended without even getting to explore the city a bit. I had just arrived and already had to leave. Instead of wasting my last few hours in Shillong sulking for not getting to visit Dawki, Mwaylong or Elephant Falls, I decided to make the most of it. I had a flight from Guwahati to Kolkata the next morning, so I had to get there before dark. I had the first half of the day to spend in Shillong, so without wasting any time, I headed out to roam around, hanging my camera on one shoulder and a fanny pack on another.

Lewduh

Police Bazaar was bustling with activity, even in the early

morning. Taxi drivers were yelling for rides, momo sellers preparing their fillings, fruit vendors stocking up their baskets and a few missionaries with banners singing a desi version of 'Hallelujah' on a mic, distributing Christian literature. Strolling through the crowd, I headed onto a busy road, wide enough for cars to pass through but entirely blocked by heaps of clothes.

'*Doh sau ka doh! Doh sau ka doh!*' (Two for two hundred!) shouted a vendor standing on the heap.

'*Sau ka doh! Sau ka doh!*' (Two for hundred!) shouted another vendor from across the street. The louder a vendor shouted, the more the people gathered.

People jumped on the heap, pulling out clothes and checking for defects. They were mostly overcoats—first copy or export rejects from fancy brands. Some winter jackets were from the army canteen. There were shoes too, selling like hot cakes.

The road gradually grew narrower as I continued along. The heaps of clothes were now replaced by little roadside shops of vegetables and other essential local commodities. I was entering a local market full of hustle and bustle and fresh organic farm produce. Fruit suppliers rushed carrying huge conical bamboo baskets on their backs with the straps hung on their heads, making their way by whistling at the crowd. I had seen these baskets in Himachal Pradesh, Uttarakhand and Assam before; here they were locally called *khaw*, as I heard. I couldn't see any tourists there other than me. Having a camera,

I was getting a lot of attention from the people around, but mostly in a jolly way. They were cheerful and appeared comfortable with the camera—another rare phenomenon. They were curiously asking me questions in their local language and giggling among themselves as I tried to reply. I couldn't stay in one place for long in that narrow alley, so I had to keep moving.

The vegetables being sold were quite novel too. Among many varieties of local mushrooms, bulbs and leafy vegetables, the chillies and lemons caught my attention. The lemons were unusually big, as big as an orange, and the chillies were as red as tomatoes. Locally known as 'Bhoot Jolokia', I was told that these chillies are the hottest ones in the world. To make their claim more concrete, they said that it was verified by Gordan Ramsay himself. Validations by white people are taken very seriously in our country.

Many small alleys intersected each other in that market. One among them had shops of only betel nuts and betel nut leaves in enormous amounts. Paan, otherwise known as 'tambul' locally, is a very big deal here. You can see everyone chewing it. It's not as complex and full of flavours like paan in other parts of India; the only ingredients used in the paan here are choona (lime), large chunks of betel nut and a piece of dried coconut. Everyone has their own paan kit with a

Khasi-style handmade nutcracker. Again, there was a separate section for these nut crackers being sold along with larger knives, axes, machetes, shovel heads and several other household tools.

While the vendors were busy setting up their shops, two women in their chequered Khasi attire surfed about swiftly, distributing tea to everyone. They walked with such certainty, as if the road were empty, while the rest of us were making our way, trying to dodge each other. They wore yellow saris and chequered blue shawls. One of the women had a bucket of cups in one hand and a hot kettle in another. She was quick in serving tea to the vendors and careful handling the cups, as though they were made of paper and not clay. As the first woman finished serving tea and headed to the next shop, the other one arrived with some snacks in a basket hung on her shoulder. It had fruits, bread, samosas and similar other titbits. Selling tea is a highly mundane job, but looking at them actively doing it was really fascinating. Every shop the ladies stopped at, they made sure to greet the vendors and indulge in some small talk.

These few hours made my trip. It was the purest form of Shillong I got to experience and document. While reading about the place, I realized how much cultural significance it held. Locally called Lewduh, or Bara Bazaar, this almost century-old market is one of the largest trade hubs of the North-east. It still retains the traditional value of being a one-stop shop for all your household needs and for the local businesses to thrive. All the travel articles about Shillong cover all its tourist spots, but there is no mention of Lewduh.

It wasn't just a quick stroll in a daily market, but a peek into Meghalaya's lifestyle, culture and social structure. The market operated harmoniously, resembling a symphony, with each participant skilfully performing their assigned tasks in flawless synchronization. The entire bazaar was run by women, mainly from Garo and Khasi tribes.* Some were carrying out their chores with their babies strung to their backs. The shared effort towards community and sisterhood was a refreshing sight. The social structure here is matriarchal in nature, putting women in charge of the majority of the economic activities. There is no place for dowry in the tribal values of the Northeast. It is wonderful to see this kind of liberty and openness in an underdeveloped region like this. In fact, the word 'underdeveloped' from an urban point of view starts to appear ambiguous at such places.

Markets like Lewduh showcase nature's abundance in its purest form. Back home, where everything is available at any given time, we're often disconnected from the origins of our goods or where they end up after we use them. Our markets, stripped of colour and character, are expensive and unfair. We've lost touch with the fundamentals that bring genuine happiness, easily falling prey to the idea of normalcy sold by someone else. The very fact that this is an 'us and them' conversation makes me reconsider the definitions of development.

I was glad to have not hired a cab and gone sightseeing alone. It's a nice feeling to find a place like this on your own, out of your planned itinerary. Yes, visiting grand monuments is great; it can save you from questions like, 'You went to Shillong, and you did not visit Elephant Falls!?' But finding a place's beauty in something so mundane makes your memories with it more personal and intimate. Having thoroughly enjoyed

---

* Andrew Gardener Marwein, Shashi Teibor Laloo, 'Lewduh Market', *Sahapedia*, January 2022, https://map.sahapedia.org/article/Iewduh-Market/10388

the role of a fly on the wall with a camera, I wished for more such days to film, find surprises and live from one moment of surprise to another.

* * *

During the journey to Assam, the faces of the people I encountered at Bara Bazar remained vivid in my thoughts. The trees changed colours as we drove closer to the cities. I reached Guwahati late in the evening. My flight to Kolkata was scheduled for the following morning. After spending a wholesome day and covering a distance of 100 km, someone in Guwahati was awaiting my arrival. It was Jyoti masi.

Jyoti masi and my mother were best friends during their college days at Kathak Kendra in Delhi. It was for her wedding that I visited Assam for the first time. I was just eight months old, so I obviously don't remember anything from that trip. Our only remnants of those moments were my grandmother's stories and the pictures my mom clicked from our Kodak camera, which was also the first camera in our family. While passing out of college, my mom made a funny pact with Jyoti masi. They agreed that if one of them had a baby boy and the other had a girl, they would arrange their marriage. Now, Jyoti masi does have a daughter, and it gets weird all the time they get on a call and tease each other using our names.

Though I was now twenty, Jyoti masi never stopped giving me forehead kisses and yelling at me if I did not answer her calls. Her family is filled with classical artists. The windows of her house are filled with plants and walls with awards. On my last trip to Assam, we had an unforgettable time celebrating Bihu at their ancestral home. She and her sister, Ranju, had a distinct Assamese tone to their Hindi and often surprised me by suddenly saying something in Marathi. I too tried my best to compliment her in Assamese.

It was dark when I reached Jyoti masi's place in Bhetapara. She had cooked my favourite meal. Simple, homely, Assamese-style rice and dal with big chunks of potato and a large, sweet water fish, rohu. We video-called Aai and chatted until late, totally forgetting that I had to catch my flight to Kolkata early in the morning.

It is a comforting feeling to have family away from home. I've had the chance to visit Jyoti masi only four times so far, yet every visit feels like a warm homecoming. There's a beautiful sense of belonging and togetherness when our parents' friends love us like their own, spoiling us with affection and care. And when we see them after years, it's like rediscovering a piece of our childhood that they've carefully held on to from the last time.

ELEVEN

KOLKATA

Indulgent

Day One, 17 November 2019

During journeys or while waiting for flights, I've always fantasized about reading a book or writing something, but thanks to my attention span, I can rarely do so. With everything happening around you, it's so hard to keep your mind in one place. I spend most of the time observing people, browsing through shops, watching workers busy at their jobs, people at the lounge, pigeons on the roof. People-watching is one of the most fun ways to pass your time; and the best way to do it is by plugging in your earphones and playing some waltz. It is astounding how you see people sync to it. It is a montage only you can watch. Be it waltz, jazz, rap or R&B, you find a frame for every genre. I am not a reader to begin with, but since saving my phone battery is a priority, I prefer to read or sketch on journeys. However, there is one problem—no matter how hard I try to read a fancy book, there is always a subconscious thought that some girl sitting across the aisle would notice it and approach me. We would spend a day in her city, walk across pavements, sit on grass and listen to a street busker. But with every flight, my hopes are diminished by the fact that my co-passengers are mostly men who are either unapproachable, sleepy, over-inquisitive or too intimidating. So, I make my peace and let my romantic notion of recreating *Before Sunrise* with someone be just that—a romantic notion—and carry on.

I landed in Kolkata with a group of corporate people bantering over which is the fastest route to reach Maidan. I had to go the same way, but I decided to step back and let them pass. Kolkata was much less cold than Guwahati, and Guwahati was not even half as cold as Shillong. My hostel, ironically named 'Bombay Backpackers', was on the topmost floor of a rustic old commercial building in Park Street, the most elite and vintage area of Kolkata. The building had an incredibly slow, greasy elevator that took ages to reach the fourteenth floor. It played an annoyingly depressing piano tune all the way. Those two-and-a-half minutes in that dingy space teleported me to a world of perpetual melancholy. I made peace with the fact that visiting this world at least twice a day was going to be inevitable.

Mornings are the best time to arrive in Kolkata; it sets you at a pace where you can nicely roam around till the sun starts getting harsh. There are several stereotypes and romanticisms attached to this city, and within my first hour, I realized, all of them are true! My knowledge about Kolkata comes from school history textbooks, short stories and mainly, films. Apart from that, during my first year, I used to talk to a girl who took great interest in Bengali culture, so much so that she influenced me to finally watch *Charulata* and exposed me to an array of independent Bengali artists. Thanks to her, my playlist had a segment of fifteen to twenty indie Bangla songs. With whatever I knew about Kolkata, I believed exploring it would be no less than reading a character out of a storybook.

I chalked out a route through whatever was walking distance from my hostel and set out for my day. From Mullick Ghat Flower Market itself, I could see the railings of the majestic Howrah Bridge. It eventually grew bigger to a point where I was standing below a gigantic structure of high bolted lines of iron pillars running till a vanishing point, disappearing in the mist. Morning sunlight fell through those railings, creating geometric patterns on the road. The patterns flickered as the vehicles passed. Brightly coloured buses and the iconic yellow taxis added colour to the road. At the peak hour of 9 a.m., I was the only person walking against the flow of pedestrians heading towards the commercial part of the city, Maidan. I guess that's why the metro too was empty while travelling from Park Street to Maidan.

Metros in Kolkata are as cheap as Mumbai locals, but less crowded and stinky (I guess). The only thing I found very daunting about Kolkata's metros was that they travel underground. Underground things make me anxious. Maybe it's the thousands of tons of concrete above my head that can come crashing down at any moment. Maybe it's the dank smell of thousands of people in a tunnel, or maybe the stereotype thriller movies have stuck in my head about how easy it was to kill anybody in a metro.

'Do check with the peak hours; metros get really crowded,' said Krithika once on a call.

'That's not a problem; I've seen worse!' I replied with an utter conviction for having a gallant experience of commuting by Mumbai locals.

Oh! I haven't told you about Krithika, right! Krithika is a photographer from Kolkata. We connected on Instagram a few weeks ago. Her feed showcased the streets of Kolkata more vividly. I had asked her for a few recommendations, and she ended up making a detailed itinerary with estimated time and costs mentioned. Taking into consideration the format of my travel series, she had efficiently curated a trip that would perfectly fit under the budget of 300 rupees. Krithika had her exams going on, so we had decided to catch up on the last day. Such people are a blessing. Knowing them, you, of course, feel sorry for your organizational skills, but then you can always rely upon them. Surprisingly, I have realized, it's never a burden for them; 'planning' is their drug. Friendships or romantic relationships are very fun in which one person is clumsy and the other one is highly organized, and they keep their thing running, steering between structure and chaos.

I returned from Howrah via ferry and spent the afternoon at Prinsep Ghat, although the place is ideally suited for evening strolls. The lush green shade of the old trees provided an excellent environment for workers to nap and couples to get kinky. Prinsep Ghat was like a lunch break during a day where everyone in the office is busy except you. A place to linger for a smoke with an occasional thought of taking a day off and joining the boatmen for a while.

College Street

According to Krithika's itinerary, the next task was to get to College Street in a yellow taxi. As aesthetic these yellow Ambassadors looked from outside, they were as normal from within. It felt no less than roaming in a kaali-peeli taking long turns across the Flora Fountain.

College Street was exactly the Kolkata I had watched in movies or read about in books. Vintage buildings, overflowing bookshops and bold, hand-painted Bangla typography filled up every corner of my vision. Sounds of vendors quarrelling in Bangla, an old Bajaj scooter passing by and piles of books being dropped created its own rhythm. The traffic waited for the tram to pass as it did, blowing its horn 'POMM POMM' and making a jittering sound that old automobiles make. The tram passed smoothly through an inch of a gap from other vehicles. Pedestrians fearlessly walked through the traffic, exhibiting

traits of activism present in
every Bangali babu. Just like
the roads, footpaths were
pretty busy too. Apart from
tiny, congested book stalls,
two categories of people
occupied the streets: 1) Slow-
paced elites who stopped at
every bookstall and laid their
hands on Marxist literature,
and 2) Annoyed proletariats
moving fast, making their
way through the former.
Shooting myself on the
street, I bumped into three
people who gave me a 'yet another
YouTuber' look.

College Street is arguably the biggest book market in
the country. The lane carries tremendous cultural value for
being home to some of the most prestigious book shops and
publishing houses. Its nostalgic value and close proximity
to universities attract both white-haired intellectuals and
students.

There was clutter everywhere—on the street and on the
sidewalk. Walls were filled with layers of old and new political
posters and overhead tram lines blocking the sky. Not even
one place was devoid of this clutter; nothing was empty. For
an outsider like me, this chaos was fascinating. But I'm sure if I
were a local, I would have developed a similar kind of tolerance
I have developed for my home town, Mumbai. Out of this, I
have sadly missed out on a lot of novelty Mumbai had to offer.

If only I could see my city the way I see other cities, I would have made the most out of it.

* * *

Indian Coffee House

Walking ahead, on the same street, was the famous Indian Coffee House. In the pre-Independence period, this was where all the activists gathered to discuss politics and plan protests against the atrocities of the British Raj. Post-Independence, the place became a hub for intellectuals, poets and artists for their palavers and powwows.* Places like these excite me more than anything else. A gleeful excitement to eat at a place full of stories and heritage paced my walk.

Indian Coffee House looked like a huge courtroom with low-hanging ceiling fans making a squeaking noise. A seven-foot-tall painting of Raja Ram Mohan Roy was hanging on one of those aged pale walls. There was a balcony upstairs, like the ones at English opera theatres. Waiters in elegant white uniforms and fan-crowned turbans roamed with the grace of

---

* Karthik Venkatesh, 'A short history of the India Coffee House: Conversation, revolutionary politics and a different way to do business', Firstpost, 13 January 2021, https://www.firstpost.com/art-and-culture/a-short-history-of-the-india-coffee-house-conversation-revolutionary-politics-and-a-different-way-to-do-business-9184321.html

exam supervisors. They took their time and did their job like artists. They were old, therefore slow, and took great offence if someone (especially millennials) pointed out their ill service. The waiters were the most Indian of the Indian Coffee House.

I sat at the table for an eternity, hoping for someone to show up. The waiters passed by my table, looking through me. I called, I waved, I waved with both my hands and kept waving. The people around me gave me looks, but not the waiters. This struggle continued until a group of foreigners entered the cafe, and all the waiters suddenly rushed to attend to them. Two waiters joined a couple of tables and one wiped them, while another ecstatically explained the menu along with the history of each of their dishes. The whole thing was highly ironic for a place like Indian Coffee House, which had been established as a response to the coffee house culture monopolized by the British at the time.* If I wasn't hungry, I'd have found that scene quite hilarious, but at that point I lost all my patience and walked to the counter.

'*Arrey bhai sahab, kab loge order? Loge bhi ya nahi?*' (Sir, are you even going to take my order?) I complained. It takes a lot for me to actually stand up for myself, but here the spirit of a Bengali babu's activism had gotten into me. It finally worked. Getting their attention was hard, but not for someone who has waited for a year to get his domicile certificate. I am the most persistent when it comes to getting work done from such systems, and I am proud of it! You either rebel, which is too exhausting, or you stick to them like a leech until your work

---

* Sridevi Nambiar, 'The Story Behind India's Most Historic Coffee Chain', *Culture Trip*, 1 March 2018, https://theculturetrip.com/asia/india/articles/the-story-behind-indias-most-historic-coffee-chain

is done and never see them again. But
waiting for twenty minutes more, all I
had on my table was a plate full of dry
noodles with a dirty ketchup sachet. Indian
Coffee House's ambience quickly jumped
from a government office to a boys hostel mess.

I chewed my meal disappointedly, regretting
not giving enough time to think about what
to order. It felt like meeting your idol, who
plays the nice guy roles in every film but is
an asshole in real life. Now it makes a lot
of sense why this place was the best spot
for activists—it made them resilient and
prepared for the worst.

However, even if the above description changes your
opinion about Indian Coffee House, you should still visit the
place. It is, of course, a great heritage spot, but the lack of
attention by its staff is something that could add more character
to your Kolkata trip. And, if you were raised in a middle-class
family, it may even remind you of your childhood.

Another thing I realized much after this trip is that it's
not fair to hold an establishment like that to contemporary
industry standards. It is after all the Indian Coffee House; it
serves a much bigger purpose. Given a choice, they could have
renovated the place with modern furniture, served fries and
hired efficient staff to maximize their profits, but it wouldn't
have remained Indian Coffee House—a classic case of Theseus'
paradox. Places like these should be given credit for retaining
their originality in the age of futile identities.

* * *

Long walks

Late in the evening, I helped Ana pack her bag. She was my roommate, and she was leaving the next day. After we were done, we decided to head out for an easy stroll on Park Street.

Park Street was exactly like Colaba in Mumbai. Fancy shops of expensive brands have made their place in the blocks of classic old colonial buildings. Flashy boards of these posh showrooms lit up the streets at night. It created defined shadows of us that slithered behind us on the cobblestones.

Now, when it comes to walks, it is crazy how your steps start to fall in sync as you talk. Or even if there is a moment of silence, your bodies still interact. How one steps ahead when turning into a narrow lane and the other one follows. Or how there is a certain hesitation to hold hands while crossing the road. Especially with a stranger you're not going to meet again. Doesn't it feel novel to not only know them but to experience yourself through them? Even if we consciously decide not to set an agenda for this relationship, we still let these non-verbal interactions decide the flow. There is nothing romantic about it; it is so human that one can feel it in the company of absolutely anyone—a child, an old man, a lover, a hater, an animal, a friend or a stranger. Although Ana and I knew enough English to communicate, the real interaction was done by how speedily we walked, where we halted or who let whom pass.

* * *

Day Two, 18 November 2019

In the morning, Ana's bed was empty. Only two people showed up for breakfast. I sat at one corner of the table, and at the other end sat a tall, blonde Italian girl. I was too nervous to start a conversation. It is the exact same feeling when you're alone in an elevator and someone walks in, so you either keep staring at the changing floor numbers or make small talk. On top of that, it had barely been ten minutes since I'd woken up, which is when one is at his weakest of social skills. So, I decided to focus on my breakfast of aloo puri.

'Would you like some coffee?' she asked. She too, I assume, must have felt the anxiety. The elevator anxiety.

'No, thanks. That's a moka pot, right?'

'Yes. That's how you spot an Italian traveller,' she chuckled.

'Are you from here? I'm Sofia, by the way.'

'No, Mumbai. I'm Indrajeet.'

'Mumbai! That is where Bollywood, right?'

'This is also how you spot a European traveller.' We laughed together.

'How long are you here for?' she inquired, sipping her coffee.

'I am leaving tomorrow. You?'

'Leaving tonight. Have you been to the Victoria Memorial?'

'Oh, I am going there today. Want to join?' I offered.

'Sure thing,' she agreed. I smiled at the thought of having company and splitting the auto fare.

Sofia was the first person I met who did not fit into a single European tourist stereotype. She loved spicy food and never got ill from it. It was her first week in India, and she could already manage to cross the roads like vendors at traffic signals. Listening to her quirky ideas, the distances felt shorter.

Trigger warning

As we were about to reach the Victoria Memorial, something happened. The footpath was secluded and covered under roadside trees. Some 10 metres ahead of us, a group of hijras was standing, busy among themselves. Seeing us approaching, they stopped talking and got ready to ask us for money. Now, in Mumbai, they often show up at traffic signals or in local trains. Some days, I hand them a ten-rupee note, and sometimes I just nod, and they move on to the next person. They are harmless; in fact, they are extremely caring and warm. Here, however, I felt uncomfortable because there were six of them walking straight towards us, tucking in their saris. For the first time, it felt sketchy to me. We both paced our walks to dodge them. As we moved closer, Sofia managed to pass through them, but somehow, I got stuck. Their plan was to make the foreigner pay but now that I was caught between, they wouldn't let me go.

'*Chalo tum kuch nikalo; tum toh yaha ke ho,*' (You ought to pay; you're an Indian) one of them said while the rest hastily surrounded me. Their eyes were as big as the red bindis on their foreheads, and their pot bellies were sticking out. I was nervous and cold; I wanted to get away as quickly as possible. From the back, I could feel their rough hands and their tight grip frisking me for my wallet. Seeing me scared, one of them held my nipples in a pinch. A sharp wave of panic ran through my entire body. I have never felt this uncomfortable before. I started sweating and my heart pumped faster than ever. I wanted to punch the front one's nose, but I couldn't muster the courage to do so. I avoid violence at all costs, but I could feel how much anger has to build up in order to resort to violence.

It was ugly. Using all my strength, I managed to push them aside and ran until a few metres ahead, catching up with Sofia without looking back. This happened within a few seconds, yet it felt like several hours had passed.

The heavy heartbeats did not stop for a long time. 'Why wasn't I mad enough to knock the person?' 'Oh. There were too many of them.' 'Why am I so short and weak?' 'I want to beat the shit out of someone.' 'Fuck them!' A bitter circling of embarrassment, guilt and angst filled my mind. My short height is something I was very conscious of during my early days. I use it as an excuse to not get into fights. I'd been bullied for being the shortest in the entire class. After years, I saw my bullies in the eyes of the eunuchs. I saw a version of my suppressed anger in them too. I have seen the aftermath of anger to believe it doesn't help anyone. But I do feel angry, about several things . . . I just don't know what to do about it.

I have always roamed around with the privilege of being a man. It's something I never had to question, never had to confront, until I did. Looking back now, I see how much of this privilege is intertwined with the way we're conditioned to view others, especially those who don't fit the norms we've been taught to accept. I never have to think twice before getting into an auto, nor do I care about roaming in a new place until late. Revisiting this today, I realize it has a small part to do with my conditioning as well. The constant disassociation and anger that comes with this feeling changes a lot within us. A substantial part of my school life was affected by bullying—the disassociation I had for myself and angst towards others. Would the hijras be experiencing anything similar while being among us yet not being seen? It's just their suppression that came out in an ugly way. They or, in fact, most people whose identities aren't acknowledged enough, must be experiencing this. So much anger and resentment could be avoided if only we were more aware and refrained from invalidating people for their differences. There is so much we try to suppress within ourselves that inevitably surfaces at the wrong place. Like this. The more you avoid or deny something, the more it gets to you. To express oneself is the most beautiful thing I have learnt in the two years of my relationship. And from here, I have nothing but empathy for everything that happened with everyone involved.

* * *

It is so grand!

I remember my visit to Victoria Memorial in bits because I was zoned out the whole time. Most of it I recall through my conversations with Sofia. Like the one we had at the foyer near the statue of the young Queen Victoria.

'This is so grand, yet full of minute details. You see the creases on her gown, Sofia?' I pointed out to her while rolling my camera steady.

'Yes, it's grand. That's the thing with Gothic monuments,' she replied.

'What?' I asked in confusion.

'It's so grand that it makes you feel so small and insignificant,' she explained.

'But doesn't it look beautiful?' I asked.

'Does it? Even though it symbolizes years of oppression?' she replied, and we both stood in silence.

The opulent beauty of the Victoria Memorial turned into a graveyard of several dark realities. The documentation of the Indian freedom movement in the museum inside vividly painted this thought in my head. This experience left me pondering how a simple shift in perspective can completely alter the moral significance we attach to a place. Despite its status as a remarkable example of Indo–Gothic architecture, the foundation of the Victoria Memorial serves as a constant reminder of the dark historical events it represents.

* * *

We walked almost everywhere. As the afternoon cooled down, we decided to take a short detour through the Esplanade area before returning to our hostel. The energy of Esplanade lies at the junction of colonial architecture and modern-day commerce. Essentially, Esplanade is to Kolkata what Colaba is to Mumbai.

On the way, Sofia's flip-flops started to bite and left blisters on her foot. My sandals fit her perfectly (okay, a bit tight), so I exchanged them with her oversized pair of pink flip-flops and walked carefully to avoid tripping. It's always at an unfamiliar place that I experience the comfort of not caring about what I'm wearing. Not that I have an elaborate wardrobe; it is just that you don't make too much effort towards pleasing people when you know you're not going to meet them again. So, you stick to the attire that makes you feel good, which, for me, majorly involves *bandi* (traditional cotton shirt), Quechua quick dry trousers and several rolls of plain black t-shirts.

At Esplanade itself was Nizam's restaurant, which had been marked in bold in Krithika's itinerary. The kathi kebabs we had there were spicy, but Sofia was just fine with it. She was enjoying her Indian meal, watching me sweat and wipe

my nose after every bite. We even
tried the biryani there. For a change,
it had an unusual amount of whole
boiled potatoes and boiled eggs in
it. It was low on spice, and the
potatoes gave it a sweetish
taste. Biryani is not supposed
to be sweet!

An interesting fact lies
behind the potato-laden biryani
of Kolkata. In 1856, when the
Nawab of Awadh, Wajid Ali Shah, got exiled by the British,
he settled in Kolkata. It is said that his fondness for Awadhi
Biryani made him take along his royal chef, but since he was
no longer able to afford meat in his biryani, the Nawab's chef
added potatoes and eggs to it. Since then, the Kolkata biryani
has had its own identity. But in my opinion, it doesn't stand
a chance next to the biryani corner near my office in Aram
Nagar, Versova.

Although everything I mentioned above sounds like a lot of
activity, it actually took place over four to five hours. We spent
the major chunk of the day crossing roads, changing metros
and hopping buses. I also spent a lot of time waiting for Sofia
while local women took photos with her holding their babies.

It is so strange yet interesting that every time you see a city
with a foreigner, you absorb it in a completely different way.
They get fascinated by many things that are mundane for us

* Homegrown, 'How An Exiled Nawab Invented The Famous Kolkata Biryani,'
  Homegrown.in, 8 June 2021, https://homegrown.co.in/homegrown-explore/how-
  an-exiled-nawab-invented-the-famous-kolkata-biryani

and are usually overlooked. Their fascination makes us notice them in a new way, and while we do it, we see how they've changed in the meantime. Especially while we ignored it under the indulgence of Western paradigms. This gaze connects us more to the culture we come from. Acknowledging our identity itself plays a role in its evolution. It is like that really old chair in your house that your grandpa once owned. It's dusty and lies in a dark corner until an artsy friend of yours comes over and compliments the

chair out of everything else in your home. Then you think, 'It does actually look great,' all the while browsing fancy modern furniture online.

I was the only person in my dormitory that night. There is no more comfort than a cold shower and changing into fresh, dry clothes after spending a tiring day amid dirt and sweat. The sheer absence of oil and stickiness on the body is itself a state of bliss. This comfort sparked a novel desire for a travel companion, someone to share these tranquil moments with. However, under the given circumstances, all I could do was note down my expenses and sort out the bills. That took a solid thirty minutes and another thirty to rewatch that day's footage. A lot of walking during the day resulted in a good night's sleep.

Day Three, 19 November 2019

Chinatown

Kolkata's Tiretta* Bazaar has been home to a small Chinese community for a long time. The immigrants from China came to India during colonial rule and settled here for work. Gladly, it was due to this that the evolution of our go-to college canteen lunch took place—Indo–Chinese cuisine, or 'desi Chinese'. Chinese cooking methods came into contact with Indian ingredients, paving the way for legendary inventions such as Gobi Manchurian, Paneer Chilli and Chinese Bhel. The intercultural confluence here was so strong that even today the Kaali Temple of Chinatown is looked after by a Chinese priest and the offering given to the deity is a plate of chow mein.

An online article I read said that every morning, Tiretta Bazaar is open for Chinese breakfast[†]. That's where I decided to start my day from. A couple from the hostel were stoked to hear about the breakfast idea and even asked me

---

[*] Aheil Banerjee, 'A slice of China in Kolkata', *Times of India*, 22 August 2023, http://timesofindia.indiatimes.com/articleshow/102932206.cms?utm_source=contentofinterest&utm_medium=text&utm_campaign=cppst

[†] Athena David, 'Eating at Tiretti Bazaar's Sunday Breakfast Market', *Goya Journal*, February 02, 2021.

to wake them up. Turns out they weren't ready to leave their beds, and I had to go alone.

The streets, jammed by noisy traffic during the day, were all quiet at 5.30 a.m. Only a few hand carts ran across. People had lit fires at corners amid the light mist and crisp cold. At Tiretta Bazaar, except for a few momo stalls, everything else was setting up slowly. They sold many other items too, but by now, I have forgotten their names. I waited for more carts to arrive so that I had options to choose from, but everything was happening so slowly that I could no longer control my hunger. A lady put six steaming momo on a plate and passed it on to me. I paid her Rs 20. Those were the biggest momo I've ever had. I hastily dipped one in the Schezwan sauce that they were served with and ended up burning my mouth. The sauce was hot too, and I had forgotten to carry water. The breakfast proved to wake me up fully.

Unlike how I expected, I couldn't see any Chinese people on the street. Except for a woman selling some sauces, there were only Bengalis serving at those momo stalls. Upon inquiring, I learnt that most people from the community have either left the country or died of old age. Dishearteningly, the shrinking Chinese community will be gone in the coming years. Even the priest at the Kali Temple. And the offering of chowmein will be just another fact they will sell tourists on walking tours.

* * *

After going back to the hostel, I finally met Krithika. 'Is that the only thing you shoot with?' That was the first thing she said, pointing at my GoPro. After that, we spent a couple of minutes in mutual admiration. She complimented my compact vlogging setup while I couldn't stop thanking her for the detailed itinerary she had prepared.

Kumartuli

'We are heading to Shobhabazar to visit Kumartuli,' said Krithika, and the next thing I knew, we were in the metro on our way. Since she belonged to Kolkata, getting to places was happening quicker. Besides, there was someone to talk to, I guess. After a really long time, I was enjoying the privilege of a plus one and not having to think about what to do next.

Kumartuli literally means 'potter's lane'. A community of artisans live here and sculpt idols of (mainly) Goddess Durga throughout the year for that one grand occasion, Durga Puja.

'Durga Puja, initially, was a thing only among the *bhadraloks*, the elites,' explained Krithika. I listened to her, keeping up with her pace of walking. 'They held pompous celebrations in their courtyards. But then, as it became more popular, artisans from the countryside came and settled here. Kolkata has a life of its own during Puja,' she added. Looking at the way they worked, one could guess the magnitude of the festival. Some idols were way bigger than life size. Some were waiting to be painted, while some were just rice stalks given a human figure. There was a specific style of carving being followed in every workshop, and there was an evident pattern in oval faces, slender eyes and extravagant headwear. So many idols of the deity were being brought to life. These will be looked at with hope, love, devotion and happiness on those designated days.

In a dark workshop, sat an old man at the only place where sunlight fell through a crack in the tin roof. He was engrossed in carving the eyes of an idol. Krithika asked him something in Bangla to which he replied, '*Cholbe*', and we stepped in. Watching him do his work was as captivating as sitting beside a river, watching her flow. My camera rolled as his hands carved the goddess with emotion, filling her with empathy, power, compassion and abundance. The divinity that they talk about is nothing but a projection of artistic expression. It thrives on prayers and collective belief. Isn't divinity nothing else but a reassurance of our own emotions?

The man's eyes looked into my tiny camera and squinted. He smiled, showing his crooked teeth, and waved with his hand smudged with paint.

* * *

On our way, we halted at a shop called Laxmi Narayan and Sons.

'This is something you'll find interesting,' Krithika said to me, and then ordered two fried patties, locally called tele bhaja.

'Now this place is pretty old.
Netaji Subhash Chandra
Bose was once a patron of
this shop. He used to leave
secret messages for his associates
here, and they would be delivered with these tele bhaja.
They distribute free tele bhaja every year on Netaji's birth
anniversary,' she said.

'The taste hasn't changed since then,' the shop owner
added. He was a jolly fellow, very keen on telling us about his
grandfather and Netaji's friendship, and shared newspaper
clippings of articles featuring his shop. Krithika and the owner
spent a few minutes speaking speedily in Bangla while I just
looked at them smiling. It's always enjoyable to watch two
people converse in a different language. Perhaps to guess what
they are talking about. Also, the snacks we had cost only Rs 6.
It doesn't get any cheaper than that!

Krithika's knowledge of her city was mind-blowing. She
had answers to all of my questions. It was thanks to her that I
had a proper plan for my trip, with everything perfectly fitting
into my time and budget. For me, it was too much organizing,
but she really enjoyed planning everything. At least, that's
what she said. She is very particular about things and prefers to
prepare for her trips beforehand.

'Krithika . . . it's such a non-Bengali name. Especially with
the "th" in it, it sounds more like a south Indian name,' I said
curiously.

'Of course, I am Tam-Bram (Tamilian Brahmin). I was
born in Hyderabad, though.'

'Oh, I thought you belonged to this place. You speak fluent
Bengali for a south Indian.'

'Actually, my family stays in Varanasi. My grandfather is a high priest there.'

'Wow! So, you're a Tam-Bram, born in Hyderabad whose ancestral home is in Varanasi and stays in Kolkata. How interesting is that!'

In this conversation, I figured out one thing. I remembered stopping at a place in Varanasi where everything was written in Tamil. From Krithika, I learnt about the Tamilian community who settled in Varanasi many years ago and have been looking after Kedar Ghat and its temples. No matter how much I travel, I will never stop being in awe of such cultural interconnections.

At a restaurant in Dalhousie Square, we devoured a plate of nicely cooked Chicken Kosha (Bengali chicken curry cooked in mustard oil) along with soft luchi (puri made from all-purpose flour). While eating, I explained to Krithika why I found Dalhousie Square intriguing. Firstly, the name has a cool ring to it; second, it was featured in Dibakar Banerjee's highly underrated film *Detective Byomkesh Bakshi* and finally, it served as the epicentre of British political power in India, right from the period of East India Company to the Queen's rule. From first reading about Dalhousie Square in my eighth standard history textbook and then seeing the place in a crime thriller film to actually being there was an interesting trajectory in itself.

We had a long day, but there was still one last thing to be checked off—the tram ride. Trams being a prominent aspect of Kolkata's heritage, it would have been a shame to miss out on

---

* Soumitra Das, 'Dalhousie Square in a shambles as its grand old buildings fall apart', *Frontline Magazine*, 17 November 2022, https://frontline.thehindu.com/arts-and-culture/heritage/dalhousie-square-kolkata-in-a-shambles-as-its-grand-old-buildings-fall-apart/article66106692.ece

that experience. I'd seen trams snaking across the street for the past two days and wondered what it would feel like to be the reason for traffic. We entered a tram that was slowly pulling off the terminus, not knowing which way it was going. On the inside, it was a dreamy wobbling box. Warm dim lights spread a shade of amber on wooden seats and rustic windows. It was that time of the day when the sky rapidly changed its colours. The lights grew prominent as the day set. I avoid using the word 'vibe', but it fits so well here. The vibe inside the tram was just like visiting your grandfather's first office and seeing the chessboard flooring he had mentioned. Apart from all the romanticism, it took thirty minutes for the tram to get on the road. All the shots were taken, and we got down even before it reached its first stop.

Kolkata is the perfect coexistence of the modern and the vintage. This coexistence not only exists in the city's infrastructure but also lingers in its day-to-day life, on the streets and among the people. I find Kolkata fundamentally quite similar to Mumbai, which is why it gives me a sense of familiarity. Maybe it is due to the crowd or the Gothic architecture, but, as a Maharashtrian, one aspect of Bengali culture I can relate to is the enormous stubbornness towards absolutely anything. Bengalis are as unapologetically moody as us Maharashtrians. Especially in trade. You ask a Bengali guy to do anything, and you are most likely to hear:

'*Hobe na.*' (Can't be done.)

I don't know what makes them so business phobic. Is it the deep-rooted Marxism? Whatever it may be, it doesn't imply they are not passionate. Bengalis are the most poetic people I've seen; they are the greatest connoisseurs of art. Their fancy towards literature, Rabindra Sangeet, Bengali cuisine and films is eternal and as ardent as their political and fashion statements. All the stereotypes about Bengali people are certainly true, and it won't change for long it seems.

The tram ride reassured me of Kolkata's colonial hangover. Even after over seventy years of gaining independence, a certain section of this city exudes an exclusive colonial charm, while its essence remains infused with the spirit of activism. Every aspect of this place holds a tale of its remarkable journey. Be it the tele bhaja costing Rs 6 with a message from Bose himself, a corner of Indian Coffee House hiding the secret meeting that led to the independence of the country, the melodious Rabindra Sangeet played at traffic signals or the eyes of Durga travelling from an artisan's workshop in Kumartuli to a sea of women in draped Baluchari saris and finally ending at the Hooghly River. Kolkata is brimming with stories, still exuding enough inspiration to ignite the creative spirits of future generations of filmmakers, writers, musicians and poets.

TWELVE

DARJEELING

*Days here are so short that one would only
remember Darjeeling under street lights.*

Day One, 26 November 2019

A sharp hue of red burst on the horizon and began to blend in with the dark sky. The sun, usually hard to look at, rose slowly like a pale, yellow dot, lighting up the land through the frolic clouds. A man sitting next to me was in total awe and couldn't decide whether to click his first flight sunrise or to enjoy it for himself. His joy and the view made me wish it was my first flight too. For my twelve-year-old self, it would have been magical. The first time I flew in a plane was seven years ago, from Mumbai to Hyderabad, with my mother. She was taking me to shoot for a TV show I'd been selected for as a child actor. Flying in a plane was a milestone, just like in every other middle-class family. My father taught us flight etiquette weeks prior to our journey. That was the only time I had paid full attention to inflight announcements and probably the last time I received attention from the cabin crew.

After landing in Bagdogra, I hitched a ride on a moped up to Siliguri and then took a shared cab to Darjeeling.

Just like the last trip, this too was going to be a long one. After shooting an episode in Darjeeling, I was supposed to head to Nagaland to attend the much-awaited Hornbill Festival. My next three days were going to be very spontaneous because my excitement for Hornbill did not let me plan enough for Darjeeling. All I knew about Darjeeling so far was from the movie *Barfi*. Apart from that, I had excitedly watched Wes Anderson's *The Darjeeling Limited*, but the entire film had only one scene with a little part of Darjeeling in it.

However, whatever little I knew about the place evoked a sense of cosiness, especially its name. Every name has a face. When you think of Ashok or Padma, your brain will conjure up a cumulative face based on all the Ashoks and Padmas you've known. Similarly, Darjeeling is such a perfect name; I felt the comfort of a misty dusk even before reaching there. But to get there, I had to survive through the horrors of the cab ride from Siliguri.

The Tata Sumo was packed with travel-sick people who kept puking one after another. My bottle ran empty, passing water to all those who fell sick—the bottle never returned with me. Cold winds filled the spaces as we passed through lush tea plantations spread across valleys. Labourers returned home with their back baskets full of freshly plucked bounty of tea leaves, army officers paddled their way through cantonments and pairs of whistling thrushes were sighted frequently.

After passing Kurseong, a horn blew, and we stopped. Looking back, we saw a black engine on a narrow railroad parallelly chasing us. The sensational eastern Himalayan toy train unveiled its flashing headlight through the smoke. Even my snobbery towards touristic affairs couldn't let me restrain the desire of a toy train ride. Letting her pass, we waited while adoring her elegance. Not just me, a tourist, but even the locals stood in awe.

I got down a few kilometres before Darjeeling at a village called Ghoom. A small settlement of narrow inclined roads, wooden houses, little shops and smiling people with pink cheeks. Most of them wore Nepali Dhaka topis (cloth hats). It was not yet dark, so I decided to spend some time at Ghoom and then cover the 9 km distance to Darjeeling on foot. After Rishikesh, Dharamshala, Shillong and other trips to hilly places following those, my endurance for uphill climbs had peaked. This was supposedly the golden age of my calf muscles. Post that, I still chose to walk, but it became easy for me to just give up and hire a cab everywhere.

Yiga Choeling Monastery was the first place I visited in Darjeeling. In the ambiguity between which exactly is the 'Ghoom Monastery' I visited both, Yiga Choeling as well as Samten Choeling monasteries. However, the only vivid memory I have is of the first one.

The priest and I were the only people in the silent, colourful sanctum. His humming and the rattle of his spinning prayer wheel were the only sounds audible. The subtle smile on the face of Maitreya Buddha in the sanctum radiated compassion in its 15-foot-tall golden appearance. The aroma of potala incense sticks intensified the calmness of the space.

Exactly contrary to this was the War Memorial for the Gorkha Regiment of the Indian Army, not very far from the monastery. It is located at Batasia Loop, from where the toy train passes, forming a loop. The loop created to ease the train's steep descent, offers a scenic view of the valley covered by tea plantations and features a sky blue acrylic cut-out that reads 'I *heart emoji* Darjeeling'. Families, newlyweds and batches of college kids huddled around to click selfies with the signage. The silent rifleman statue at the Gorkha Memorial appeared strikingly contrasting to its chaotic surroundings.

Watching flocks of people rushing to visit Batasia Loop, I sat cosy at a restaurant on the other side of the road, slurping hot thukpa. I had thukpa for the first time in Rishikesh, but this one tasted far better. Freshly chopped spring onion and soy sauce added a nice flavour to its mildly savoury stock. Like many other businesses, this cafe was run by a young Nepali couple. The guy cooked while the girl sat at the counter. Well, it wasn't exactly a counter; it was just a stool with a red, soy sauce-stained cloth on it. Above it was a photo frame of Batasia Loop during winter, clad in snow. Interestingly, the cafe didn't have a name. There was just a board with 'Restaurant' written on it in bold letters, and that was it.

Just as in Shillong, the Youth Hostel Association of India has a property in Darjeeling too. Since they were my saviours in Shillong, I had booked my stay here too. It is also the base for Sandakphu Valley and nearby treks. Although I paid Rs 400 for a bunk bed, I had the entire dorm room to myself. In fact, besides the receptionist, the cook and me, there was nobody in the building, thanks to the off season. We could actually set the building on fire, and no one would care. I badly wanted to take a bath, but now that the evening was getting even colder, I couldn't dare to dip even my toe in the water. Rapid physical movements were the only thing going to keep me from this freezing cold, so, not wasting any time, I dropped my backpack in the room and set out for a stroll.

Two roads

It was dark by now. Hopping on the railway tracks, I followed the main road, which further diverged into two lanes. The one heading the slope was bustling with locals in thin coats and Dhaka topis. The only shops here were selling meat, groceries and cheap tea. Footpaths under dim street lights were blocked by food carts and heaps of winter coats. People walked speedily and didn't stop at a shop for long—they knew what they wanted. The scenario drastically changed after I took a turn for the upper lane, also known as Darjeeling Mall. Fancy shops selling premium Darjeeling tea and Kashmiri handicrafts attracted tourists ambling on the pavement, warmly lit by slender street lamps. Here, among the crowd of rich families and young couples holding hands, I was roaming alone without being able to interact with anyone.

It gets really tough to interact with people at such popular tourist destinations. It's either Indian couples who are not interested in engaging with a stranger or families that are so busy among themselves that they barely care about anything around them. Even the locals have developed their own script to deal with the tourists. Every time an outsider walks to them for a conversation, they put on their performance mode and stick to their usual lines like, 'My grandmother herself handpicks tea from our garden! You want to see?' Or 'How much does your camera cost? You are a YouTuber? Come inside, show my shop.' This was followed by flexing about being once visited by a semi-popular Youtuber I have never heard of. Darjeeling Mall was all of this.

Returning to the hostel and sitting alone in my room with no network after a day of minimal human interaction and the freezing cold made me homesick on Day One itself (yes, it can happen). After spending hours staring at the dim light bulb in my room, I finally made up my mind to step out and make a call. I roamed around the building holding my phone upwards in search of a signal, ending up finally getting some at the terrace. Struggling with chattering teeth, I talked to my parents. They were quite agitated for me not calling home since I'd reached here. I quickly exchanged highlights of the day with my girlfriend and even called friends whom I rarely text or, at least, when I am not sober. In the piercing cold, I spent an hour not only smiling but giggling and repeatedly asking, 'Okay, can you hear me now?' My palms, feet, nose and ears had frozen until they turned numb, but it was a fair trade. In the contentment of a fulfilling day, I returned to my room and fell asleep, pulling not only on my own quilt but also joining the quilts of the other two beds.

* * *

Day Two, 27 November 2019

A breezy morning from the terrace of Keventer's cafe gave a bird's-eye view of the market coming to life. From those little clusters of wooden houses, the clock tower rose like a beacon. A heavy breakfast of greasy bacon, soft sausages and eggs did a great job of driving the cold away from my body.

I signed up for a tea tour today. While most people are very anal about their beverages, here I am a no-nonsense coffee drinker ready to explore the Champagne of teas—the Darjeeling Tea. Actually, more than the tea itself, I was excited about its process of plucking that they have shown in ads since ages. The romanticized visual of a happy woman plucking fresh green tea leaves and tossing them in her basket. Turns out it was not the harvest season, so all we were shown were dusty machines in a huge hall. There were no happy women plucking anything. Only a worker arguing with the staff for her wages, if that counts. I had also missed out on a lot by showing up late. I paid Rs 100 to *imagine* how tea is processed and have three sips of their premium flavours. It was bland in the most European way possible.

But then again, when was tea even Indian? Roughly 150 years ago, after having a tough time with China over the tea trade, the British decided to cultivate tea in parts of India.[*] Tea, being a highly consumed commodity by the European elites at the time, slowly began to gain popularity across all classes of Indian society. Tea boards in India, in fact, gave door-to-door demonstrations on how to make it. A mere decoction of boiled tea leaves went on to become India's popular beverage, chai, with the addition of Indian spices and herbs and was served outside factories and offices. I am damn serious when I say a cup of chai has the power to generate genius ideas, kickstart businesses, cure art blocks and shape the country's politics. However, the tea I had on the tour was nothing like the chai I've been drinking all my life. Where are the milk, sugar, ginger and cardamom? It was just

---

[*] 'History of Indian Tea', *Indian Tea Association*, https://www.indiatea.org/history_of_indian_tea

coloured water. But then again, this didn't let me stop from getting the free samples. I did take them with me.

Namu Myōhō Renge Kyō

As it got dark, life in the valley started to settle down, smoke from houses made its way through the chimneys and the inclined lanes of the mountains turned silent. Far away, the Buddhist Peace Pagoda calmly stood against the backdrop of a splendid purple sky. Its glowing white dome made it seem like a *peace* pagoda in its truest sense.

I rested on the stairs under the moving shadow of the tranquil structure and settled for a pause. Barbets and woodpeckers warbled in the distant alpines. From the Japanese temple nestled in the woods a few metres away, a rhythm of drums echoed. The standstill of time broke when five monks in flowy lemon yellow robes appeared from the temple and approached the pagoda. They chanted Buddhist hymns and played a disc-shaped instrument with a long bamboo handle. The disc was made of leather and had hymns printed in Japanese. It made a rippling sound after hitting it with a bamboo stick. The monks banged it in the interval of one second, in a set of four to complete the chant with three bangs. Calmly, in a melodious rhythm, they carried out their rituals and making a few rounds of the pagoda, they returned.

Enchanted, I followed the monks back to the temple. A simple wooden structure, with its sanctum surprisingly in the attic. In a corridor hung a yellow cloth that read 'No Nuclear Weapons in Our Beautiful World'. A 'Japanese' temple saying that is quite understandable, I thought. Taking a turn after a short flight of spiral stairs was a sight of sheer bewilderment. Colourful tassels, golden gongs, murals of fire-breathing dragons and curly clouds. The vibrations of drums filled the space and formed a bubble of shimmering celebration.

All the while I didn't utter a word, nor did my hand instinctively reach my phone. There was nothing running in my mind. I was not wondering about where to have dinner or if there was anything else left to visit. There was no thought right from worrying about the broken buckle of my backpack to fear of failing college. I have never felt or seen anything like this before. Enchantment wouldn't be the right word; perhaps awareness, of nothing spiritual but of the little things—the drums, their echoes fading back to silence, dragons, fire, unclenched shoulders, cold breaths, the warmth of the mattress, the smell of varnished wood. Crisp, substantial awareness.

Gently and subconsciously, I could feel my breath syncing with the rhythm of the hymns. I would have never landed here if I was slightly late or early. If not for this, the peace pagoda would have been yet another monument to tick off. My disappointment for a dull day at the tea estate vanished as it got me here right on time. 'Let things happen to you'—a quick reassurance made me hopeful of my trip ahead.

One of the monks smiled and gestured to me to take a seat and join their chanting. I sat down on a mat and was given the disc-shaped instrument. We all followed the rhythm, reciting the prayer written on a board: *Namu Myōhō Renge Kyō*.

* * *

Day Three, 28 November 2019

Visiting a Miniso shop was the oddest thing I did today. Not that I had nothing else to do, but there is something about such shops; they have a certain minimalist put-on that, ironically, ends up making you fall prey to consumerism and buy things you'd rarely use. But this time, at least, I got something I badly needed—a good toiletry pouch. I was tired of returning home to find toothpaste smeared all across my books and charging devices.

The Darjeeling Himalayan Railway

On my very third day in Darjeeling, I had been walking the pavements of Mall Road like a local. Listening to a distant street musician while eating fresh bread at Glenary's bakery, it struck me that I hadn't been on the toy train yet. So far, I'd done everything a tourist could do, so I might as well do that.

I was honestly avoiding the toy train only for the fact that it was absolutely mainstream and hence expensive. But since it contributes so much to Darjeeling's identity, I decided to add it to my vlog. In the last two days, I'd seen it pass so many times that I thought I would regret not riding it.

Built by the British in the nineteenth century, the Darjeeling Himalayan Railway has been an attraction for many years. This narrow gauge train that runs alongside roads, valleys, street markets and almost everything else in these parts is enough to get one intrigued. Its railway station is much smaller in comparison to others. Except for the penguin dustbins, the premises resonate an old English aesthetic. The tariffs mostly varied between whopping Rs 800–1500. (If you think that's not a lot of money, you can actually take a train back to Mumbai at that cost.) But there was this one passenger train to Ghoom sharp at 4.30 p.m., which cost only Rs 104. Perfect. I decided to travel to Ghoom via train and get a connecting cab to Jalpaiguri.

I had three more hours at my disposal in Darjeeling, so I walked to the Shri Mahakal Mandir nearby. I was glad I didn't read about this place before visiting when I met with an unusual sight. As the name suggests, Mahakal is clearly a Shiva temple, but interestingly, it has many elements of a Buddhist shrine. Tibetan prayer flags tied across huge bells covered the surroundings, spreading like creepers on a nearby sacred banyan tree. At the entrance of every Shiva temple, there is always a Nandi (bull), but here, along with a Nandi, stood two tigers, carved in the Tibetan style, guarding the way. But the most astounding sight was seeing a Buddhist monk sit beside a Hindu priest next to the Shiva linga. They greeted everyone with a warm smile and carried out the rites together.

Buddhism,* with its fundamentals strikingly in contrast with Hinduism, was actually in confluence with it here. Both the cultures were so beautifully blended together that one could hardly tell that the scholars of these two schools of thought used to have tough debates at one time. Everything we were taught about Buddhism and Hinduism in our philosophy class fell in contrast to this scenario.

After stepping out of the shrine, I took a seat on a bench and observed the devotees. They removed their footwear with one hand while holding a pooja thali in the other. Before entering, they spun the Tibetan prayer wheel and chanted 'Om Namah Shivay'. It struck me how Buddhism, a religion that doesn't believe in a god or life after death, coexists so closely with the predominantly polytheistic Hindu practices here.

This blend of different beliefs made me reflect on the nature of religion and culture. While many think religion is the force that unites people, these fascinating crossovers suggest otherwise. It seems that culture, rather than religion, is what truly binds people together. Culture fosters a shared sense of participation, creating connections beyond doctrinal differences. Religions are often defined by their texts, but cultures are shaped and inspired by the people themselves.

---

* G.B. Nandan and Nasir Ahmed M. Jangubhai, 'The Comparative study between Hinduism and Buddhism', *International Journal of Humanities and Social Science Invention*, 5 May 2013.

I spun the prayer wheel for one last time and prepared to leave. While I was tying my shoelaces, a dog fiddled around and later followed me all the way, fascinated with the enamel mug hanging on my backpack.

The train was just pulling into the station when I got there. The light of the engine flooded through the mist and faded a few metres ahead. Due to it being the off season, the platform had fewer tourists and some local vendors. I was sharing my berth with two skinny schoolboys way taller than me. They were indifferent to the amazement and generously gave me the window seat. The train cruised slowly, making its way, catching everyone's attention from the markets cluttered near the tracks. The tourists mostly gazed at us and waved in awe. It was funny to be on the other side of this experience after seeing it for the first time when I arrived. The train gained speed after leaving the town, but even at that speed, a bicycle could've easily sped past us. The golden light of the evening shone against the black engine, the rhythm of its wheels synced with its blowing horn and the carpets of tea estates vanished in the horizon. Sticking my elbow out of the window, resting my chin on it, I absorbed all of this with the awe of an eight-year-old. Of course, the Darjeeling Himalayan Railway was a hype but it's certain that the mountains I remember watching during this ride wouldn't have been the same any other way. Here's a tip—as you grow up, there are very few moments that allow you to have a childlike amazement, and especially on a solo trip, where you are an absolute stranger, it is a must to live each one of them. That's rare.

* * *

Late in the evening, I reached Jalpaiguri, a small town in West Bengal. Although only three hours away, it is not at all similar to Darjeeling. Jalpaiguri was a gloomy city at night, and finding a decent hotel room was a scarier task. Anyone I looked at made me feel like his would be the last face I would ever look at. My gut feeling didn't let me go out after getting a room, because of which I even skipped my dinner. The first thing I did was take a hot bath, which I didn't do in the last few days. The shower didn't work, and the bucket weirdly smelt of alcohol. I thought over it a hundred times before taking on a blanket and then ended up sleeping without one.

I have made peace with the obvious fact that not every trip is going to be life changing. In fact, the purpose of travelling is entirely defeated when we expect a drastic revelation out of it. During this trip, it was the least I'd interact with anyone, but I didn't spend a single moment feeling lonely. Apart from exploring a new place, I also spent time with myself, living moments that would remain with me on days when a pandemic locks me in from the world, and on days I have nobody to make a call to or at times when being alone itself feels unfamiliar.

I have often found myself conflicted between the desire for solitude and the urge to escape from it. Travelling solo and living through days of experiencing both extremes helped bridge the gap of this conflict. Not that I have learnt to live by myself (in fact, being an absolute extrovert, I don't believe I can), but let things like solitude, longing, companionship and social interaction each play their part.

My train to Dimapur was early the next morning. I couldn't think of anything else but be anxious about not missing it at any cost. In fact, an even worse fear was to prepare myself for a twenty-seven-hour long journey. Technically, my trip wasn't

over, but I had no time or enough mental space to let the last
few days sink in. That night was about bidding goodbye to
one city and preparing for the next. The only way I can recall
Darjeeling is through the episode I shot, every time a cup of
green tea is served or when Binita didi from our office shares
about her days in Darjeeling with a smile on her face. And the
name—yes, it does sound cosy.

THIRTEEN

NAGALAND

Nagas: The people best to party with; the worst to mess with.

The rail journey from Jalpaiguri, West Bengal, to Dimapur, Nagaland, took an entire day. My co-passengers were a family of three (presumably Assamese) who couldn't sit idle without standing every other moment to fetch things out of their bags, a skinny guy sleeping on the upper berth who never woke up the entire journey and a stout missionary who sat half-assed on an empty seat. It was his panic over losing his luggage that woke me up early in the morning.

The Wai Wai cup noodles I bought at New Jalpaiguri Station were my saviour throughout the journey. I had them for breakfast, lunch and dinner. It is unfortunate that after returning to Mumbai, I couldn't find them anywhere because once you eat Wai Wai, there's no going back. It wasn't until recently that I managed to find them at a grocery store. Now, every time I take a bite of Wai Wai, it takes me back to this journey.

Where is Teja Palace?

Covering the distance of 678 km in eighteen hours, I reached Dimapur at 11 p.m. and had another 71 km to go until I reached Kohima. An overnight road trip would have been risky, so spending the night in Dimapur made more sense.

The hotel was already booked and was not more than 100 metres from Dimapur Railway Station, but there was a new problem. My phone had lost network and nobody at the hotel was answering calls; all I had left was to rely on the locals for directions at 11 in the night. My Mumbaikar syndrome has caused me a spectrum of inconveniences due to my assuming that every other city would be awake until midnight. Dimapur was nothing like I had imagined. There was no life outside the railway station. Roads were deserted, and uncannily, the only shops outside the station were the ones selling coffins! Walking through an alley of coffin shops with minimal street lights at 11 p.m. while having no clue about your hotel is not a great first hour of your trip.

I paced out of that area till the main road, where I spotted three workers wrapping up their day at an omelette cart. They gazed at me with suspicion as I approached them. After asking, the three of them gave me three different directions for The Teja Palace hotel. I asked an autorickshaw guy and a beggar too, but no one knew exactly where the hotel was. Anxiety crawled upon me as it had been forty minutes since I began frantically searching for my hotel on the empty roads of Dimapur.

'What's the matter?' asked a security guard at an ATM, seeing me freak out.

'Do you know where Teja Palace Hotel is? SBI colony? Any idea?' I asked panting.

'No. SBI colony is right where you came from, but I haven't heard of any Teja Palace so far,' he said, and I left to continue my search.

'Wait, where are you going? This is Nagaland! Let my friend come; he will take you to your place,' he scolded me. It really got me bad when he said, 'This is Nagaland', with a wrinkled forehead! Soon after that, a person showed up and led me to a narrow alley where a big white building stood boldly, cutting all the darkness with its bright halogen lights. There were seven colourful flags welcoming me at the gate of The Teja Palace after such a manoeuvre. In the first hour of my trip, a stranger nearly saved me from spending the night at Dimapur Railway Station.

* * *

Day One, 30 November 2019

'Kohima! Kohima!' yelled the cabbies outside Dimapur Railway Station. I got into one of those nine-seater Tata Sumo cars and left after there was no more space to fit even half a butt. I was glad to have left early in the morning; except for a few Army jeeps, government convoys and media vans, the roads were empty. Everyone was heading to Kohima for the same reason—the Hornbill Festival.

Ever since the Hornbill Festival started to get international attention, the state government has also taken it more seriously. All through the year, Nagaland's tourism is at its peak only during Hornbill Festival, making the most money from this sector. Annually held from 1 to 10 December, Nagaland showcases its cultural heritage to the world. Hornbill Festival had been on my list for the last three years and if not for this series, I would've had to wait till my thirties to afford this trip. It was sheer luck.

Nagaland lies on the farthest end of the north-east of the country. Over centuries, its valleys have been home to diverse indigenous tribes. There are nearly seventeen different tribes[*] with unique traditions, diverse dialects and extreme lifestyles. Even today, despite rapid globalization, Nagas have managed to retain their ethnic identity. However, I had no imagery of Nagaland through films or books. Weirdly, I was more intrigued by it due to the inaccessibility of its culture.

It took us three hours to reach Kohima through an excruciatingly bumpy and dusty road. Meanwhile, I had sprained my neck, the dust wouldn't stop my sneezing and a thin, itchy layer of dirt formed on my skin every three to five minutes after I rubbed it off. I could hardly feel my legs anymore due to carrying my backpack on my lap all the way because I was

[*] 'Nagaland Profile', *Official State Portal of Nagaland*, last modified on 8 May 2024, https://nagaland.gov.in/pages/nagaland-profile

too afraid to put it on the deck and get my
friend's camera cracked. I hadn't eaten
anything except the sunflower seeds I
got on the highway. They tasted like
hay when I first had them. Turns out I
was eating them the wrong way. A co-
passenger showed me the right way by
breaking open the shell and then eating
the seed inside. Now, it tasted much better—nutty, salty and
a bit sweet.

Neitho

Neitho welcomed me in Kohima. She was a friend of my
political science professor. Neitho was the first person in
Nagaland I interacted with. With every initiating conversation,
I judiciously used words to articulate. What if I say something
offensive? What if my behaviour comes out as racist? Should
I be asking about the headhunters? What would her take on
separatist movements in the state be? Or should I just start
off by complimenting her coat? Yes, Neitho wore an overcoat,
seemingly looking like she had been wearing it every other
day. A side bag sunk down her shoulder by the weight of two
visibly fat books. In contrast to that, she also chewed paan,
but that was so subtle, she didn't let me notice her spitting it
out. Meeting Neitho made me realize just how hard my trip
would have been without any local help. Like assembling a
shelf without an instruction manual.

The festival was going to commence the next day a few
kilometres away at Kisama village, so I decided to spend
the day with Neitho. We strolled on the streets of Kohima

inquisitively exchanging all that we knew about our cultures, of which she had a lot to bring to the table.

'Why did you speak to that cafe owner in English? Isn't he a local?' I asked after we got ourselves some coffee on the way.

'Yes, but he's from a different tribe.'

'So, does every tribe have a different language?'

'Yes.'

'And can you figure it out?'

'No.'

'Really? Not even a bit?'

'No, they are very different from each other.'

'What tribe are you from?'

'I belong to the Angami tribe. We are the locals of Kohima.'

'But you said you're a Christian?'

'Christianity is my religion, and Angami is my tribe.'

The more we talked, the more I learnt about the Nagas, the city, the food and most importantly, the reason why it would be so tough to find a vegan here.

More than the war memorial and state museum, the daily market was the most fascinating place to stop by. It was similar to the one in Shillong, except they sold a bizarre plethora of living insects and animals. An average stall in the market would consist of some indigenous spices, cakes of rock salt, crickets in a basket, silkworms, wriggling mealworms, some chillies on the side, chunks of honeycomb with larvae in it, cages of rabbits kept below, rats, quails, pickles, ducks, frogs tied in plastic pouches, fresh fruits and nice mushrooms. The boundaries of what can be called food, friends, animals and pests appeared blurred in the Kohima market. Honestly, these are quite normal things to exist, but when they are put together, it can be a difficult sight. I, however, in my explorative mood, found it exotic.

Neitho spoke on everything my camera pointed at. 'These blood worms are the most expensive ones . . . These mice are very beneficial medically . . . These bamboo chunks are used in cooking; their smell is the strongest among all the bamboo shoots . . . This thing is grown here, and that thing is known for its bitter taste . . .'

Although all this seems so outrageous and taboo, nobody had a problem with me shooting. In fact, they were the most cheerful on camera. In a sense, it's fair because if we were fed frogs all our life, we would not really consider it any different from other food.

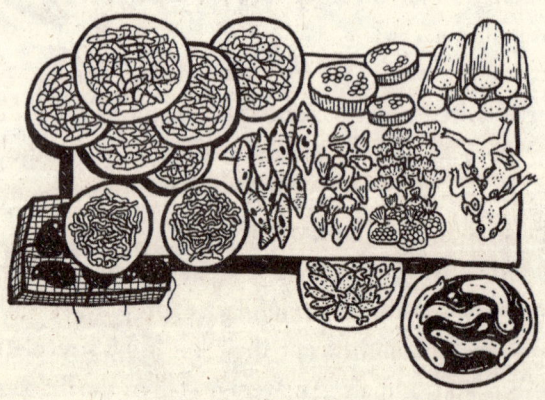

* * *

Around this time, I had exhausted my last memory card and had to buy a new one. I was thankful that this didn't happen in

Kisama village, though. I was still new to the idea of backing up footage on a hard drive the very same day.

Bidding goodbye to Neitho, I left for Kigwema, the village next to Kisama, where my homestay was. I've had a hard time trying not to jumble up the names of different places—Kigwema, Kisama, Kohima and Khonoma.

The bus vanished, rolling down the mountain after dropping me on a long road of Kigwema. Kohima glittered in the valley. Along the road, there were fewer houses, spaced at a distance of 100 metres each, with courtyards full of flowering plants. Dense woods covered the uninhabited patches of land. The calm of serene dusk took away all the weariness and lulled me into absolute solitude. I could hear my cold breath.

Surprisingly, I didn't even panic when my phone lost network. Out of sheer instinct, I walked up to a stranger's house and rang their doorbell. An old man opened the door. Upon my requesting, he not only helped me with the directions but also sent his son to accompany me to my homestay to make sure I wouldn't get lost again.

Ketho, my host, had gone out to buy groceries, so her brother checked me in. While I was in Shillong, a friend from the hostel referred me to Ketho's homestay. She and her brother ran their old ancestral house as a homestay during the Hornbill Festival. They were still busy preparing for their business. Ketho's brother was done fixing bulbs and was now making beds. Being the first guest, I got the best room. A minimalistic set-up of two beds, a table and a little window made just the right place to unwind. Cute cacti planted in paint buckets and cup noodle containers gave the courtyard its desi cottage core aesthetic.

On the other side, Ketho's sister lived with her husband and their toddler son, Jivvy, in a wooden house. He was always playful and didn't shy away from meeting new people. He had small eyes, chubby red cheeks, a nose with dried green mucus and hands that were dirty all the time. I, who usually don't get along well with kids, made him run laughing throughout the courtyard.

Bamboo Shoot Pork

Ketho had already arrived while I freshened up. She was preparing dinner in the kitchen downstairs when I went to greet her.

'Hey! Sorry, I was at the market when you arrived. Welcome! You are our first guest!' she said, wiping her hands to her apron. 'It's so cool you've travelled so far on your own. First time in Nagaland?' she curiously asked, raising her eyebrows behind her big round glasses.

'Yes, it is my first time! By the way, beautiful house! I met your nephew. We are good friends already.'

'I know, right. He is the USP of our homestay. This place actually belonged to my grandparents. I live in Kohima. I work there as a journalist. No one lives here now, so we open it for tourists during the Hornbill Festival. These are the craziest ten days of the year.'

'I am sure.'

'This time, everything happened last minute. It's just two of us running this whole thing,' she explained in her distinct Naga-accented English.

'No worries. Maybe I can help you cook?' I insisted. By now, I too was subconsciously adopting a thing or two from her accent.

'Can you cook?' Ketho asked.

'I'd love to. What are you preparing?' I affirmed from all the knowledge Neitho imparted to me in Kohima Market today. Besides, in that freezing cold, the kitchen was the warmest place to be in. My fleece did its bare minimum to keep me warm.

'So, the rice is cooking, and now I am preparing bamboo shoot pork. It's pretty easy actually,' said Ketho, letting me work under her supervision.

Her actions were swift and precise. While she boiled the meat in a big pot, I cut chillies and garlic and strands of fermented bamboo shoots. Ketho went outside and brought a green, round thing from a vine in her backyard garden. It was a local vegetable known as chow chow, or chayote. She then cut it into pieces and boiled it separately. I kept looking at how fruit from the backyard quickly made it to our meal. Apart from being this organic, one thing to observe about Naga cuisine is that it's highly primitive. There is very little sautéing, frying, tempering, marination or complex use of spices. Most of the ingredients are boiled and eaten with rice, or sometimes raw.

While the pork simmered, we started a nice bonfire in the courtyard and poured ourselves some fresh apple cider.

'It's cooked!' Ketho said, smelling the aroma coming from the kitchen. Ketho, her brother, two of her friends and I sat around the fire with our meal, digging our fingers into the steaming hot heap of rice and tender pork fat with big chunks of chayote on the side. This counted as my first actual meal in Nagaland. Taking part in the cooking was the best way to familiarize myself with Naga cuisine. It was by far the best pork I had ever had. The chayote and the bamboo shoots, with their strong aroma, added more flavour to the soft texture of the pork.

I could never stop fantasizing about the magic of regional food. The way it travels through places and generations. After language, it is by far the only way to communicate between cultures. Some tastes are familiar while others are new; it is this exchange of diverse tastes that brings us closer to places and people.

Ketho remained the entertainer all through the evening. After so long, the stars were clearly visible and flickering brightly in the sky. It was a moment of smiles and giggles. Watching people's eyes sparkle while they shared their lives and felt heard. An old ancestral house had turned into a home. I was finally where I always wanted to be.

* * *

Day Two, 1 December 2019

Hornbill Festival 2019

I had pictured this day in my imagination so many times. A mix of excitement, novelty and being finicky to make sure everything goes perfectly kept me awake until late the previous night. The early morning of 1 December had to be the coldest morning ever. But in spite of that, public buses were full of life, filled with colourful tribesmen, lively singing all the way instead of sleepy, unwilling school kids. All the colours gathered at the huge gate of Kisama village. Tribal spears and bison skulls hung on the gates resonated with a 'Do not mess with us' undertone. My excitement got me too early to the festival venue, where everyone was still preparing—shops were setting up, carpets were being rolled open, media crew securing their spots and performers were arriving from their respective villages. Day One of the Hornbill Festival had a glow of newness on everyone's faces.

The main ground was surrounded by sixteen different types of houses prominently built from bamboo, but too big to be called shacks. Let's just refer to them as 'pavilions'. These sixteen pavilions represented the sixteen major tribes of Nagaland. They were prototypes featuring the lifestyle of each tribe, with its respective tribesmen mingling in their ethnic attire and preparing its traditional food. Interestingly, almost all the houses, although slightly different from each other, had their cooking area right in the centre. It also efficiently served as a heat source. It was as primitive as a big pot on a fireplace and chunks of meat hanging up on a rack exactly above it, slowly being smoked. Around the pot, there were baskets full of corn and thick grains, while the walls were decorated with various weapons and animal skulls hung on them. Smoke from the pot danced in the sunlight slipping through bamboo cracks. The aroma of delicious meat spread across the pavilion.

Men wore fancy headgear attached with tail feathers of hornbill birds. Some even had wild boar tusks and tiger nails on them. One could never stop gazing at them with novelty. A round metal disc covered their genital areas, which, I suppose, was to protect them from getting hit by . . . maybe arrows. The metal disc was attached to a handwoven fabric hanging on a sturdy belt. The belt had a wooden slot at the back to keep their traditional weapon, *dao*, a long-handled machete with a straight blade, broader at the end for greater impact. It performed a variety of tasks, right from snapping twigs to chopping off heads. Apart from daos, many men wielded long, furry spears and oval shields. Tattoos on the wrinkled skins of some old folks told stories of the ugly battles they fought in their early days. Their attire's purpose was to make them look intimidating, but their cheerful smiles had an altogether different story to tell.

While the men wore clothes compatible for battles and hunting practices, women's attire was more elaborate and suitable for household chores and farming. They wrapped a thick, striped Naga shawl around their body along with bright ornaments, designed primarily from animal bones, beads and feathers. Tasselled floral headbands worn by women from the Sumi tribe were eye-catching. Most of the neck jewellery consisted of a thick belt of beads arranged in a pattern of red, white and black. Sometimes, with a variation of a few cone-shaped metal pieces in between. I was obsessively crushing over Naga girls, not just because of their chic attire but the way they pulled it off. They could probably drape themselves in grey curtains and still look charming. I was so close to asking a Chakhesang girl out for a morning coffee, but seeing all the other men in the league with spears and swords around, my chadness obviously took the back seat.

With all the tribesmen hanging out in groups, flaunting their vibrant drapery, the pavilions collectively looked incredibly vivid. The Konyak pavilion was all red, the Ao pavilion was white, while the Sumi and the Samteng pavilions were blue and yellow, respectively. Initiating conversations and recording reactions, a sudden, distant yodel caught my attention. It was the Angamis teasing their neighbours, the Aos, and they yodelled back. Soon after that, tribesmen at the Chakhesang pavilion gathered in a circle at their courtyard and hopped together singing '*Aaaa Hei! Aaaa Hei!*' beating their spears. At the same time, another drum emerged from a pavilion. Its increasingly high tempo sounded like multiple drums being played in synchronization. Upon approaching, I saw people standing on both sides of an enormous 15-foot hollow wooden log laid down flat and beating it with wooden hammers alternatively in a rhythmic pattern. The goosebumps on my skin justified why it was used to declare wars. The energy was at its peak!

By now, every pavilion had something or the other going on. With my camera rolling, I kept hopping from one place to another, struggling not to miss anything. Changing lenses felt irritating, and people who obstructed the field of view easily got on my nerves. After filming almost everything, I made sure to set aside my camera to see the festival outside of my preview screen. Some tribes were dancing, some were singing and some were beating drums, but it was the Konyaks who did things differently. Amid the merriments, a loud gunshot drew everyone's attention. Among spears and swords, the Konyaks went ahead and pulled out their handcrafted flintlock rifles. The gunmen were tall and skinny. They loaded their rifles with utmost precision and fired up in the sky blithely. The air filled with the acrid aroma of gunpowder and the echoes of cheering Konyaks along with their shots, as though it were a way to declare who was the most badass of them all. In the olden days, the Konyaks were ferocious headhunters[*] and were considered the most brutal tribe of Nagaland. They believed that the person who had chopped off the highest number of heads of enemy chiefs was the mightiest of them all.

Out of curiosity, I asked one of the tribesmen to let me hold his rifle. A massive boost of adrenaline gushed through my body as I held it. I could just see how any weapon could make you think less and make you more impulsive. 'Now shoot!' the man said. He had already loaded it. 'Shoot? No! I can't shoot it,' I said, hunching my shoulders forward. I didn't see that coming at all. 'Go, boy! Shoot!' yelled the tribesman again, this time even louder, and almost on reflex, I pulled the trigger. The rifle shot up in the air and jerked back, jolting me away from my place. Handing over the rifle back, I made sure I didn't shit my pants.

---

[*] Sugato Mukherjee, 'The Last Headhunters of Nagaland', *The Diplomat*, 4 April 2018, https://thediplomat.com/2018/04/the-last-headhunters-of-nagaland/

* * *

The evening inauguration ceremony did not have even the slightest essence of all the madness that happened in the day. It was a formal event of speeches, politicians, news coverage, entourage, awkward silences and mic glitches. The chief guests were given spears and made to wear their traditional headgear. Imagine a group of people in black suits struggling to keep huge feathery things on their heads and collectively hitting the gong while sweating and somehow smiling every time they realized the presence of cameras. 'This is bullshit!' muttered an uncle sitting next to me. 'Why must these bureaucrats be invited everywhere?' I didn't know what to say, so I nodded and got back to my camera, which was barely shooting anything in that low light. But his agitation was valid. Time is at its slowest while listening to ministers' inaugural speeches. The overall persona of this 'cultural event' was contradictory to the festival's wild energy. The Nagas gathered on the ground were standing still while the guests spoke. They were now shivering as the hornbill feathers on everyone's headgears were visibly flickering.

The speeches were followed by a variety of dance performances from all the tribes. A commentator shared his two cents over everything throughout the performance. His voice silenced the drums. It was still an interesting sight to watch because the dances reflected the traditional lifestyles of the tribes—something I'd never seen before.

When we imagine 'cultural events', they are either religious or focused upon complex ideas like spirituality, folk tales or classical art. However, these performances were super specific and conventionally primitive. The Nagas didn't bother to explore the depths of complex expressions but stuck to the portrayals of basic daily life stuff in their dancing, such as farming, hunting, victory dances or something as simple as striking fire. The males demonstrated conflict and victory while the females played supporting roles, for example, distributing beer to the warriors after a deadly war or just winnowing grains.

The Nagas danced in ecstasy, and so did the hornbill feathers on their headgear. The strong bond Nagas shared among their communities and the collective effort towards their tribe's survival reminded me of the social contract theory I learnt in college. They had inherent rules and systems developed to keep the tribe together. It was quite evident from their lifestyle that they had seen enough inter-tribal battles and natural hardships to shape these systems.

Their performances, although very simplistic, had an insightful subtext. It showed how all our thoughts, theories and ideas boil down to something so basic. How any conflict (physically hostile conditions in this case) makes us resort to our inherent survival instinct. Yet, it is paradoxical that the fulfilment of these basic trifles leads to more profound needs. The idea of survival can be subjective for us and the Nagas but what I truly believe is that no matter how much we uplift ourselves from the daily trifles and throttle humanity to think about God, existence, science, world peace, nuclear energy, sustainability, we would even then, still be surviving.

Enough of my mental masturbation.

Day Three, 2 December 2019

Heads up

Cuisines with unfamiliar flavours take some time to be liked. Especially Naga cuisine, which stands out as quite unconventional. If you are a vegetarian, you would faint. But if the feeling of 'Let's try this for once; I am never getting this anywhere else', doesn't leave you, you must totally go for it.

I had made up my mind to go wild this time and taste whatever was served on my plate, but after what I saw at the Angami pavilion, I lost my appetite, and all the zest for my food excursion vanished. Right at the gate of the Angami pavilion was the giant head of a *gayal* (wild bison), as big as a gym ball, placed on a rock that was smeared with its fresh blood. The dead gayal's eyes were closed and its tongue was hanging out of its mouth, dripping blood.

'This is mithun! Nagaland state animal! We have this guy on our menu today!' said a guy coming out of the house. He then grabbed its head by the horns and flipped it over. Now it was resting on its horns with the cross-section of its neck disturbingly visible.

'Too much blood spilt from the neck, now no spill. No dirty . . . hahaha . . .' he said as the blood started dripping through its nose. The gayal's oesophagus was as wide as a bangle.

'You want to click a photo? Go ahead, it won't bite,' the guy said, pointing at his 'little pet'. How could one be so normal after chopping off something that big? A quick theory sprang in my mind: The moral choice of which animal to kill and which to not is directly proportional to its size and the amount of blood spillage. Hence, it is easy to move on from the deaths of chickens, pigeons, rats, insects and fish.

On a separate note, although a shock, it was still enthralling. So, yes, I did end up clicking a few pictures.

* * *

Don't think twice, it's alright

The food expedition started off with a crispy starter of silkworms. For a long time, I stood near the shop staring at those fried worms. Ten on each stick for Rs 50. I wondered whether the poor annelids would have severe self-esteem issues if they knew that their shit is so much more expensive than themselves. Surprisingly, it was the most popular item on the menu. I made my judgements looking at people's faces as they ate.

'Come on, bro! Try it. You only live once. Try, try! They aren't too bad,' said a performer, seeing me sceptically staring at those dead silkworms. He wore a denim jacket over his ethnic attire and was highly drunk.

'Don't think too much, just take one and pop it.' Saying this, he actually took one off the skewer and tossed it in his mouth.

'See? . . . not bad.' He then passed the skewer to me. Taking a deep breath, I popped one too. Moment of silence. I chewed it thrice and then swallowed it.

'That's actually not bad,' I replied. Seriously, it was as tender inside as it was crispier on the skin, even if a bit salty. Imagine how a prawn would taste with the texture of French fries. (Apologies for ruining both.) It still tasted much much better than capsicum. Later, we both finished all the worms on the skewer, and I somehow managed to escape before he offered me anything else.

Food was being prepared on a large scale, and I could smell different aromas passing through every pavilion. By the afternoon, I was hungry enough to have a proper lunch. At the Ao pavilion, volunteers were running around with bowls of steaming hot rice. They served pork almost everywhere, with perhaps varied tastes. Without letting my indecisiveness kick in, I secured my seat amidst the hustle and bustle of the Ao pavilion. A volunteer shortly brought the food on an attractive bamboo plate decorated with a banana leaf. 'Taste, taste! Tell me if you like it,' she smirked. It was a lot of rice served with juicy chunks of pork fat. Even before tasting it, its umami smell filled up my senses with hunger. The sticky, hot rice had a distinct taste of its own, and the pork! The pork was tender and miraculously juicy. It had a singular, strong meaty flavour with subtle notes of pepper and garlic. On the side were some boiled leafy vegetables and a tiny amount of tremendously hot chilli paste. I was glad I had shot most of the festival pre-lunch because it turned out to be a very heavy meal.

This scrumptious meal restored my confidence to try something else. And by something else, I mean the most underrated dish on the Ao menu—snails. As nobody else was ordering it, I went inside the kitchen to have a look. (Yes, the kitchens were accessible.) There were just two people cooking everything, and that too with utmost hygiene. One of the cooks took a few snails out of a hot utensil, demonstrated how to eat it and passed one to me. I looked at the thing and then at the cook, and she grinned. I tried doing the exact same thing she did with the snail, but I couldn't suck out anything and had to give up. The cooks certainly had a great time watching me make a fool of myself. But I'm glad it didn't happen because slimy is my least favourite sensation.

I couldn't dare to tell all of this to my vegetarian mother, but she obviously got to know after the video was released. It took me a Mysore Masala Dosa and an hour-long lecture on 'You become what you eat' for this to pass. Ever since, she makes sure to bring this up as my lowest point, in our silly arguments.

Visitors were spectators everywhere else, but at the food courts, there was equal participation. Everyone was curious, mingling among each other and indulging in great food. A sweet camaraderie between cooking, serving and eating went on for hours. It was like a mega potluck for all the tribes of Nagaland. Honestly, the hesitation towards trying Naga food is perhaps not due to its choice of ingredients but their shape. Something like silkworms can be easily consumable if they don't look like silkworms, but instead, like momo or tarts.

Although Mumbai is a metro city that offers all sorts of cuisines, from Persian to Thai, it is still hard to find dishes like smoked pork with axone in its most authentic form. It is nearly impossible to achieve this taste without smoking the meat above the stove for hours or having the right kind of ingredients. Tribal food, although having a rich legacy in India, sadly never made it to popular cuisines. Today's food excursion was way out of my comfort zone, and if you ask me whether I would eat this again, I would probably not. But being part of an altogether different lifestyle was an experience I will never forget. If you set aside the thrilling part of it, Naga food reminds us of the flavours of boiled ingredients, fewer taste combinations and homegrown vegetables.

* * *

I was finally done with my shoot and it was time for the biggest job that I'd been assigned—getting souvenirs for my office colleagues. A lot of people had asked for very specific items, and I, too, was very excited to take home some stuff. 'I am not into shopping' is what I say when I mean I am broke and have zero space in my bag. But this was one of those rare occasions, because everything being sold there was handcrafted, aesthetic, tasty, novel and, importantly, hard to be found anywhere else.

Naga shawls, being the most expensive ones, sold like hotcakes. There were stalls of ethnic Naga jewellery, tribal bamboo cutlery, spears and daos. Fabindia aunties roamed around hunting for the best fabric for their curtains. After merely browsing through all of these, I headed straight to the other section where they were selling all the edible stuff. There was a great variety of local pickles, wines and dried wild fruits. I purchased seven packets of dried wild apples, three packets of sweet prunes and a bottle of Naga king chilli sauce that was served at lunch earlier. My office WhatsApp group turned into an online flea market. People ticked their favourites in the photos I had sent, and after a lot of chatting, bargaining, exchanging, variety showing, photo clicking, resending and cash tendering, I ended up buying a lot of things without even thinking about the fact that I had just one tight backpack to fit it all. Shopping certainly isn't my thing, I realized with two heavy tote bags on my shoulders.

By night, everyone moved inside the pavilions. Fresh rice beer in bamboo mugs was being passed around, people made space and got cosy around the fireplace. Two new friends and I sang along with the Aos, and Ketho joined in later. We saved seats for friends who got up to refill their beer or take washroom breaks, exchanged smiles with strangers and synced our tunes to words we barely knew the meanings of. For us, it was all gibberish. For hours, no one really dared to get out into the cold. The warmth of the room with a light buzz of the rice beer turned up as a sweet goodbye hug to the Hornbill Festival.

Day Four, 3 December 2019

The previous day's loot was scattered all over the room. I spent a good hour fitting everything in my backpack and still had two bags to carry separately. My return journey was going to be very anxiety-ridden because I tend to forget most of the extra luggage other than my backpack. The Hornbill Festival would continue until 10 December. Since it was my last day in Nagaland, I decided to get away from the celebrations and spend the day in the normalcy of Kohima city. I bid goodbye to Ketho. Little Jivvy certainly did not want to leave me and ran all around the kitchen with half-chewed food in his mouth that his mother was trying very hard to feed him. He saw Ketho giving me a hug, and he hugged me too as I was tying my shoelaces. He said something that sounded like 'Munana', which, hopefully, means 'I will miss you'. I was followed up to the highway by the dog of the house and later got a lift to Kohima from a cheerful young biker.

Kohima

Kohima was just how I had seen on Day
One—cold, busy and mysteriously
intriguing. The daily market that
Neitho had taken me to was the first
place I visited. In fact, that was the
prime reason behind my returning
to Kohima. I spent the majority of my
time there, curiously shooting absolutely
everything that I found new, weird, gross,
unusual, tasty, fresh, aesthetic and colourful.
For an outsider, the sight could be one of
disgust, but the locals didn't care any less,
being very well aware of our inhibitions
towards it. Frogs in plastic pouches watched the customers
haggle. Rats in cages kept under the tables would know people
through their footwear. Each one counting down its days of
being together. The markets of Kohima did have the cinematic
value of a Wong Kar Wai film.

Kohima's tribal culture has a prevalent tradition
of sustainability. Hardly anyone would know the word
'sustainability', but they have been practising it for generations.
They use bamboo in every possible way as a substitute for
all the single-use plastic or non-biodegradable items. It
is something they use to make literally everything: bags,
toothbrushes, door latches, water pipes, washbasins, houses
and probably even submarines, rockets and teleportation
devices! Bamboo is used in abundance. Nature nurtured the
tribes of Nagaland, and their gratitude towards it can be seen
in their lifestyle.

In the early days of Independence, the North-east faced several issues of infiltration, militancy and civil conflicts.[*] Although one requires an inner line permit to enter Nagaland, the atmosphere here felt pretty safe; at least it did in Kohima, which is by far one of the biggest cities in the state. In the markets especially, I noticed that the locals were genuinely very warm and not just due to a big festival getting them a lot of attention. They appeared extremely kind, joyful and keen, not only on sharing about their lives but also knowing mine. Under the 'curious tourist' card, I was given several freebies to taste, fresh honey straight out of the honeycomb being one of them.

It was only 3 December, and the streets and shops were already decorated for Christmas. Although the locals of Kohima belong to the Angami tribe, they follow Christianity. I have heard stories of rampant conversions by missionaries in the nineteenth century, as a result of which almost 90 per cent of the people in Nagaland today are Christians[†]. There are churches on every nook and corner, but the most confusing thing for me was that every tribe has its own church. What could possibly be different in each church? And how do people still identify with their tribe even after converting?

I found the reason when I walked into an Ao tribe church. Sitting in the big empty nave, I grabbed a copy of the Bible from a bench pocket. The verses were translated to the Ao

[*] Sayak Basu, 'History of separatism in the conflicted northeastern state of Nagaland', *Deccan Herald*, 26 February 2023, https://www.deccanherald.com/elections/history-of-separatism-in-the-conflicted-northeastern-state-of-nagaland-1195265.html

[†] Imtimangyang, 'A brief historical account: Christianity among the Ao Nagas of North-East India', *National Journal of Multidisciplinary Research and Development*, 3 September 2017.

language. I recalled what Neitho said about the distinctness of all the tribal languages. It was for that reason that each tribe has their own church. I also found out that none of the tribal languages have their own script because the text in the Bible was printed phonetically in English. I could have just googled it or asked some person around, but here, I just had to have my quick, 'proud explorer' moment.

The morning in Kohima seemed like a usual routine, a rather fast-paced one. Oblivious to the fact that they had visitors for the festival, the locals carried out their chores without making it seem like a performance. Like how we kids acted on school inspection days. People frequently ran into known faces and greeted them with cheerful heckling. The old people especially were the bullies of the town; they had seen kids grow, some leave their homes and some return. They have seen this place go through the aftermath of the deadly battle of World War II[*] to modern-day conflicts of separatism.[†] Their relationship with violence may have been one of the reasons they hold onto their identity this strongly. Some of them bear scars of these times on their wrinkled faces, hidden by smiles of welcome. Kohima, more than the mountains, was its people.

* * *

---

[*] Anbarasan Ethirajan, 'Kohima: Britain's "forgotten" battle that changed the course of WWII', *BBC*, 14 February 2021, https://www.bbc.com/news/world-asia-india-55625447
[†] Basu (2023).

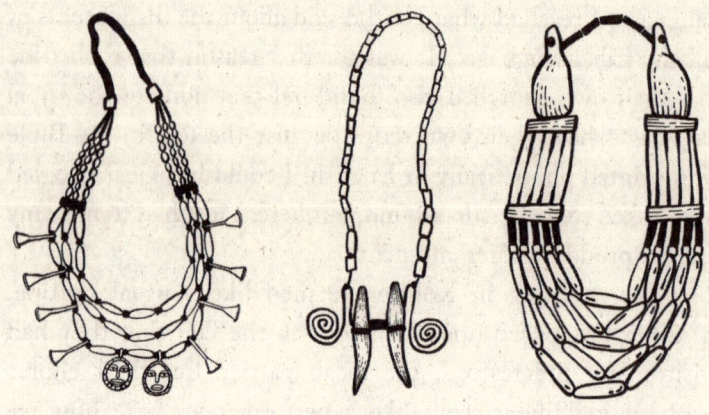

Goodbye

Before leaving for Dimapur, I spent some time at Fifa Cafe, reading a book and sipping hot ginger ale. I was too unwilling to leave Kohima and had found my comfort under the low-hanging, warm dim light of the table. When it was time to go, I finally prepared myself and got up to pay the bill. Seeing my overflowing backpack, Kini, the cafe owner, was curious about my travel.

'You've come solo? How old are you?' she asked, surprised. She had a contagious smile. Her slender fingers caught my attention every time they tucked in her hair behind her ear.

'Twenty. It's no big deal though; I have been travelling every month.' Both of us knew I was trying to sound all cool but failing terribly.

'So . . . Leaving?'

'Umm . . . Yes.'

'Come on, I'll walk you to the cab stand,' she said, putting on her long beige coat.

'And here, this is a gift from Kohima,' she offered me a jar of beef pickle.

'Kini, this is really nice, but I actually don't eat beef,' I replied hesitantly.

'Oh, then have this one,' she said, passing on a jar of chicken pickle. It was the sweetest note to leave Kohima on. We shared an awkward hug at the taxi stand amid the cabbies yelling for rides. I packed the pickle safely at the side of my backpack. I saw Kini walking back to her cafe as my cab turned towards the highway. The lights of Kohima blurred as we drove away from it and eventually diminished into the folds of the moonlit peaks.

* * *

I reached Dimapur late at night. It was exactly how it was when I arrived—apocalyptic. I have never seen the damn place in daylight, but I was glad my train to Guwahati arrived on time and I didn't have to wait for long. My flight to Mumbai was at 4 p.m. the next day, and our production head, while booking the tickets, made sure I had enough buffer time in between, but it so happened that the overnight train journey got me to Guwahati way ahead of time the next day, and now I had nine dreadful hours to pass. At the airport, I was done with trying out perfume samples, browsing self-help books and repeatedly going through the cost of snacks in the first two hours itself. I had also finished all the wild prunes I bought the previous day. I ate so many of them that at one point it nauseated me.

Sitting at a charging point, I waited for my flight to arrive. I had lost all my social battery to mingle with strangers. This entire trip (Darjeeling and Nagaland) was so novel that I barely could take a break to process the experience. It was almost a week later, after returning home, that I realized how far I was. My life in Mumbai was in stark contrast to my days in the North-east. In my imagination, I often juxtaposed the markets of Kohima with those in the cities, the bamboo cutlery with flimsy plastic spoons, looking at things at a wider expanse to mosaics of the sky through tall buildings, crossing roads, asking for directions, waiting for metros, etc. Both scenarios had their own perks, but having witnessed them, I can confidently say that we are merely the byproducts of places we come from. Travelling serves as a medium to observe and, more importantly, absorb these diverse nuances of human experiences. It allows us to evolve by introspecting, reaffirming our own roots and ultimately cultivating respect for the origins of others.

FOURTEEN

KOCHI AND ALLEPPEY

Curries, coconuts, cats and canoes

'Are you sure about this?' asked Anusha. She was already expecting this.

I nodded with hesitation.

'You want to stop, especially when it's doing so well?'

'My assignments from the last two semesters have been rejected due to lack of attendance. My professors need to see my face enough for them to let me sit for final exams.'

'*Aur fail ho gaya toh?*' (And what if you fail?)

'I am doing BA, Anusha.'

'Then why are you even taking a break?' She knew it was not just about exams.

There could have been other options to keep this series going. Maybe we could have prepared a bank of episodes for the next two months and taken a break or rescheduled our content calendar. But there was something else that bothered me other than my college attendance.

The format of Budget Backpacking had become restrictive. We had all gone on autopilot mode while working on it. Although the series still remained the hero content on the platform, we could see it getting repetitive at a point and losing its value. There was rarely any scope for exploring anything new in its narrative. I missed experimenting with different formats, working in teams and most importantly, having the freedom and control of being behind the camera. Watching stories unveil themselves rather than me telling them had become a newly emerging ambition. Especially after what I shot in Nagaland and Shillong.

Personally, I was also drifting away from the idea of short-term travel. It lacked the true essence of backpacking and eventually got physically taxing. With this shift, it would keep getting harder to sustain this series. The feeling was so bitter to even suggest closing it that I kept delaying this conversation with Anusha for more than a month. My hesitation kept creeping out of every word I spoke.

'So, you want to call it a season?'

'Yes! I think I can shoot a nice last episode, like a season finale.'

'Then, let's aim for Kerala.' Kerala, because it was highly requested. 'We can join you this time. Paula, Sarang and I.'

'Finally!' I sprang up in excitement. I always complained at Anusha for not being there for any of our shoots, and it was finally happening!

'You better not fail now!' said Anusha, with a smirk.

I was about to shoot the last episode of a year-long series. A bittersweet wave of emotions kept me worried if at all life would have anything in store after this as well as hopeful of newer opportunities to evolve.

* * *

I was the earliest to show up at the airport.

After the initial excitement wore off, I had a realization. The people I was going on a trip with had certain characteristics: 1) They were my bosses; 2) They were significantly older than me; and 3) They were long-time best friends with each other. I wasn't nervous because of my age, but rather because it would be my first time sharing my solo trip with my superiors. It felt similar to having your father, who taught you how to drive, accompany you on your daily commute. Or when your girlfriend says, 'Aww, you want to make me a painting? I want to see how you do it.' I could already foresee the challenge of fitting in and the difficulty of avoiding saying something stupid in a desperate attempt to appear cool. It's interesting how we often have romanticized ideas that sound wonderful until they actually come true.

For a week, I was hoping I'd fall sick or that Kerala proclaims itself a separate nation or that Bha2Pa shuts down!

Basically anything that could lead to this trip being cancelled. But here I was with my apprehension at my boarding gate, preparing myself for a hopefully sane trip. The bridges were already burnt to a crisp, and there was no going back now.

Day One, 3 February 2020

Paula, Anusha and I had landed in Kochi the previous night itself. On our way to the hostel, we had already spotted places to eat, even under the street lights. Sarang was shooting in Ahmedabad and was arriving at midnight. I, who had taken on the responsibility of checking him in, slept through the night and realized my defeat when I woke up to see him sleeping under my bunk bed. I had booked a four-bed dorm in Zostel Fort Kochi so that we could have a whole room to ourselves. The last time I had been here was two years ago, when it was newly opened. I had drawn a backpack on its memory wall when it was fairly blank, but it no longer looked like that.

All four of us had been to Kerala earlier, so we thought it would be better not to stick to an itinerary. By this time, I was convinced about the idea of having no plans. In any case, Kochi is not the kind of place you go about ticking monuments off your list; it requires one to slow down. After all, it's a town run by people who walk in *mundu* (lungis).

A sumptuous Keralite breakfast at Lucky Star Cafe got us charged up to brave the humid climate of Fort Kochi. Food is one reason I am sceptical of travelling in groups. My aunts would go to Paris and still want to eat kande pohe. But with people equally open to tasting local foods, it's enjoyable hunting for such eateries and evolving our palates. We relished the bonda, appam, idiyappam and several serves of kadala (brown chickpea) curry. It was a treat, indeed. And the cost? Rs 320 only!

Fort Kochi

Fort Kochi is separated from its mainland Ernakulam, the central business district of the city of Kochi, by Vembanad Lake. Clerks, vendors and fishermen frequently commute via ferries connecting its harbours. As a traveller, one must be a part of this crowd, and you might find yourself unexpectedly thrilled at the sight of a robust cargo ship docking at the harbour (or maybe that was just me).

Back in colonial times, spices and coffee brought from the mountains of Munnar were loaded on ships and exported from the ports of Kochi. The city's medieval history saw the rule of the Varmas, who later allied with the Portuguese, then the Dutch and eventually the British. As a result, Kochi's architecture and culinary scene showcase the diverse influences of these three powers. Adding to the cultural richness of the region are the iconic Chinese fishing nets along the coast. A harmonious coexistence of Hindu, Catholic, Jewish and Muslim communities make Kochi something more than just a set of aesthetic houses, clean roads and great curries.

We opted for walking, as like Puducherry, Fort Kochi is a town that lends itself well to cycling or leisurely strolls. Despite the increasing heat, Sarang managed to keep our spirits high with his dad jokes and occasional exclamations of 'Stand here, this will make a great picture!' Whenever we found ourselves basking in favourable lighting, Sarang would swiftly appear,

urging us to strike a pose, resulting in new
photos for our social media feeds. On
the bustling streets, he seamlessly
switched between doing that
and petting street cats. God!
He found so many of them.
For those who follow
him on Instagram, it's no
surprise that 80 per cent of
his stories revolve around
his mischievous cat, Mogambo,
and their conversations in Marathi.

ക്രന്നോ

The lanes of Fort Kochi are not just a blend of cultures
but also a captivating mosaic of modernity and vintage charm.
Artists from the famous Kochi–Muziris Biennale have created
such colourful graffiti at every nook and corner that one is sure
to stop and chuckle over their quirky subtext. Fort Kochi, from
a wider view, must surely look like an Edward Hopper painting
that was given to Andy Warhol for its final touches.

Again, thanks to the Kochi–Muziris Biennale, the town
resembles a giant art gallery. Apart from aesthetic houses and
minimalistic cafes, many old structures have been revamped
into beautiful art spaces and galleries. We took our time and
explored several art houses in the area at our leisure. We roamed
around separately, but I remember this one big 5x5 painting at
Aatma Art Space that attracted all four of us. We sat gazing at
it in enchantment. Hung on a scrappy, rustic wall, it depicted
a big bubble full of vague objects: cars, houses, Gandhi, a
cupboard, Marx, Savitribai Phule, the Ramayana, villages,
cities, class conflict, temples, mosques, flowers, machines,
murder, birth, cattle, forests, UFOs, chairs, windows, etc.

Collectively, it seemed like a blend of everything that's helped change society. It was partly disturbing and partly hopeful.

I find modern art exhaustingly challenging to comprehend, but about that specific artwork, even if one ignored its poignant say, its imagery was engaging enough for one to remember it at a glance. Our senses are as stupid as we are; sometimes, we can't remember things even after looking at them every day, and sometimes, even a glance is enough to keep them preserved in our memories until death. Untitled, the painting was on sale for Rs 3 lakh.

A lazy afternoon at the apocalyptic Marine Drive turned up the hunger within us.

We had done a good amount of walking around all these galleries, we realized as we sat down for a hydration break. The age gap of the group was quite evident seeing how consciously these hydration breaks were taken. For lunch, Anusha and I shared a creamy vegetable stew while Sarang and Paula had beef. For the first time, there was beef on my table. Now being a brown guy from a harmlessly right-wing family, I can't really describe the feeling of seeing the forbidden so close. It would likely be a milder version of how a monk would feel at a strip club. I'm not very religious, but neither did I feel the urge to taste it. It was just my moment of feeling eerie on seeing beef curry next to my plate.

We witnessed the sunset by the Chinese fishing nets, sharing our seats with the egrets occupying the heights, feasting on the fresh catch. The lazy ones grabbed their catches from the fishermen's crates. Paula and Anusha were strolling through the fish market while Sarang and I sat on the pier watching the fishermen wrap up their day. He had clicked a few good photos of the sunset and put his phone in his pocket by now.

Throughout the day, Sarang was the most energetic among us, despite having flown in at midnight and running on limited sleep. Even though Paula and Anusha had spent a lot of time with him, he still had new stories to share. He never ran out of them, nor did he repeat any of them.

Yet, amid this flamboyant joy, an undercurrent of restlessness permeates his behaviour. It is rare to see Sarang sit idle. He is always up to something. This restlessness often leads him to nervousness and anger. Nowadays, in the office, he smiles less. I usually see him 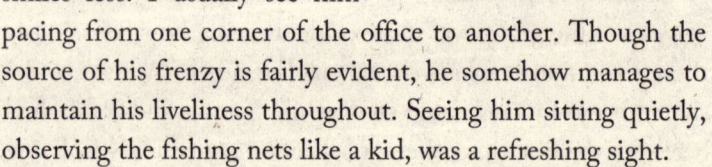 pacing from one corner of the office to another. Though the source of his frenzy is fairly evident, he somehow manages to maintain his liveliness throughout. Seeing him sitting quietly, observing the fishing nets like a kid, was a refreshing sight.

Day Two, 4 February 2020

Pazham pori

I cheated today. On bhakarwadi. If I were asked what's the best snack to have with chai, my answer would undoubtedly be bhakarwadi. But today, we discovered something otherworldly. The best snack contributed by Keralites to mankind—pazham pori. These divine banana fritters go perfectly well with both chai and filter coffee. The one we had on a roadside cart this morning gave the ultimate pleasure. It was sweet and crispy, soft on the inside and appealingly golden yellow on the outside. Anusha translated the recipe that the chechi at the cart patiently shared. I tried making it after returning home. Sadly though, even after following all the instructions, it lacked something. Nevertheless, I at least learnt the correct pronunciation.

* * *

Mattancherry

'What? Mattancherry?'

'Yeah.'

'Doesn't it sound like a creamy dessert topped with glossy little cherries?'

'OR, could it be a mutton preparation?'

'Cherri means street in Malayalam, so maybe it could actually be Mutton Street?'

Bundled up in an autorickshaw, we had this conversation on our way. This was just one of several such stupid conversations we had in the day.

Although we went to Mattancherry for its beautiful Jewish settlement, a strong aroma of mixed spices stopped us a few metres before and dragged us into the courtyard of a huge house. It was too big to be called a house but too simple to be called a mansion. Massive batches of pepper and clove were kept for sun drying. A few men in colourful lungis appeared from the

PAZHAMPORI

Banana * Fritters

Duration : 15 mins
Grade : Easy

① Choose ripe bananas of Rajeli type. Peel and cut them in 4 halves each.

② Dip the cuts in the batter of

- Flour (1 cup)
- Rice flour (1 tbsp)
- Sugar (1 tbsp)
- Water (3/4 cup)
- Pinch of salt and turmeric powder.

③ Heat up some oil in a Kadhai.

④ Deep fry till they turn Golden brown

⑤ Take out the fritters and pair with some filter Kaapi.

warehouse with sacks of cumin, looked at us and continued to spread it out in the sunlight. One of them ritualistically pointed at the top floor where they sold their spices. And we followed. A scary little flight of narrow stairs led us to a room full of spices neatly arranged on shelves. Fine-quality cinnamon, cardamom, cloves, bay leaves, pepper, nutmeg, cumin seeds, coriander seeds, poppy seeds, red chillies and many more spices attracted not only cooking enthusiasts but also people like me who love to just indulge in their aromas. As we grow older, we 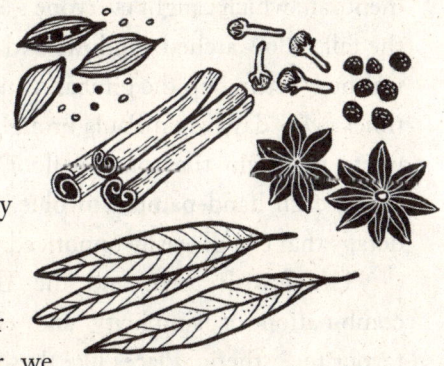 think our tastes will eventually become profound but there is still a part of us that gets excited seeing new shapes, colours and smells. That was me right there.

An uncle at the billing counter sold a set of surplus products by triggering the insecurities of his customers. 'Madam! Take this Ayurvedic oil. Best to prevent hair fall; you need it the most. Oye, you black shirt boy! What is this? Is this all you got? Take some more jeera for your mom. Akka, you won't get this anywhere else. Get some of those turmeric sticks; they're good for your immune system. See, you're getting old. Ayee, try on this special formula. An overnight cure for pimples!' He was unstoppable.

Our hands were instantly engaged with a bounty of spices. Carrying those bags everywhere and not losing them was an added effort for the day.

The Jewish town started from a few simplistic white houses and ended at an even simpler structure, but as we entered, that

plain white block suddenly turned all glitters and shimmers.
The small structure was nothing short of intricate, splendid,
delicate and breathtaking. It was the Jewish synagogue. My
eyes didn't wish to waste time even blinking, and I observed
everything minutely. Old wooden benches surrounded a golden
menorah, which caught everyone's eyes at first glance, and then
the tall yellow arched windows and low hanging chandeliers. I
was busy setting up the gimbal, which I did almost a thousand
times every day, when Paula brought my attention to the little
white porcelain tiles on the floor. There were hundreds of
them, each hand-painted in blue. Paula has an eye for such
details that can go easily unnoticed.

The Jewish town and the Dutch palace were a rare
combination of simplicity and elegant charm. That's my
favourite aesthetic. Places like these are a great example of the
equilibrium of design and utility. Having achieved symmetry,
each house retains its uniqueness.

* * *

We had spent our day like typical tourists, and we were goddamn
loving it. We hoped to get an airy corner at Kayees restaurant,
but it was full. We couldn't stand the scorching heat outside with
our bags full of spices, so we decided to spot tables that were
about to be vacated. We stood near people who were about to
finish and waited impatiently until one of the tables got empty.
It wasn't just us; every table had a group of hungry men standing
next to it. When we go to a restaurant in Mumbai or Pune,
it's likely that people will recognize Sarang from BhaDiPa and
gather around him. (He has quite a fan base.) But here I could
see him casually standing next to men who were belching and

scratching their bellies without having to worry about running into fans, enjoying his anonymity to the fullest. Getting to eat the Kayees' special mutton biryani was our only goal.

Take note that if you're dining at Kayees, especially for its iconic mutton biryani, never hurry. And make sure you head straight to your hotel after your meal because it's sure to put you in a food coma. Our lethargy made us extremely late for our train to Alleppey. We ran as fast as we could, carrying our heavy backpacks. Anusha was the only person to bring a suitcase, which slowed her down. I bet that must have been Anusha's most adventurous thing on this trip.

Covid-19?

We rushed since trains in south India usually arrive on time, but also forgot the fact that they are still Indian and hence unpredictable. Constant announcements about safety measures on the outbreak of novel coronavirus in English, Hindi and Malayalam silenced every other sound on the station. From Day One, the four of us were receiving messages from our followers to stay safe. The first case of Covid-19 in India was found here in Kerala a few days ago. Nobody knew anything about it, but still, everybody around us was discussing their theories.

'Is it that big of a deal?'

'Maybe . . . They said the virus doesn't survive in hot temperatures, and here it is!'

'But then they also say that China made it up to sell face masks at Miniso stores.'

'Only 2 per cent of the population has it, but 2 per cent of Kerala's population is not a small number.'

'Don't worry guys, I am carrying masks for all of us,' Anusha said, taking out a packet of surgical masks from the front pocket of her daypack. Anusha was the most organized person among us. She had everything, right from a bottle of hand sanitizer to a plan B if aliens sabotaged our trip. On the train, we were the only people wearing face masks and ultimately the objects of many people's attention. It was tough to keep them on as they smelt like hospitals—the smell I hate the most. None of us had the slightest idea that these masks were soon going to be an everyday thing.

* * *

We saw Alleppey in the hue of a purple sky. Our two-storey hostel was probably the tallest building in the neighbourhood! It had a legacy of once being the police headquarters, then an office for All India Radio, later a primary school and now a backpacker's hostel. The lush green courtyard highlights the white building amid quaint houses situated on the roads crisscrossing the backwater canals. From the time it was built, in 1930, until today, the place has undergone very menial changes. Classrooms were converted into dormitories; the kitchen was set up in the computer lab, while a small compartment for the school security guard was now the reception desk. It was just us and a few European backpackers on the floor.

It was an exhausting day, as we had walked a lot. But still, after taking our showers, the tranquillity of Alleppey tempted us to get out for a stroll across to the beach on the next road. I played the song 'Cherathukal' from the Malayalam film *Kumbalangi Nights* because it perfectly fit the mood, and we weren't too far from Kumbalangi either. The shared silence grew more comfortable as the song progressed. Though we didn't understand the lyrics, the melody comforted us, much like a lullaby that reminds you of the warmth of coming home after a long time. I recently looked up the meaning of the first stanza:

> *Cherathukal thorum nin theyormayaay, tharaathe pom*
> *charuvam ummakalaal, chuzhalunnoree kuttakoorirul,*
> *kaziyolam njaneriyam*

It translates to: I shall remain in lamps as the blazing memory of yours, till the end of this darkness, created by the kisses un-given.

It was exactly how we were feeling. The weariness, not of the trip but of the anxious uncertainty, seemed, for that moment, to be taken care of.

We finished listening to the entire song on a wooden bench at a small beach shack and returned after the breeze changed its course. The calmness on everyone's faces was an instant reassurance that choosing to visit Alleppey was a good call.

Day Three, 5 February 2020

Alappuzha, aka Alleppey, is a district 50 km south of Kochi, water-bound by the Arabian Sea from the east and its backwaters surging towards the other side through numerous scenic canals. Flocks of munias fluttered around the rice paddies while several egrets and herons feasted on fish at the water bodies. Alleppey is far quieter and greener than Kochi and attracts a rich crowd of tourists for its sensational houseboat experience across the backwaters. These houseboats are no less than luxury hotel rooms, equipped with all the amenities and services enough for an average family person to spend all their savings. However, some houseboats offer Ayurvedic massages to relieve that stress. Damn, this can totally go in a Conde Nast blog.

Agreed, Alleppey has beautiful canals, but it pisses me off when a travel blog claims it as 'Venice of the East'. NO! Alleppey is Alleppey; there is absolutely no need to Westernize its identity. 'Pune is the Oxford of the East' or 'Shillong is the Scotland of the East'. WHY? Ever heard 'Switzerland is the Kashmir of the West'? Sounds weird, right? It is annoying how we still package our cities to comply with Western tastes. It's not just fashion or beauty, but sadly, Western aesthetic standards have also crept into our geographies. Funny how an intangible part of our land still remains colonized.

Canoe

Our main objective to add Alleppey to our plan was to go boating in the backwaters, but not on the houseboats because: 1) They were ridiculously expensive and we were on a tight budget; 2) Houseboats being huge in size cannot enter narrow canals; and 3) Their fuel residue pollutes the backwaters. We were looking for canoes. Canoes that locals use to commute across the narrow canals. They are: 1) Manually operated by oars; 2) Not so mainstream; 3) Cheap; and 4) Tiny due to which they can be taken in the most pristine villages of Kuttanad.

Rashmi, the hostel volunteer, overheard our conversation and intervened to share her expertise. She gave us all the possible options to find canoes, along with a crash course on negotiating the price. After renting two mopeds, we left on an adventure to satisfy our yearning for boating in the backwaters. We surfed through long roads, chasing high-swinging coconut trees, watching out for and protecting our heads from falling coconuts, bridges crisscrossing singing canals, small hamlets, endless rice paddies and thick-moustached men in mundus occupying the empty bus stands.

Sitting in the back seat, I multi-tasked by shooting B-rolls, navigating the GPS, adjusting my oversized helmet and trying my best to catch what Anusha was saying. On a windy bike ride, she decided to narrate the story of her upcoming book to me. Meanwhile, I also fixated on some interestingly unique town names we passed by—Nedumudi, Kottayam, Changanassery, Champakulam, Pullangady. Cute.

We slowed down after seeing Sarang pull over near a canal bank. He and Paula had spotted a canoe. An old boatman was chilling on his wooden canoe smoking a beedi. After trying our best to explain to him what we wanted, he called one of his friends, and voila! We had two canoes for the four of us to do a backwaters tour. This may sound very simple, but we had actually stopped several times to inquire about these canoes and were almost losing hope as no one had an idea.

The boatmen agreed to take us in the canals for an hour at Rs 200 each, which was a great deal. The canoe bobbed as we stepped in. Unlike the engine-driven houseboats, the canoes didn't make any noise. With a nice rhythm of oars rowing through the still waters of the canals, the boatmen took us inside the backwaters of Kottayam.

'*Kuttanadan punjayile* . . .' sang the boatman as he rowed from the scorching heat to the cool canopy of palms. That song travelled further, becoming my earworm for the rest of the day. The canal narrowed down gradually and was now covered with floating water vegetation, on which Indian pond herons perched looking for their hunt in the water.

'So, Indra . . . How was it?' asked Anusha after the rowing stopped.

'It's going great.'

'No, I mean travelling. It's been a year. How does it feel?' she asked, putting me in a spot.

'Umm . . . I don't know,' I replied, terribly failing at articulating my thoughts.

'Is it?' she probed.

After a moment of silence, I turned to her and said, 'I've never felt this alive before. I feel happy and humbled. Thanks for this, Anusha.' I never thanked Anusha for being so positive and trusting all the time. We met daily at the office, but then I thought it would be awkward to just randomly walk up to her and say 'thanks'. Especially since I used to be extremely terrible at conveying my emotional side to people. I thought I had very little of it, but moments like these kept proving me wrong. However, I still feel it was a missed opportunity to have a heart-to-heart conversation with her. My hesitation for vulnerability had led to many such missed opportunities. There is always so much to tell her that I hide behind my worry of encroaching on her space. I feel I only take from her.

'You should actually write about it. Like a collection of your travel stories. Maybe a book,' she said in a casual tone. Or maybe not.

'A book?'

'Yeah, a book.'

* * *

Tipsy

On our way back to the hostel, we stopped at a country bar to taste toddy, a local fermented liquor popular in rural Kerala. We had the greatest connoisseur of liquor with us, Paula McGlynn, and it was she who initiated the plan. She knew the best of the liquors and the correct methods to consume them. She even carried her whisky glasses and a cute sample container to observe the drink's reaction after a few hours.

The local joint we visited wasn't at all like the one you start picturing after hearing the words 'country bar'. It was a minimal set-up of three airy huts amid the green rice paddies waving in the wind with flocks of wetland birds swinging around. Being all this, the place was named 'New York Todi Place', and all the time we wondered what was so 'New York' about it. Our imaginations ran wilder as we got tipsy. Along with crispy tapioca and dry fish, the toddy we had was strong and smelt obnoxious yet tasted a bit sour with a sweet-ish aftertaste. We realized our state of drunkenness only after we got off the chairs and stood up.

* * *

We reached our hostel early in the evening, around 5 p.m. Sarang and Paula had their train to Goa that night, while Anusha and I were flying back to Mumbai the next morning. We had to return to Kochi that very night.

During the journey from Alleppey to Kochi, no one spoke a word. My mind soared through the salty winds as we drove parallel to the coast. With each passing moment, the realization of this journey drawing to a close slowly settled within me, leaving a bittersweet lump in my heart. Before this, I only thought of these trips individually, but for the first time, I was astounded to perceive this entire experience as a cohesive journey. It reminded me of trekking, where you focus only on the few metres ahead of your trail, surpassing numerous hills along the way. It is only upon reaching the summit that you comprehend the distance you have covered. All of my trips with their shares of triumphs, disappointments, lessons, reassurances, friendships forged, people missed and time spent alone boil down to one emotion—belonging. Belonging, irrespective of geographical boundaries and human relationships. These two, of course, heavily influence our sense of belonging, but the further I travel, I have always come home to my people feeling more grounded.

Although I didn't share my travels with anybody else, this moment almost felt like a goodbye hug from an actual person. A farewell to several versions of me that evolved and interchanged many qualities within this process. It was a tough choice to pick one of them to take back home. The insanity, weirdness and functioning on pure instinct are going to be tough to preserve in the deafening noise of the city and its ever-changing face. These escapes were breathers for me from constantly being influenced by crowds, their tastes and opinions. I was certain I would yearn for this more than anything else.

As we drove closer to the city, the sky gradually turned dark, settling me to come to terms with this parting.

After reaching Kochi, Sarang announced, 'I am going to make you eat the best French toast you've ever tasted in your lives.' After surviving three days at only Rs 3000 (each) and braving the humid weather in this hectic trip, we decided to reward ourselves with a fancy dinner. He took us to a cafe called French Toast, right beside the Cuckoo Club, which he had visited several times for his stand-up comedy gigs. I can't recall the name of the dishes we ordered; they were too gourmet to remember, but the taste—the taste was something else! The tender and creamy French toast instantly melted in my mouth, flooding my taste buds with flavours of cinnamon, egg and honey. Every bite savoured was worth the physical exhaustion from the last few days. That meal was by far the best memory I have with the three of them. I can't help but flex it every time our office conversations turn to nostalgia.

Day Four, 6 February 2020

Lounge shenanigans

We crashed at Anusha's friend's house in Kochi the previous night. I don't remember when I dozed off while sorting out the bills. Early in the morning, we left for the airport hoping to get some time to indulge in the airport lounge service; basically, browse through magazines, treat ourselves to a fancy breakfast and get pampered on massage chairs. Standing in the security queue among serious corporate types, I constantly kept looking at my watch. Anusha was already done checking in and was waiting for me on the other side. Time was slipping fast, and the odds didn't seem favourable. My backpack reached before me through the conveyor belt. I saw the cop's face change at the security monitor.

'NOT NOW!' I muttered after he got out of his chair and held my backpack. After making it to the other side, I was asked to empty everything.

'*Yeh kya hai?*' (What are these?) asked the guard.

'Camera batteries.'

'*Aur ye? Yeh machine gun hai? AK47?*' (What is this? A machine gun?) he grinned.

'*Nahi sir, gimbal hai.* For my camera.'

'Gimbal? Camera stand? Okay, okay,' he confirmed. 'Camera, why? Film industry?' He was being friendly at a very wrong time.

'No, sir, for shooting YouTube videos, sir.'

'Arrey waah! YouTuber! My nephew is also a YouTuber. He makes gadget videos . . . Unboxing.' I instantly regretted mentioning YouTube. 'Give me your number; you give him some tips.'

'No, sir, this is different. I've got to catch my flight. Thank you, sir. Bye, sir.' I somehow managed to escape. This usually never happens; it was the bloody gimbal's fault. If you're a videographer, you'd agree that gimbals are the most counterproductive gadgets ever. They are heavy and complex and cease to do their ONE job exactly when it's crucially needed, which is balancing.

By the time I was found clean, the boarding gates were already open.

'Anusha, let's just go now; we can skip the lounge,' I said, feeling guilty. I was sure she was pissed with me.

'*Arrey, chal, jaate hai!*' (Come on, let's go; we'll make it!) she said rather adventurously; something I didn't see coming.

Looking at the buffet, it seemed like a very good decision. A plethora of scrumptious food tempted our hungry bellies—sandwiches, fruits, cornflakes, sausages, salads, croissants, pastries and a whole other section for beverages. Accommodating everything on our plates, we totally forgot we had a flight to catch, and while we were busy feasting on our breakfast, our names were finally announced.

'This is the final boarding call for . . . Mrs Anusha Nandkumar and Mr Indrajeet More. Please reach gate number 5. I repeat . . .' I have never dared to pull off such a stunt because I have seen people breaking down for missing their flights, but seeing Anusha in her adventure spirit, I decided to follow her. Grabbing the coffee and stuffing my mouth with melon cuts, we rushed towards gate no. 5. Through all the discipline-loving south Indians at the airport, Anusha ran dragging her suitcase, while I followed her balancing my coffee. We finally boarded, and I chewed the melon in my mouth, finished the coffee and tried to ease into my seat with a plane full of agitated passengers looking at us.

* * *

This was the only time during the whole trip that I got to be alone. All my thoughts, rational and irrational, were waiting to flood in. I have always found social interactions extremely daunting, especially with seniors. An entire trip with them would be absolutely unthinkable. But throughout our time in Kerala, none of that happened. I chuckled thinking about my anxiety before coming to this trip. I had spent the last few days in the company of three wacky teens, surrounded by discussions of good films, nice art, great food, dad jokes and nostalgic memories. It was the only time I met Sarang, Paula and Anusha outside their work mode, and now I kind of understand what keeps them young. Probably someday I may have to diverge paths with them, but wherever I go, a bit of this 'eccentricity' will never leave my craft.

A part of me is still indulgent in this series, but I need to prepare myself to move ahead and get on to newer things. It won't be as fascinating as hosting a travel show, but as long as there is newness and creativity in it, it's worth the effort. Although the series is coming to a close, I am sure there is much more travel waiting to happen. In fact, now in a more desirable way and with newer challenges. If I were not hosting Budget Backpacking, I would have learnt a deeper understanding of all the 'whys of travelling' much later in life.

The uncertainty of what 'next' still haunts me. But maybe that's the beauty of it. If thought the other way around, it would be an absolutely boring road to travel through. Out of this fear, what I vouch for the most is the fun of finding out things, falling for people, growing with them, longing for some while appreciating the ones who stay. None of this would be experienced if everything was certain and definite. As I age through my twenties, I am sure I will grow more practical, maybe grumpier, lonelier, inevitably wiser and happier, but the life that lies in between excites me more.

FIFTEEN

SOUVENIR

As I write this, my heart is heavy for the first time, thinking about all these trips finally coming to an end. I now understand the unsettling feeling of parting from a journey as described by other travellers. I had never felt it before. I always headed home detached. The thought of the edit lined up ahead would occupy me as soon as I boarded my journey back home. For that entire year, I barely had enough time to decompress and reflect on any of those trips. I was either travelling, supervising editing, going to the office, chasing assignment deadlines or trying to attend lectures. For a nineteen-year-old, life was running at full pace.

However, now as the pandemic hits, amid the scary uncertainty lying ahead, I have nothing else to do but seek refuge in the comforting memories of my travels. I finally see this journey as a cohesive experience that I'm still trying to make sense of as I continue writing. Perhaps a few years later, I will find these few pages extremely cringe-worthy, but I will proceed and leave my future self to deal with that embarrassment. Over the years, I have actively kept myself from rationalizing every detail of my life experiences. But as an average audience, my fixation on perfect closures won't let me leave this hanging.

My exposure to travel was only through solo backpacking. We never really went on family vacations, nor was I part of those summer holiday conversations my schoolmates had after school resumed. But I do not resent that. I hardly have a good template for an ideal family travel. The ones I see while on a trip are just loud and obnoxiously demanding. Also, my family isn't the type to go on vacations; for us, dal makhani at Bhagat Tarachand is the most we could do. We just spend enough time together until we head into a disagreement.

For me, travelling started barely a year before hosting this show. My first trip was supposed to be with a friend. We had both recently turned eighteen, but since his parents changed their minds at the last minute, he couldn't make it, and I had to go alone. Since then, it's been this way, and I quite like it.

I doubt it will change. Maybe if I fall in love again, I will take my partner on a trip. That is the best litmus test for romantic compatibility—when you see each other in the ugliest, oiliest and most tanned states. That's when you see each other's most raw sides—the way you each manage your time, the way you each see things and most importantly, what you each choose to see. Vedika and I went to the Serendipity Arts Festival in Goa the following year, and that's when I realized we might not have a future together. Yes, we did break up eventually.

I am still in awe of the fact that a travel series, which started as an experiment, would shape some of my most core fundamentals. What began as a spontaneous adventure has evolved in ways I never imagined, impacting even the seemingly most irrelevant parts of my life. This journey has transformed how I consume art, appreciate food, choose music, explore languages and engage in conversations. It has also significantly altered my relationship with myself. I've learnt to create space for romance and friendships, and, more importantly, I've come to enjoy my own company. I spent almost a year feeling lost—unsure about my job after graduating and struggling to cope with a break-up. However, over time, I realized that the lessons I learnt during that period have given me the confidence to trust my instincts and navigate life's challenges with greater assurance. This year kept reminding me of the inevitability of change and uncertainty, and amid that, what stays, stays.

* * *

The year 2019 was the shortest as well as the longest year I have lived. In this same year, I camped on a beach, camped amid snow-capped mountains, watched sunrises in the East and sunsets in the West. I roamed the ancient bylanes of some of the oldest civilizations and explored new-age settlements like Auroville. I collected pinecones while hiking through the Himalayas and ate dosa with podi after a hectic day in the South. I hung out with a BBC producer right after grabbing chai with the housekeeping team of a hostel. Taught almost every European the word 'chutya'. Prayed in temples, monasteries, churches and mosques. I hugged thousands of goodbyes, celebrated the birthdays of the most random strangers, flirted a bit, painted a few cafe walls and overheard too many stoned metaphysical discussions in hostel common areas.

Despite these eventful experiences, a major part of my backpacking memories consists of extremely mundane tasks. If you ask me to recall my most vivid memory, weirdly, it would be of waiting. Ironically, travelling is more about waiting than moving—waiting for buses, trains, lifts, check-ins, sunsets and places to open. The waits turn into longing, yearning for familiar faces, familiar touches and to find new patterns within. This waiting time is when I spent the most time with myself.

The wait, no matter how boring, allows you to observe the most irrelevant details about a place—perhaps the uniqueness that even the locals have grown accustomed to seeing. It's during these moments of boredom that you might stumble upon an epiphany. The boring part is necessary because you have no idea how it will surprise you. It is indeed true that travel makes you step outside your comfort zone and embrace change; sit alone at a restaurant; it's not about the destination, it's about the journey and all of those done-to-death inspirational quotes you see on Instagram posts. However, these moments are spread out over a lot of waiting, longing, figuring out emotions and anxiously dealing with uncertainty. If you try to escape the wait, you might as well miss the magic.

In Kolkata, I roamed around the entire Victoria Memorial feeling nothing, but while waiting for my bus at Dalhousie Square or walking past Writer's Building, I couldn't stop thinking about the way the British carried out their business here. The Indians employed here must have been a good group of educated youth. Were they also oblivious to the fact that Bengal was going through a deadly famine during World War II?

While waiting for the Ganga aarti to commence at Dashashwamedh Ghat, watching the kids run around flying their kits, I wondered if they would grow old only to row boats for the tourists or migrate to a metro city to live a better life. Whatever better means to a migrant's life.

In Gokarna, after coming back from Paradise Beach, sitting under the shade of a grocery store waiting for my bus, I was so bored that I couldn't help but watch the dejected faces of the fishermen wrapping their nets by the shore. It didn't seem like they had caught anything. Then one of the boatmen raised his head as he heard the horn of a trawler in the deep sea returning with a bounty of fish.

Watching families in trains exchanging food—all curries, some with a tomato base while some were coconut-based. Hand-painted typography on shops, in Devanagari, Gurmukhi, Tamil and Bangla. The Kumar Sanu music in local buses across the country. Slurs. Scammers. Stalkers. People returning home from work. Spotting couples in co-ord sets at airports. (I don't get the obsession of wearing co-ord sets while flying.) Ads displayed on screens at the boarding gates. Listening to locals speak in their native language. Observing rocks. Spotting birds. Collecting a perfect stick during a hike. All of this has occupied a major part of my wait during my travels. I doubt I would notice all this if I were not travelling solo. It wasn't any grand adventure or a profound epiphany that enriched my travels, but such tiny, mundane, silly, personal moments I spent with myself, observing within and without. The magic lay in these little details that I managed to live in the rush of shooting as a one-man crew. For me, all the memories of these trips are from when the camera wasn't rolling.

No matter how much I vlog, certain moments can never be truly captured. Even if I try, I doubt my efforts will reach people as effectively as those snappy, quirky, clickbaity vlogs. The more content I consumed (both mine and others'), the more my disappointment, angst and confusion grew. Over time, I became increasingly distant from vlogging as a medium of storytelling, especially since I had never watched a vlog before going on a trip myself. Vlogging is undoubtedly a great form of documentary filmmaking, but no matter how hard I tried, I couldn't stop myself from mentally editing the video while shooting it. In doing so, many beautiful ways to tell a story were lost. These vlogs became mere products to be assembled on the editing table, nothing more.

However, it was through this series and these mundane encounters that I discovered what truly makes me happy while creating content. Nothing brings me more joy than capturing stories and uncovering new ones during the editing process. It's like solving a puzzle. I was initially unaffected by all the responses I received during the series, for it was people from across the screen whom I could see or smile at. But even five years after that series ended, when someone walks up to me across a crowded train and shares details about their first solo trip they did after watching my vlogs, it moves me. I had absolutely no idea whether it would even inspire ten people to go backpacking solo. This is more than enough reassurance for me to keep creating.

* * *

This same realization is the reason behind my disassociation from modern notions of travel and its portrayal in pop culture. They only serve the juicy part of the sandwich, which in most cases is either oversimplified or unnecessarily deep. The thick, dry sides of intense yearnings are what people realize only after they get out of their houses. I admit, it was only after having extensively watched *Yeh Jawaani Hai Deewani*, *Zindagi Na Milegi Dobara*, *Dil Chahta Hai*, *On the Road*, *Into the Wild* and *Motorcycle Diaries* that I was inspired to travel. Not denying they're great movies, but if you ask me now, I have newer reasons to travel, and I would certainly not regard these references as entirely true.

Daily, I scroll through videos titled 'I quit my job and now I am travelling full time'. As if travelling is the outcome. How can it be an outcome? I feel we have successfully commodified the idea of travel itself and put it on a pedestal that nobody talks about its impacts on other facets of our personal lives. We fancy the spontaneity it offers, but our fear of uncertainty keeps us in denial of all the ugly things we might face. Backpacking, no matter how romanticized, is always like watching the first cut of your film. You cannot skip the fluff. But as you watch through the fluff, you see the highlights more vividly, and eventually a story is built.

In today's world, it's unrealistic to expect life-altering events from your travels. However, the attempt to explore this facet of ourselves makes us more familiar with our individuality. It opens up the possibility of being surprised, even amid the constant bombardment of information. I believe that the more we travel, the more we discover new versions of ourselves. We become more malleable to new experiences while gaining clarity on what we don't prefer. Travel engages our most basic human instincts that we've lost touch with—our curiosity to hunt for new opportunities, our reflexes to identify potential threats and recognize our shared struggles that make any place feel like home.

Every time I have gotten home, I have been a new person, and even that has changed as any trip has taken time to digest. Your habits change, and your methods of seeking information and meanings change, but you always come back to those very few sets of fundamentals you consciously stick to.

I find 'travel' as an experience more or less like reading a book or watching a film. You find a few chapters interesting, get blown away after reading the entire thing in one go or sometimes, you just don't know how to feel about a book, but as days pass, you subconsciously start relating to it. Most of the time, you re-read an old book after years only to find it novel again.

* * *

At that age, I would have never been able to afford to travel so extensively. It is certainly a privilege (it is not something you HAVE to do; you could watch a movie or read a book instead, but since you are reading this book, let's assume you are privileged enough to travel), and hence the stories we are told about our lands are by the privileged.

We still have an outsider's gaze at our own country. Our definitions of 'our people' are highly subjected to different contexts. We lack a homegrown perspective on our collective identity. (Which is also why we end up buying the ones enforced by ideology, but I won't share much on this.) We try to fit Western concepts in our contexts, and maybe that's where we find it difficult to empathize with our own people. Our languages, foods and landscapes are much more than just a 'land of colours'.

I was busy shooting inside the silk lane of Varanasi, where I saw villages of artisans keeping alive a craft for generations; it made me wonder how limited and funnelled my sources of inspiration have been. It upsets me to see how the advertising industry, social media content and mainstream cinema are so out of touch with their largest audience. The aspirations they have set for us are hollow and unapproachable.

Although we share different languages and differ in our food habits, landscapes and beliefs, it's time we start acknowledging these differences and how we fit in our community. We may develop a sense of belonging to our places and ultimately respect those of others.

We do not need 'tribal-themed villages' to promote tourism, while we already have actual tribal communities that deserve to take up space in the mainstream world. This gap would only create privileged niche markets that exoticize such parts of our culture while the underprivileged communities would still be on the receiving end of our industrial debris. Our cities would all look the same. The locals and migrants would keep deferring on languages. Our farmers' markets would be replaced by apps and food that taste the same, and all the metro cities would look like they're manufactured on an assembly line. Our individuality and collective reflections won't match at all. Our rate of consumption would be at the expense of overexploiting our own natural resources and ethnic identities. We hope and aspire, but in fear.

Finding answers to all these questions I still haven't come to terms with a dilemma. All these culturally rich places are highly devoid of modern infrastructure and urban opportunities. It is great to see the self-sustaining markets of the North-east, the highly intricate traditional Kath Kuni houses of Himachal Pradesh or the fishing communities of Kumbalangi. How will these regions be impacted if they gain easy access to transport, media and international brands? Their wanting all these facilities is valid too. Because none of us can relate to the hardships they may be facing on a daily basis. Would their place look the same as mine? Would they get a little bit meaner? In most realistic circumstances, these regions would only keep getting emptier, leaving only the elderly and the children while the cities get overcrowded.

Our ingredients, scripts, art, films and relationships add up to our individual identities and also influence our collective behaviour. A feeling of belonging will let us actively claim public spaces and adapt rural sustainability practices to urban opportunities. The more we sit with ourselves and observe our vulnerabilities in a new place with its own cultural characteristics, we shall then start to relate to each other more globally. We certainly are a land of colours, but sadly, that's the only thing we are conditioned to see. We are a land of colours, layers, tragedies, triumphs, diverse ecosystems and ideologies co-existing. We are a land of beaches, plateaus, mountains, forests, hectors of farmlands and factories. We are a land of beliefs and misbeliefs. We are a land of the Buddha, the Vedas as well as the Charvakas. We are a land of Dalits, Adivasis, the urban middle class and migrants. We are a land of tigers, elephants, hornbills, bees and fungi. The more we empathize the more we question, the more we feel, relate, exchange and ultimately evolve.

In several places, people are still very fascinated by Mumbai. Their eyes light up every time I tell them I am from Mumbai. Their words are full of hope and curiosity. I always feel that things would have been very different for me if I were not from a city. All of this would have been slightly unapproachable. But maybe I would have dreamt more intensely.

I have revisited a few of the places in this book, some in the same year, but the experiences have always been different, and the more I explore, the more I am reassured that every place has a character of its own. A soul, a sound, a flavour. It has its own pace, which it also manages to put you into. Its history, its trade and its ever-evolving culture influenced by its people keep adding to her character. I began critiquing all the unnecessary romanticism and ended up having one. But let me have it for a while. At least it is not borrowed.

If I were not travelling, I can't imagine how else I could have done what I do. Although a lot of travel habits changed. After this series, I preferred to travel much slower and longer. Enough until I could at least smile and greet three people while on a walk. It pretty much cut down the clutter and indecisiveness that I struggled with earlier due to lack of time. Ever since the pandemic, I've only volunteered during backpacking. It ranged from bartending at a hostel in south Goa, documenting a sixty-year-old Himachali mudhouse in the forests of Jibhi to conducting comic workshops in Auroville and Bir.

I find my life in Mumbai to be extremely dull and predictable. I figured this when I was nineteen, which makes me even more worried. Initially, I thought I might either have to move out or find a new way to enjoy it. It is humid and expensive, the libido is always at an all-time low, the uncertainty is scary and even if I stop, everyone is running so fast that it barely feels like a break. But most importantly, there is so much happening that I do not get the luxury of being bored, and the more I travel, the more I realize how rare this is. So, at this point, I have managed to salvage my relationship with this city. I enjoy the wait of travel and the mental capacity to think creatively, slow down and dive back into work. I can see myself doing this for a while and enjoying it fully.

The feeling of coming home is the most basic of our needs; in fact, developing a feeling of home for a place is more rewarding. It innately lets you take charge of things in your control and navigate life better. More than an escape, it has always been a process of coming home to your people with a widened capacity to love and evolved sensibilities to be loved. Every time I hug my mother to bid her goodbye, her shoulders feel weaker. However, her equally zestful smile from the safety door makes all the weariness disappear when I return home. I cherish those smiles as my souvenirs. My father sees me as his young self who can now afford to see all that he wanted to see.

I'd travel farther and longer, yet it would still be just an attempt to find a home. My home, after every trip, keeps adding souvenirs of habits, beliefs, interests and new-found facets of love. My home gets bigger for people to accommodate and feel comfortable; it gets warmer for new ideas to be talked about and ambitious to be dreamt fearlessly. For hands to be held passionately and faces buried in a loved one's neck for a bit longer. The extra fluff gets discarded, and everything gets simpler and more accessible.

It is worth the travel if it is to come home.

ACKNOWLEDGEMENTS

Having spoken so much about the 'power of randomness' (that I also explicitly mentioned in the Preface), this book itself is a great example of it. For someone who could barely fill a page in school, writing a book was a far-fetched idea. Parallel to this travel series, certain things aligned perfectly for this book to be completed.

First of which, getting my first job at BhaDiPa. I might not be doing any of this if I hadn't been introduced to content creation with such freedom. I wouldn't be writing my first book if I weren't doing the travel series in the first place. I would have never met Anusha Nandakumar, who is the biggest reason why this book came into being. It was she who first suggested that writing a book isn't that foreign an idea and since then has been a constant support throughout all the drafts.

I am grateful to Sarang Sathaye and Paula McGlynn for trusting me with so many projects to experiment with, and the entire initial team of BhaDiPa—Chaitanya Golhar, Prajakta Salbarde, Sagarika Joshi and Anuja Bhandare—who edited the travel series, and my dear friend Divya Kharnare, without whom I might have remained too lazy to even apply for the internship.

In this same journey, I met Vedika, my first girlfriend. There was no reason for our paths to cross if not for that Chopta trek we signed up for. It was she who edited a structured manuscript from a mess of words. She has seen me and this book at our ugliest and still chose us. 'I can see this ending up somewhere nice,' she said when the book was barely ten pages.

In 2019, with the travel series and its growing reach, I met many people with shared interests. Meera Krishnan being one of the closest. Though she helped edit the rest of the drafts, I'm more grateful to her for teaching me to look at the world with love and empathy to become a better writer and film-maker. Our mutual support for each other's work still inspires us to do more.

I also met Tanvi Abhyankar, the editor of this book's proposal, in a similar way—an audience-turned-friend through our mutual love for travelling.

After being rejected by almost all major publishing houses for an entire year, I finally decided to take the self-publishing route. One evening, during a sulk session over beers, Tanvi suggested reaching out to Aparna Piramal, an author she followed on Instagram. With absolutely no hope of expecting a reply from someone of her stature, I wrote to Aparna, and to my surprise, she responded. It wasn't for the book though but to make a video of her kitty party the following week.

If I had never met Tanvi, I wouldn't have known about Aparna, she wouldn't have invited me to shoot her party, we wouldn't have gotten to talk, she wouldn't have sent my proposal to her editor at Penguin Random House, and I wouldn't have received that mail from Anushree Kaushal, who liked my manuscript and signed me a month before quitting her job.

After that, Gurveen Chadha and Manali Das from Penguin's editorial team worked on it for another couple of months. Their objective vision and experience eventually shaped this book.

During these years, I met Rohit Khedkar, Mayur Mengle and Yadna Kanvinde, some of the finest visual artists I know. Their homes were always open to me, especially on days when home wouldn't feel like one.

Given how my procrastination could have potentially shelved this book, it was really bold of all these people to give me their time, efforts and support. I will be forever grateful to each one of them.

Extreme gratitude to my supportive community of audience who chose to give their precious attention spans to my work.

And lastly, the same to my Aai Baba (Smita and Milind). You were the first two artists I've ever known. Thanks for choosing your passions that inspired me to pursue mine.

REFERENCES

'Amer Fort', Tourism Rajasthan. Last updated May, 2024. https://www.
tourism.rajasthan.gov.in/amber-palace.html#:~:text=One%20
of%20the%20top%20tourist,sandstone%2C%20and%20
with%20white%20marble

Banerjee, Aheil. 'A slice of China in Kolkata.' *Times Of India*, August 22,
2023. http://timesofindia.indiatimes.com/articleshow/102932206.
cms?utm_source=contentofinterest&utm_medium=text&utm_
campaign=cppst

Basu, Sayak. 'History of separatism in the conflicted northeastern
state of Nagaland.' *Deccan Herald*, February 26, 2023. https://
www.deccanherald.com/elections/history-of-separatism-in-the-
conflicted-northeastern-state-of-nagaland-1195265.html

'Battle of Talikota.' *Jagran Josh*. October 9, 2014.
https://www.jagranjosh.com/general-knowledge/battle-of-talikota-
1565-ad-1412077564-1

Binayak, Poonam. 'A Guide to Fontainhas, Goa's Latin.' *Culture
Trip*, December 22, 2022. https://theculturetrip.com/asia/india/
articles/a-guide-to-fontainhas-goas-latin-quarter

Britannica. 'History of Goa.' *Britannica Encyclopedia*. Last updated
May 5, 2024. https://www.britannica.com/place/Goa/History

Britannica. 'Puducherry.' *Britannica Encyclopedia*. Last updated May
5, 2024. https://www.britannica.com/place/Puducherry-India

Britannica. 'Hippie Subculture.' *Britannica Encyclopedia*. https://
timesofindia.indiatimes.com/city/goa/the-hippie-who-got-goa-
the-globe/articleshow/49875431.cms

Chatterjee, Satischandra, and Dhirendramohan Datta. *An Introduction to Indian Philosophy*. New Delhi: Rupa Publications, 2007.

Chiu, David. 'The Beatles in India.' *Rolling Stone,* February 14, 2021. https://www.rollingstone.com/feature/the-beatles-in-india-16-things-you-didnt-know-203601/

Cogswell, Ned. 'The History of the Hippie Cultural Movement.' *Culture Trip*. December 13, 2023. https://theculturetrip.com/north-america/usa/california/articles/the-history-of-the-hippie-cultural-movement

David, Athena. 'Eating at Tiretti Bazaar's Sunday Breakfast Market.' *Goya Journal*. February 2, 2021. https://www.goya.in/blog/eating-at-tiretti-bazaars-sunday-breakfast-market-kolkata-chinatown

Das, Soumitra. 'Dalhousie Square in a shambles as its grand old buildings fall apart.' *Frontline Magazine*. November 17, 2022. https://frontline.thehindu.com/arts-and-culture/heritage/dalhousie-square-kolkata-in-a-shambles-as-its-grand-old-buildings-fall-apart/article66106692.ece

Ethirajan, Anbarasan. 'Kohima: Britain's "forgotten" battle that changed the course of WWII.' BBC. February 14, 2021. https://www.bbc.com/news/world-asia-india-55625447

Goyal, Anuradha. 'Finding Kabir- The poet and saint in Kashi.' *India Tales*. January 7, 2013. https://www.inditales.com/kabir-in-kashi/

'Hawa Mahal.' *Rajasthan Tourism*. Last updated May 4, 2024. https://www.tourism.rajasthan.gov.in/hawa-mahal.html#:~:text=The%20five%2Dstorey%20building%20looks,%E2%80%9CPalace%20of%20the%20Winds%E2%80%9D

'History of Indian Tea.' *Indian Tea Association*. https://www.indiatea.org/history_of_indian_tea

Homegrown. 'How an Exiled Nawab Invented the Famous Kolkata Biryani.' *Homegrown.in*. June 8, 2021. https://homegrown.co.in/homegrown-explore/how-an-exiled-nawab-invented-the-famous-kolkata-biryani

Imtimangyang. 'A Brief Historical Account: Christianity among the Ao Nagas of North-East India.' *National Journal of Multidisciplinary Research and Development.* September 3, 2017.

'Isar Lat.' *Tourism of India.* Accessed https://www.tourism-of-india. com/isar-lat-or-swargasuli.html

'Jaipur's Hawa Mahal, an iconic piece of architecture and its history.' *Times Travel.* June 28, 2023. https://timesofindia.indiatimes. com/travel/destinations/jaipurs-hawa-mahal-an-iconic-piece-of-architecture-and-its-history/articleshow/101334904.cms

Kissa, Lydia Thomas, and Aristidis Matsoukis. 'A Study of the Role of Hinduism on Agriculture in Relation to Climate Change: The Case of India.' *Researchgate.* December 2019. https://shorturl.at/ amzF3

'Manikarnika Ghat.' *Tour My India.* https://www.tourmyindia. com/states/uttarpradesh/manikarnika-ghat-varanasi. html#:~:text=Manikarnika%20Ghat%20is%20one%20 of,Scindia%20Ghat%20and%20Dashashwamedh% 20Ghat

Narayanan, Renuka. 'Kashi, In step with history.' *The Hindu.* November 13, 2021. https://www.thehindu.com/features/ magazine/Kashi-In-step-with-history/article59835333.ece

Nambiar, Sridevi. 'The Story Behind India's Most Historic Coffee Chain.' *Culture Trip.* March 1, 2018. https://theculturetrip. com/asia/india/articles/the-story-behind-indias-most-historic-coffee-chain

Nandan G.B., Nasir Ahmed and M. Jangubhai. 'The Comparative study between Hinduism and Buddhism.' *International Journal of Humanities and Social Science Invention.* May 5, 2013.

'Nagaland Profile.' *Official State Portal of Nagaland.* Last modified May 8, 2024. https://nagaland.gov.in/pages/nagaland-profile

Norbu, Jamyang. 'Tibet in India: A people's history of the Tibetan resistance.' *Frontline.* July 22, 2023. https://frontline.thehindu. com/books/tibet-in-india-a-peoples-history-of-the-tibetan-resistance-book-excerpt-echoes-from-forgotten-mountains-by-jamyang-norbu/article67094048.ece

Pereira, Andrew. 'The Hippie Who Brought Goa the Globe.' *Times Of India*. November 22, 2015. https://timesofindia.indiatimes.com/city/goa/the-hippie-who-got-goa-the-globe/articleshow/49875431.cms

Pradosh. 'Hampi, Pattadakal and Aihole.' *Bombay Nomads*. September 5, 2011. https://www.bombaynomads.com/cms/2011/09/hampi-pattadakal-and-aihole.html

Pritam, Ruchi. 'On the Ramayana trail – Kishkindha at Hampi.' *Pragyata*. February 6, 2018. https://pragyata.com/on-the-ramayana-trail-kishkindha-at-hampi/

Rajora, Neha. 'Cultural Landscapes of Amber, Rajasthan.' *researchgate.net*. August, 2013.

'Rishikesh.' *Uttarakhand Tourism*. https://uttarakhandtourism.gov.in/destination/rishikesh#:~:text=Rishikesh%20is%20commonly%20referred%20to,to%20learn%20yoga%20and%20meditation

Standage, Kevin. 'Manikarnika Ghat – Breaking the Cycle of Death and Rebirth.' *Kevin Standage Photography*. May 18, 2020. https://kevinstandagephotography.wordpress.com/2020/05/18/manikarnika-burning-ghat-varanasi-banaras-kashi/

SNS. 'The Fascinating Story of the "City of Dawn", Auroville.' *Statesman*. January 22, 2022. https://www.thestatesman.com/travel/fascinating-story-city-dawn-auroville-1503040512.html#google_vignette

Venkatesh, Karthik. 'A short history of the India Coffee House: Conversation, revolutionary politics and a different way to do business.' Firstpost. January 13, 2021. https://www.firstpost.com/art-and-culture/a-short-history-of-the-india-coffee-house-conversation-revolutionary-politics-and-a-different-way-to-do-business-9184321.html

Vijay, Samyuktha. 'Awakening Devotion: The Life and Works of Tulsidas.' *Historified*. February 21, 2024. https://historified.in/2024/02/21/awakening-devotion-the-life-and-works-of-tulsidas/

Scan QR code to access the
Penguin Random House India website